BLACK EDUCATIONAL LEADERSHIP

This book explores Black educational leadership and the development of anti-racist, purpose-driven leadership identities. Recognizing that schools within the United States maintain racial disparities, the authors highlight Black leaders who transform school systems. With a focus on 13 leaders, this volume demonstrates how US schools exclude African American students and the impacts such exclusions have on Black school leaders. It clarifies parallel racism along the pathway to becoming teachers and school leaders, framing an educational pipeline designed to silence and mold educators into perpetrators of educational disparities. This book is designed for district administrators as well as faculty and students in Race and Ethnicity in Education, Urban Education, and Educational Leadership.

Rachelle Rogers-Ard has over 28 years' experience as a classroom instructor, non-profit administrator, program manager, Adjunct Professor, and district administrator. Currently, Dr. Rogers-Ard is the Executive Director, People, Leadership and Development, with the Alameda County Office of Education and the founder and co-lead for the Grow Your Own Collective.

Christopher B. Knaus is Professor of Education at the University of Washington Tacoma. A global critical race practitioner, Dr. Knaus focuses on disrupting the intersectional racism of colonial schools and colleges, and investing in Black and Indigenous educational systems.

BLACK EDUCATIONAL LEADERSHIP

From Silencing to Authenticity

Rachelle Rogers-Ard and Christopher B. Knaus

Routledge
Taylor & Francis Group

NEW YORK AND LONDON

First published 2021
by Routledge
52 Vanderbilt Avenue, New York, NY 10017

and by Routledge
2 Park Square, Milton Park, Abingdon, Oxon, OX14 4RN

Routledge is an imprint of the Taylor & Francis Group, an informa business

Library of Congress Cataloging-in-Publication Data
Names: Rogers-Ard, Rachelle, 1965– author. | Knaus, Christopher
Bodenheimer, author.
Title: Black educational leadership : from silencing to authenticity /
Rachelle Rogers-Ard & Christopher B. Knaus.
Description: New York, NY : Routledge, 2021. | Includes
bibliographical references and index.
Identifiers: LCCN 2020019618 (print) | LCCN 2020019619 (ebook) |
ISBN 9780367466169 (hardback) | ISBN 9780367466138 (paperback) |
ISBN 9781003029960 (ebook)
Subjects: LCSH: African American school administrators. | African
American school administrators—Anecdotes. | African American
students—Social conditions. | Educational leadership—United
States. | Racism in education—United States. | Discrimination in
education—United States.
Classification: LCC LB2831.82 .R64 2021 (print) |
LCC LB2831.82 (ebook) | DDC 371.2/011—dc23
LC record available at https://lccn.loc.gov/2020019618
LC ebook record available at https://lccn.loc.gov/2020019619

ISBN: 978-0-367-46616-9 (hbk)
ISBN: 978-0-367-46613-8 (pbk)
ISBN: 978-1-003-02996-0 (ebk)

Typeset in Bembo
by codeMantra

To the many, many children who grow up without being able to learn from powerful, authentic Black school leaders and to the many, many Black educators who feel they cannot be who they are and keep their jobs.

CONTENTS

FIGURE AND TABLES

Figure

Tables

ACKNOWLEDGMENTS

Both authors would like to thank the participants in this book, extremely powerful educators whose Blackness makes them visible targets in an anti-Black world. We survive because your dedication and daily love help cultivate health and sanity for so many children and adults alike. To say that this book would not exist without your voices, resistances, and knowledge is too cliché; you are each authentic administrator educators who do not give up on a vision of Black affirmation. Your work, your struggles, and your wins, however small they may seem, are what sustain resistance against white supremacist schools.

We would also like to thank Matthew Friberg and Jessica Cooke at Routledge Education for making this entire project possible and for providing affirming support throughout. All love to Jordan Gonzales at Academic Mechanic for centering justice in words, particularly through helping us finalize the book. Jordan's critical editing, indexing, and super thoughtful feedback reflect decades of friendship and family, and we trust him to help us clarify what we think we are trying to say. And for the book's beauty, we acknowledge Marc Bland, artist and photographer extraordinaire. Your artistic vision was the missing piece, as always.

We particularly want to thank the many who reviewed early drafts and provided words of affirmation, edits, and endorsements to keep on. These include Billye Sankofa-Waters, David Stovall, Bettina Love, Steven Thurston Oliver, Lewis Diuguid, M. Christopher Brown II, Bobby Humes, Tyson Marsh, AJ Goines, Ramona Burton, and Sara Rosenfeld. As with any book, there are many who influenced our thinking that go unnamed, yet we recognize our work is the direct result of community.

Dr. Rachelle Rogers-Ard's Acknowledgments

I would like to acknowledge all of the Black men and women upon whose work I stand. I honor and remember my great-aunts, who were educators in Houston, Texas, modeling culturally responsive practices before it was du jour.

Special thanks and heartfelt appreciation to my co-author, Dr. Christopher Knaus, who truly models what he writes and teaches; he uses his privilege to create opportunities for others. To think that ten years ago, I told him I wanted to publish, and he said, "Let's go!" From that time to now, he has been consistent in demonstrating collaboration, thoughtfulness, feedback, and integrity. While our beliefs differ, our commitment to developing work-related kinship is the same. For that I am incredibly grateful.

To the educators who shared their stories with us, you are my heroes and she-roes. And, for a few of you (and you know who you are!), I absolutely love you; you make me want to go to work each day.

Finally, to the wonderful and amazing humans I birthed, who are the reasons I get up each day: thanks for dealing with my craziness while trying to get this book together. You are my foundation, my heart, and my air. Book #1 complete!

Dr. Christopher B. Knaus's Acknowledgments

I would like to acknowledge the honor that collaborating with Dr. Rogers-Ard is. Dr. Rogers-Ard's passion, insight, patience, and commitment to being who she is, in a world that continually talks, walks, and rolls over Black women, is contagiously life-affirming. From our first conversation about Critical Race Theory in the office of what may have been the last Black Mayor of Oakland, I have been and continue to be awed by Doc's fabulousness, humility, and dignity. No one can move an audience like you, Doc; through song, music, talks, and plain honesty, your modeling of helping people grow gives me faith in humanity. I am eternally grateful for our friendship and shared investment in each other's growth.

I'd also like to honor the dozens and dozens of critical Black educators who have helped inform my thinking about racism, survival, and life beyond oppression. These include numerous Black teachers and administrators, former students, community leaders, and a range of advocates of color. Several recent students have also helped expand my thinking of Pacific Northwest anti-Blackness, including Dr. Conrad Trayvon Webster, Kenderick Wilson, and Beleqsa Tamaami.

Extra love and public affirmations are always due to President M. Christopher Brown II, who encouraged me to conduct this research and was gracious with a postponement of our other writing projects. Family of the highest order, Dr. Brown provides a continual reminder that Black leaders can maintain their authenticity with emphatic commitments to justice at the most executive levels. President Ronald Rochon, in addition to almost 25 years of mentorship, models incredible presence and patience while centering purpose in executive leadership roles. I am also eternally thankful for my BFF, President John Mosby, who takes authenticity to a whole new level, helping disrupt the false and harmful expectations of how we so often stereotype Black leaders.

Particular critical love and recognition is due to Dr. Venus Evans-Winters, who continues to allow me to call on her with last-minute conference requests and is always willing to share in the mentoring of awesome colleagues. For modeling loving, Black-affirming leadership within a hyper sexist leadership context, I appreciate Nososi Ntshuntshe for welcoming me into Sinethemba Secondary, a township school in Philippe, South Africa. Thank you as always to my fierce mentor, Geneva Gay; our too-infrequent chats always ground me in the work of loving care. The School of Education at the University of Washington Tacoma provided necessary funds to keep me returning to the Bay Area, and I particularly thank Jarek Sierschynski and Dean Rachel Endo for assistance, advocacy, and affirmation. Dr. Mona Johnson-Bissonnette, as always, was super influential, particularly around the focus on trauma and school leaders.

Last, and always most important, Dr. Cyndy Snyder continues to be my light and breath, an eternally patient coach as I hold other people's traumatic experiences with my own.

FOREWORD

Black Leadership in the Uncertain Time of Now

On March 11, 2020, the World Health Organization declared the novel coronavirus known as COVID-19 to be a global pandemic. According to the US Center for Disease Control (CDC), a pandemic is defined as an "epidemic that has spread over several countries or continents, usually affecting a large number of people." I have never lived through what has been classified as a global biological pandemic, yet I continue to live under the social pandemic of white supremacy. Because racism is *everywhere at all times,* white supremacy should be considered a pandemic that has spread over "several countries and/or continents" over the last 500 years. While I am unsure of the ultimate impacts of COVID-19, I remain deeply concerned as to what this could mean for people who are without the necessary resources for survival and sustenance. In the midst of panic-stricken residents who have emptied grocery stores of food and supplies, those who are unable to purchase items for their survival are left without access to life-sustaining resources. The city of Wuhan, China (thought to be the origin of the virus), has operated in quarantine since late January; K-12 schools and universities across the globe have closed; and cities and nations are closing borders and operating under curfews, and, in worst-case scenarios, are under makeshift quarantines (currently referred to in the US as "shelter-in-place"). Unfortunately, the lessons of history inform me that those who are poor, Black, Latinx, Indigenous, South-Asian, Arab, immigrant, differently abled, female-identified, housing/food insecure or some combination of these do not fare well in such conditions.

As a Black person born in Chicago in the early 1970s, the social pandemic of white supremacy has remained consistent. Given my understanding of white supremacy as *the perceived views and values of white Western European-descended, Protestant, able-bodied, cis-gendered, heterosexual, able-bodied, men* as normal, right, and good, everyone else who does not match those descriptors has been excluded and/or marginalized. Where some may think pandemic comparisons to be unfair, I would remind them of what it means to be a descendent of kidnapped Africans living in a world that often considers you to be criminal before you are human. For those who pay attention to the visibility of police violence on Black bodies in daily living and in schools, a conversation with Black people in the US would alert you that this type of sentiment and behavior is nothing new. In fact, the rest of the world (which includes white people in the US) are just catching up to these realities.

Marc Lamont Hill discusses the struggles of supporting young people living under extreme precarity. Michael Dumas calls schools "the site of Black suffering." Sonya Douglass Horsford reminds us that Black folk who held leadership positions often felt as if they were advocating for "learning in a burning house." *All* of these scholars are correct; when faced with these realities and contradictions of schooling, the work becomes even tougher for the critically conscious educator. Yet our understandings of justice-centered classroom teachers are considerably more developed than our visions for a justice-centered school leader. We are clearer in the content, disposition, and pedagogy needed to support classroom teachers who are committed to justice, but we often find ourselves struggling in terms of what it means to prepare and support a justice-centered principal and/or superintendent. When we experience a principal that demonstrates a deep understanding of justice in thought and action, we are shocked at how rare they are in their commitment to the education of young people through deep community engagement, content knowledge, authentic instructional support, and knowledge of political economy.

Deepening the contradiction is the fact that we are clear that these school leaders probably *did not* learn their justice-centered approaches in a traditional college of education. In fact, in many discussions of educational justice, the school leader is positioned as the enemy, willfully demonstrating a commitment to upholding the hegemonic forces of the state or local school district. Ever-present in the over-reliance on standardized test score performance, historically rooted in eugenics, corporate charter school proliferation, blaming families for their current condition, and Black population loss in urban centers, the job of working in a schoolhouse in a leadership position instantaneously makes you an agent of the state. If we understand the aforementioned to be true, what does it mean for the people who operate in the role of principals and superintendents in K-12 schools?

The Black critically conscious school leader must be willing to think and act in ways that are fugitive and abolitionist. They must be willing to operate in-between the rules, regulations, and compliance of the state. If you take this seriously as a critically conscious school leader, you must vigorously advocate for students who may have undocumented status. You must tend to the needs of your students who are housing insecure. You might have to purchase industrial washers to make sure your students have clean clothes. When the state demands that you must discard them, reminding them of their permanent disposability, you must take into account the fact that sometimes, these rules and regulations don't work for our young people. Instead, it calls for the justice-minded school leader to think about what it means to abolish the conditions that have historically isolated our students and families in the name of "progress" and "duty." Reading was considered "too dangerous" for the descendants of kidnapped Africans. It was "too much" for those who were wrongly imprisoned to claim their humanity. The rules and regulations of the settler state in 1619 remain similar to the "rules and regulations" that govern schools that serve Black students who are surviving white supremacy in the form of poverty and isolation in 2020. Many schools and school systems remain steadfast in their commitment to constrict before they will let our youth embrace freedom dreams. Their draconian nature criminalizes them before it allows for any semblance of education. When young people push and ask questions of the school, they are thwarted. Any school leader that understands these things to be true must shift their understanding to work for the people they say they care about if those people are Black and/or members of historically marginalized groups.

The point here is to not paint the grimmest picture of the current moment. Instead, I understand that the radical imaginary is birthed from an understanding of now (the current social, political, and economic moment) to push us to work with others to build a different future. I am grateful for Rogers-Ard and Knaus's willingness to engage discussions on the real-world work of Black education leaders, breaking free from the order and compliance of the school to begin to embrace education. They have dared to act fugitively in the way suggested by Dumas: *they are not free, but they have made a decision to run.* Like the kidnapped Africans before them, they are not running from something. Instead, their process develops clarity on where they are running and with whom they are running. In the end, these critical Black educational leaders are trying to get free because a hefty salary and new social position does not purchase your freedom. Under these conditions, the "rules" and compliance issued by the state must be broken. They are unacceptable. We've known this for too long. Where the realities of COVID-19 appear to be temporary, the pandemic of white supremacy remains. It is those like us who will cease its function. This book serves as documentation of the kind of work needed to make this a reality.

Until Victory is Ours,
David Stovall, PhD
Chicago, Illinois
March 15, 2020

INTRODUCTION

Introduction

This book, written by two educators, researchers, and colleagues that span K-12 practice and university-based educator preparation programs, is an outcome of a long-standing working relationship that became a steadfast friendship. While we have collaboratively written this book, it is also the accumulation of shared experiences working within racist schools as an African American female teacher, district leader, dual district and University-based practitioner-scholar, and a white male teacher/higher education practitioner-scholar. Our relationship spans race, gender, spiritual and religious differences, as well as vast differences during our formative years, which we have both documented elsewhere (Knaus, 2011; Rogers-Ard, 2007). Our professional relationship stems from our shared commitment to disrupting systemic racism so that we can help foster transformation towards hooks's (1994) framing of education as the practice of freedom. This work could have happened only because of the huge amount of trust each participant had for us as researchers.

This book is a culmination of three years' work with Black educational leaders across the Bay. We are so grateful for our participants' willingness to be extremely open to us, to share their stories—their hurts and their trauma—so that others may be better prepared to create more lovingly affirming spaces for Black leaders. While we began our work focused on supporting children of color, specifically Black children, we increasingly centered Black teachers, and soon thereafter, Black school leaders. As we navigated our own professional spaces, we directed our concerns toward the number of Black leaders we knew who were struggling—not with children, but with their values being tested in racist educational spaces. When we began to listen to educators' stories, we decided to bring a few of them together to create a safe space where these leaders could vent. With home-cooked meals, bowls of fruit, and plenty of hugs, we began our regular sessions with brief check-ins. By the third check-in, we realized how rare opportunities to be human are for Black educational leaders. In reflecting on our sessions, these Black leaders clarified their investment in authentic dialogue, and we knew then that these leaders' experiences should be shared with a wider audience.

Each time we asked a leader to share how they were feeling about their choices, contexts, and challenges, we were honored and reminded of the great risk each person took. We encouraged and invited a white male into this affinity space because of the ways in which Chris has continuously written about, reflected on, and demonstrated his own self-awareness around race, patriarchy, and the collective isms that make this Black survival difficult. Chris has done tremendous race work around privilege; his writings (2007, 2014, 2019) outline both an analysis of our country's racist policies as well as the effects of those policies on him personally. Chris continually pushes for increased thoughtful dialogue around racism in classrooms, at friendly gatherings, and across hostile higher education settings. He approaches people of color from a place of humility and has spent many years cultivating true friendships and living in spaces where white people are uncomfortable. In other words, Chris talks the talk and walks the walk. This is not to say that Chris automatically receives the "Black stamp of approval"; his relationship with Rachelle, a Black woman, has not been without bumps and bruises. However, both of us agreed early on to call out and name situations and actions that created tension and threatened the tenuous trust that we were building.

Furthermore, we also committed to deep, honest conversations about our triggers so that we meaningfully integrated racial healing into our relationship. Chris models what is critically important for white people to understand: it is not up to people of color to create space for white folks to discuss race or to educate and hold white people's whiteness. Instead, we argue and live that white folx must demonstrate cross-racial solidarity by building authentic relationships with people of color and communities of color that challenge racist behaviors and systems. Simply put, welcoming a white, male person into this sacred space of Black educational leaders was a rare phenomenon of which we are aware and grateful. Thus, we lead with a reminder to white people that reading and writing all the books in the world is insufficient to engaging in and with communities of color in critical, anti-racist human work.

Relatedly, while some of the focus group participants were invited due to their relationship with Chris, Rachelle's reputation as a staunch supporter of Black leaders directly shaped the spaces we created. Rachelle's foundation in faith, in the healing power of song and music, and her continual commitment to affirming Blackness—particularly as a leadership strategy—helped participants get excited about their involvement. Indeed, many participants knew what being in community with Rachelle would be; they knew our conversations would be surrounded by food, healing laughter, and a sharp seriousness in mapping survival strategies. Because Rachelle continually reads, holds space in her office for all people to enter, be affirmed, and also be challenged (and to leave with a book or two), participants knew what they were getting into by committing to talk with us over the course of a few years. Thus, because of who and how Rachelle is, we were able to hold space for honest reflection, for transparent sharing, and for tears to flow so that participants *and* researchers could hold each other, model what we believe professionalism should look like, and honor the spirit of Sankofa by looking back to move forward, collectively.

Why Now

The rise of COVID-19 and the impact of holding anti-Black media clips capturing intentional violence in our hands has shifted our everyday experience. As multiracial coalitions protest in resistance to pandemics of racism, health disparities, and continued anti-Black violence, the work of supporting Black leaders is even more essential. Many, if not most, of the students we support have been (or currently are) Black educators on the pathway to the classroom, school, or district leadership roles, and our day-to-day realities are influenced dramatically by lived racism, both by us differentially, and by Black student/educators we collectively support. Thus, while we endeavored to write this book about the daily experience of Black leadership, we wanted to answer our own questions about why (and how) African American leaders stay in professions seemingly designed to murder their spirit while diminishing the Black children we share responsibility for growing within a racist anti-Black world.

We soon realized that many of our discussions—researchers call these interviews—with the Black school administrators whose stories grace this book were rooted in the need to be heard, to express voices critical of the daily experience of being a permanent target from white racist colleagues who were also self-proclaimed allies. We realized that the need to share was as important as the need to develop camaraderie around coping strategies and ways to navigate and build a community of support to encourage constant effort to transform from systemic, intersectional racism. These participants reported facing all manners of racism, including intersectional sexism, heterosexism, ageism, lookism, classism, and the ever-present reality that sometimes, one never knows if an interaction or system is racist, or just bureaucratically anti-human. Thus, in our discussions around coping mechanisms, we began to answer questions around what Black school leaders were dealing with, as well as how to strengthen methods of coping against the onslaught of anti-Blackness from every direction.

As we began making sense of these discussions, we recognized the intensity of need could not be greater; opportunity gaps become wage gaps which become entire communities displaced by white wealth, all while schools struggle to effectively provide a colonizing education to Black students. We also recognized the need for continual code-shifting: Black school leaders need to speak one way to white teachers, another way for Black teachers, quite often another way for other educators of color, and entirely different linguistic codes for huge ranges of students, parents, families, district leaders, politicians, university faculty to whom these leaders relied upon for required credentials, and for coaches, union leaders, police and probation officers, legal teams, and a host of other professional, community, and youth-centered advocates. In short, these leaders were forced to engage in dozens of Englishes, continually choosing which cultural nuance to add to which audience, all while aiming to balance personal and professional authenticity. Even among those who claimed to not code-switch, to always be who they are in every setting, language shifts were practiced almost unwittingly; as normalized as racism is in schools, so too were strategies to navigate situational and systemic racism.

Underneath these code-switching, navigational approaches rested the point we return to at each page: racism and white supremacy shape every interaction, at almost every single moment. Regardless of the percentage of African American students, these Black educational leaders always represented as the *only*: the only African American leader, the only African American person in the room, the only African American woman, the only African American person who spoke Spanish, the only queer African American person, the only educational leader fighting for and with Black students and Black communities, often even when they were in rooms full of Black educators. This isolation reinforced a structural lack of professional mentorship. Indeed, these Black leaders could not shake an exhausting daily reality:

> For large numbers of Black students, the lack of an active Afrocentric leadership perspective in schools, a perspective that 'equates the very identity and humanity of African American people with literacy and education' (Perry, Steele, & Hilliard, 2003, p. B11), has resulted in disastrous consequences . . . .
>
> *(Foster & Tillman, 2009, p. 11)*

These disastrous consequences rest within the nuances of sentence construction, for it was and is all too rare when these school leaders get to pull away their many layered masks and simply talk how they talk, and say what needs to be said.

The journey of this book begins with Chapter 1 as an introductory framing of US schooling as anti-Blackness, clarifies applied Critical Race Theory, and presents our orientation to educational leadership. Chapter 2 provides background on research methods and introduces participants. Chapter 3 discusses pathways towards becoming school leaders, highlighting the systemic lack of engaged, culturally responsive classroom teachers, school leaders, and district personnel that participants took as personal responsibility. Chapter 4 clarifies how these Black leaders have seen Black children positioned by other school teachers and leaders, framing concerns about the health and well-being of Black children. These concerns about Black children not being seen as who and how they are directly impacted the development of anti-racist, community-centric leadership identity. Chapter 5 reflects a prevailing loss of professional space and security as seen by the silencing of Black educators all while they are expected to balance racist expectations. Chapter 6 presents our framework for Black school leadership, which centers Authentic Leadership as a foundational purpose of school districts, clarifying five elements of HEART: honesty, empathy and equity, accountability, reflection, and trust. We conclude by situating this framework as a way to restructure district leadership pathways and development processes to recognize the cultural strengths of leaders of color, particularly Black leaders.

These nuances were what led us to write this book, to honor Black school leaders by cultivating conversations about navigating through and transforming from the societal onslaught of intersectional racism to become effectively anti-racist, pro-Black, pro-children, and pro-society. We argue the entire edifice of schooling must transform to protect Black lives, to prepare Black students to stay alive, to navigate racist systems, and to ultimately transform from racism to a healing, affirming society. We hope that this text can be used to help support Black educational leaders to arm children to survive the world that is, not the world that white people presume exists for all children as it does or did for them. If we are to truly change the world, we must support, listen to, hear, interpret, and create spaces for Black educators leading the charge.

1

BLACK LEADERSHIP WITHIN ANTI-BLACK SCHOOLS

"It's a war for the souls of our children."

– André (High School Principal)

The scream-song sound of children playing in the school's courtyard had slowly resided, as children reluctantly dragged their backpacks towards their parents' waiting cars. One lone child remained behind, however, and Rosie ruefully shook her head, knowing the routine to come. As she rushed down the stairs to meet the child with open arms, the child, maybe eight years young, jumped to her. Rosie caught the boy, swung him in two full circles, and then landed him next to her while still holding his hand. She walked him into her office, where the principal chatted with the Parent Teachers Association (PTA) representative. Rosie walked past the two white women and guided the young boy into a chair in her office, then placed a book in his hands faster than the two white women could roll their eyes.

The only Black administrator—and just one of three Black people out of 37 employed at the 35% Black-enrolled elementary school—Rosie was used to adults dismissing children who sometimes did not have a family member pick them up on time. Rosie was also aware of the many systemic reasons that led to the children being picked up later than was convenient for the majority of white teachers and administrators, who rushed home as soon as possible after school. The continuously high unemployment rates, the history of redlining to exclude Black home ownership, the lack of a reliable mass-transit system, the gentrification pushing Black families farther from their children's schools; Rosie knew well that poverty and racism directly shaped the reality that some Black parents were not able to pick up their children at exactly

4:30 each afternoon. But what frustrated Rosie the most was the rolling of the eyes, the white dismissal of children and families navigating a racist, unequal, often hurtful world by the very educators paid to support them.

This white dismissal of Black children had been built upon a foundation that Rosie had long been used to. As a self-identified Black butch queer New Yorker, Rosie had a rough landing in the Bay Area, which she had thought was progressive and more open to Black and queer people. But after a decade as an administrator in the whiteness of Bay Area schools, Rosie was burnt out. "I was just taking care of a lot of white teachers," Rosie reflected, "and never fully taking care of myself, or even really the children, cause of what they had to face from their teachers." Rosie had forged a culture of affirmation for the majority Black and Latinx students, but creating and maintaining a positive climate within a largely anti-Black staff and community took a toll on her health. Ultimately, Rosie decided that the toxicity of white-led schools was simply too much.

> It's really about being proactive and asking yourself, "How can I be my best self to serve?" And that's a question that I've never asked myself because I was always good at it, so I just did it. But I didn't ask about the self-preservation, I didn't think about the longevity. Because I was like spoiled saying, "Man, I'm good at this, I've got this on lock, so I'm good, I'm just gonna keep going the way I'm going." And then Bam! I'm in the hospital getting a foot chopped out of my colon.

Rosie spent much of her eleventh year as an educator laying on her couch recovering from stress-induced body trauma and corrective surgeries, which gave her time to think about being an educator in spaces designed to silence who and how she is.

"I think part of it, too," Rosie reflected, "is that you keep looking for a silver bullet. I know that was part of my own ignorance. You're looking for that school [that cares for children of color]. And it doesn't exist." Shortly after recovering, Rosie finished out her academic year and then stepped away from schools. She relocated back home to New York and spent a year re-evaluating her professional options. With 15 years of professional leadership that included being a school leader, Rosie had faced too much cumulative toxic stress. After years of being the only Black school administrator in a white-centric school system—which is to say, any public school system in the United States—Rosie's body forced her to accept what she already knew.

> I mean I know the academic side of it really well, I know the literature, I know the research, I live the experience. But to deal with that all, I really had to get spiritually zoned in, which is definitely a work in progress. It's another reason why I'm moving home. My parents are very, very active in the Bahá'í community. And I'm going home to learn from them and heal, too.

We open this book on Black[1] educational leaders with Rosie leaving school administration to find a space of healing in order to thoroughly frame the impact of Black leadership within white-framed schools. Rosie did not leave schools until cumulative stressors and intersectional racism impacted her body to the point of debilitation.

While many teachers leave before this damage is done, recognizing the toxicity within their first few years of teaching, many who join the ranks of administration eventually internalize these racialized stressors in their bodies, hearts, and minds. Our focus is on Black educators like Rosie—committed to equity and justice, to culturally responsive approaches, to critical care of children and families of color—and also interested in leading effectively, in creating schools that help children learn how to navigate and transform society to address our environmental, social, economic, and violently destructive ways. And we begin with Rosie's need for healing as a foundation to explore school leadership within a context of violence that specifically targets Black educational leaders.

Through our own professional and personal lived experience, we have come to know well how toxic educational spaces intentionally enact demeaning violence upon women, people of color, and most particularly, women of color. The African American and Black students who attend schools in large urban centers across the US are often mentored by the few isolated women and men of color who desegregate predominantly white faculties; these students grow up living violence as a normalized, othering everyday reality in schools. Black students are taught to embrace demeaning, dismissive values, to tolerate societal oppression, the violent devaluation of women of color, the violent policing of Black youth, all while being told to be strong, to excel, to rely on personal grit to overcome via a silent, subservient acquiescence to the day-to-day violence against young people's humanity.

Yet this book is not a primer for well-meaning white educators, professors, or educational leaders. Indeed, our focus is not to help colleges of education more effectively prepare leaders to better manage Black educators. Our aim is not to encourage districts to offer more professional development or one-off speakers who challenge the mainstream on Friday afternoon from 3 to 4:30 pm, only to return to the same systemic silencing on Monday. To be sure, we ground our fundamental argument in the belief that school systems are designed to silence children and educators of color (Knaus, 2011). Thus, in order to survive the continual attacks against Black people, people of color, poor people, people with disabilities, the full spectrum of queer and trans communities, indeed, even against our planet, we must transform educational systems (Love, 2019). Since we have not yet transformed systems, though, authentic Black leadership within oppressive systems is not sustainable. This argument builds upon critical race theory's notion of the permanence of racism, reflecting ongoing Black leadership that has continually challenged schools as intentionally maintaining whiteness that, in turn, is designed to silence Blackness (Capper, 2015; Khalifa, Dunbar, & Douglas, 2013).

We offer a challenge to the ongoing recruitment of Black (and of color) educators and leaders as necessary but insufficient, with a caveat on longevity and well-being of the educators being recruited into toxic, anti-Black systems. Because of the pervasive intersectional oppression that operates as the foundations of school and district practice, school systems are not sustainable for authentic, healthy Black educational leaders. In turn, this systemic critique poses challenges for district and college efforts for recruitment—for who benefits when Black educators are retained within systems that ultimately cause them harm? Indeed, what does retention look like when the longer one stays within a leadership role, the more racism operates like a cancer, causing real bodily harm to educational leaders of color, particularly Black women? The vast literature on Black women's health disparities directly links racism and poverty to shortened life spans, and the socioeconomic benefits of climbing the leadership ladder do not seem to impact survival or health rates, as the pain of navigating racially hostile climates accumulates in Black bodies (Assari, 2018a, 2018b; Love, 2019).

Our focus centers the Black educators who continually recommit to nurturing a critical presence, to navigating the onslaught against their humanity. We center Black leaders to increase awareness of personal strategies to survive and transform societal attacks against Black communities. We highlight Black leaders who intentionally persist through the same violent anti-Black context specifically so that they can push back, create pockets of resistance, so that they can position themselves as change agents with what André's opening quote names: the war for the souls of children. We center the experiences of critical Black leaders precisely because, like Rosie, such leaders are systematically silenced; many are pushed out well before they can become school leaders. The pushout process for many would-be educators and school leaders begins before school, in newly gentrifying communities that economically exclude Black families. And this process continues across the P-20 spectrum, culminating for many in high school, when students of color simply choose to no longer accept racism and sexism as the foundation for learning. We are thus concerned with and committed to Black educators who remain in their local schools despite gentrification pressures that geographically push them further from their children. In particular, we are concerned with those who move from classrooms to school buildings and district offices, in full recognition of the systemic nature of the war against the souls of Black children.

In what comes next, we clarify how US schools perpetuate anti-Blackness as part of the fabric of education. We then analyze racism along the pathway to becoming teachers and school leaders, framing an intentional educational pathway designed to silence and mold educators into perpetrators of an educational war against Black children and communities. We apply a critical race theory approach to overview Black school leadership within the everyday operation of colonial schools, illustrating how critical race theory can be applied to shape conversations around authenticity within racially hostile school systems.

We then situate Black educational leaders as intellectual guides and critical voices in the fight against schooling as the primary method of sustaining intellectual, cultural, and social white supremacy. This chapter thus aims to provide intellectual hope for explaining and responding to Rosie's prioritization of her health and survival, and offers a shift from her leaving the field after over a decade as a clarion call to transform school systems immediately. Until we transform the way the US thinks of schools, educational leaders will remain predominantly white precisely because of the toxicity Black children and Black educators face as they simply survive within school systems that value, affirm, assert, and normalize whiteness.

US Schooling as Anti-Blackness

To clarify the complexity of Black educators who intentionally occupy leadership roles in opposition to the colonial intent of US school systems, we begin with the historic purpose of schooling in the US. The enslavement of millions of Africans at the hands of intentionally oppressive European settlers provided a foundation for recognizing that, to the US government and wealthy whites, the existence of Black people has been framed as an economic benefit to white people (Dancy, 2013). Indeed, Black people were brought to the US to serve white people, so that white people did not have to work as hard for dramatic economic benefit, and ultimately, schools were created to teach this subservience (Freire, 1970; Woodson, 1933/1990). While many have argued that the United States has not spent sufficient time engaging in honest reflection on the lingering problem of racism (hooks, 2003; Taylor, 2016), this lack of thorough engagement reflects an intentional outcome of formal education in the US (Macedo, 1994). Schools in the US were founded upon the socially constructed principle that white people, and particularly white men, are far superior to everyone else, and far superior at just about everything (Dyer, 1997; Lipsitz, 1998; Mills, 1997). This notion of white supremacy has been implemented as an ideology through US schools (Epstein, 2008; Macedo, 1994; Valenzuela, 1999); indeed, we take as a central assumption that without schools, racism would not have been justified and implemented so effectively, across the past several hundred years and into the foreseeable future. In short, the colonial purpose of schools, resisted across untold classrooms and communities, retains an intentional fostering of white supremacy and anti-Black racism (Love, 2019).

The white supremacy upon which the US was founded similarly remains the foundation for public schooling within the United States, shaping curriculum, pedagogy, school design and scheduling, and processes for professional certifications needed for entry and career success (Au, Brown, & Calderón, 2016; Knaus & Brown, 2018; Sleeter, 2012). Thus, the dramatic, sustained educational inequalities and inequities in the provision of all aspects of schooling, despite continued documentation raising alarms over the past centuries, aligns with the white supremacist purpose of schooling (Spring, 2018). The US has historically excluded those not socially or legally defined as white from schools across its history, including Italians, Jews, Polish, Irish, and especially indigenous, Latinx, African Americans, women, those variously defined as poor, and a host of children often derisively classified as students with disabilities (Lipsitz, 1998; Spring, 2018). Individuals and communities have fought for access into these racist school systems, knowing full well that school success increases opportunities for economic wealth, even if such wealth is limited in comparison to whites (Lipsitz, 1998; McLaren, 1999).

As some racialized groups were eventually granted inclusion into schools, and, in turn, were re-constructed politically to be considered white, African Americans, however, along with indigenous communities, have not been fully integrated into the scope and sequence of public education (Ignatiev, 2009; Sleeter, 2012). Indeed, schools have intentionally maintained a colonizing mission. The first schools served as the primary method of enforcing intellectual, cultural, linguistic, and social acquiescence to whiteness, with indigenous nations (including Mexicanos in what was then Mexico) being violently forced to tolerate colonial schooling, with rape, molestation, and torture a daily part of attendance (Adams, 1995; Spring, 2018). Meanwhile, Black people, enslaved to provide the economic foundation the US continues to thrive upon, were forcibly kept from participating in early colonial schooling systems, instead resorting to clandestine classrooms, hidden from the white people who would otherwise punish Black learning (Williams, 2005). The US justified this differential access through the continual need for free (and later, cheap) labor, demonstrating a commitment to ensuring Black people not be included in the American project (Singh, 2004). Thus, schools were assimilationist tools, intentionally melting all cultures into one—focused on capitalistic greed and individualism framed as freedom (Macedo & Bartolomé, 1999).

From the inception of schools, those excluded by law or by practice were framed as uncivilized and uneducable (Spring, 2018; Woodson, 1933/1990). Today, students who remove themselves or are removed by educators are discussed in similarly dismissive language, with exclusion from schools justified by zero-tolerance disciplinary policies meant to police Black behavior that does not reinforce whiteness (Caton, 2012; Love, 2019; Payne & Brown, 2010). For many students of color, particularly African Americans, leaving school before graduating is frequently due to the simple reality that they do not have positive experiences in school (Goodman & Hilton, 2013; Knaus, 2011; Rumberger, 2004; Vega et al., 2012).

The sinister intentionality of the US purpose of schools is thus an intentional denial of cultural history, language, oppression, and ultimately, humanity for all but those socially, legally, and politically determined to be worthy, which is to say, accepted by whites (Epstein, 2008; Woodson, 1933/1990). This denial has directly tied to early definitions of educational and intellectual success, which frame just about everything white as good and everything Black as negative (Dyer, 1997). Let us be clear—challenges to the globally oppressive nature of whiteness are not new. As Richard Wright (1956) argued over 60 years ago,

> The systems and the manners of it have varied, but there has not been a Western colonial regime which has not imposed, to a greater or lesser degree, on the people it ruled the doctrine of their own racial inferiority.
>
> *(p. 151)*

It is no coincidence that the first feature-length film in the US, *The Birth of a Nation*, depicted Black people in horribly offensive caricatures, just as the nation was implementing what became known as public schools. Thus, while racially privileged, segregated schools were created to instill racist beliefs in white children, less-resourced schools—equally segregated—were created to instill internalized racism into Black children (Watkins, 2001). Meanwhile, the nation touted efforts to keep whites adhering to white supremacy, in part through stereotypical Black images, conjured for the sole purpose of convincing white people that they are, at a minimum, better than Black people (hooks, 1996). While corporate mass media has continued its anti-Black mission, schools have been implemented as the default societal tool to ensure adherence to what Mills (1997) refers to as the Racial Contract, the social commitment to dolling out economic, housing, food, and health supports only when in the service of white supremacy.

James Baldwin (1985) further argued, " . . . the history and the situation of Black people in this country amounts to an indictment of America's legal and moral history" (p. 13). Our purpose is not to clarify this indictment in full, as that has been done comprehensively elsewhere. Our focus instead is to frame, as a foundation, the role of schools in the US as the central means through which whiteness has developed in direct opposition to Blackness. This foundation has led to the implementation of measurements of success at school that intentionally align with white, middle-class linguistic codes and norms, extending the Eugenics movement through the arm of schooling designed to convince multiple language speakers, recent immigrants, and in particular, indigenous and Black people that who they are, how they think, and why they even exist should be challenged by the day-to-day of what is commonly referred to as schooling (Au, 2009; Delpit, 2012; Rogers-Ard & Knaus, 2013).

A tangible result of this intentional dismissal of Black thought, language, experience, and reality is systemic silencing of Black people through legally enforced participation in schools. Indeed, public education in the United States was designed to question the very existence of African American thought, thus requiring a curriculum, pedagogy, and school design that systemically silences Black children and educators alike (Knaus, 2019). This silencing, built into every aspect of schooling and enforced by law to be taught to all children, has shaped and exacerbated the physical and intellectual wounds caused by settler colonization, slavery, and the continued conditions of oppression today (Adams, 1995; Ginwright, 2016; Woodson, 1933/1990; Wright, 1956; Yellow Horse Brave Heart & DeBruyn, 1998). The normalization of whiteness as the way to act in a classroom is supported by the limited presence of nuanced, multicultural perspectives that contradict the Western curricular narrative, the shaming of the multilingual nature of people living within the land now settled and claimed as the United States, and the framework of disciplinary procedures designed to police behavior (Macedo, 1994; Saltman, 2003; Sleeter, 2012).

Thus, contemporary schools mirror the historical context of US settler colonialism. In addition to legislating apartheid inequalities, colonial America institutionalized a legal context that criminalized not just Black learning, but also Black teaching and decent buildings in which to teach (Tolley, 2016; Williams, 2005). The extremely violent reaction to Black people found guilty of trying to learn (Davis, 2015) contributed to the mainstream white (and other groups of color) perceptions of African American knowledge as less relevant and less intelligent than white cultural norms that continue through many white teachers' resistance to multicultural education (Evans-Winters & Twyman Hoff, 2011; Howard & Milner, 2014; Sleeter, 2001). Thus, common sense has meant ways of thinking for those who would identify as white, not sense common to people trying to survive white oppression. As the mandate of public education began to spread and legally require all residents (and eventually citizens) to go to school, the commitment to framing Black people, thought, experience, and expression as less than white was intentionally legitimized through an alignment of K-12 and higher education. Only those who succeeded, by formal assessment and grades, to approximate whiteness were deemed smart enough to graduate (and in turn, be hired as educators). Pathways towards becoming an African American educator in predominantly and historically white schools and colleges have thus historically meant navigating a racist system first as a student, and then upholding that same system as an employee barely tolerated by white infrastructures.

Because of this intentional segregation, however, Black communities took advantage of the space to nurture their own educational visions and interpretations. Left to their own devices, Black educators in the late 1800s built educational communities, fostered critical consciousness, and crafted notions of education that centered liberation as the purpose of knowledge (Tillman, 2004b; Williams, 2005). Rather than navigate and uphold the educational infrastructures of racism, however, Black resistance to whiteness took root in K-12 curriculum and pedagogy (Au et al., 2016; Fairclough, 2007; Walker, 2001). Indeed, while vastly underfunded in comparison to white schools, Black schools were often the only public space for Black communities to develop and communicate systemic challenges to these oppressive constructs, and in the few teachers who navigated white educational infrastructures, lessons for both navigating whiteness and overthrowing systems of racism went together (Walker, 2000; Williams, 2005). So, too, with Historically Black Colleges and Universities; while many were founded by white philanthropists, these institutions often claimed space for critical thought to develop and spread (Brown, Donahoo, & Bertrand, 2001). Despite the best attempts of public leaders and contemporary colonial administrators, schools and colleges became spaces, even if just temporarily, where Black educators could intentionally resist the impacts of colonization through the critical education of Black children (Brown & Davis, 2001; Foster, 1997; Ricard & Brown, 2008; Walker, 2001).

From the beginning of schooling then, Black people challenged the notions of "educator" and "education," adopting a community-centric approach out of the necessity of survival (Walker, 2000; Williams, 2005). Much of this resistance was crushed by the impact of *Brown v. Board of Education*, which white supremacy interpreted as justification for the closure of Black schools and removal of Black educators (Bell, 2004; Hudson & Holmes, 1994; Tillman, 2004b). As Tillman (2007) clarified, "The firing of African American principals led to the silencing of voices and exclusion of specific racial, social, and cultural perspectives that were critical to the education of Black children" (p. 55). The closure of Black schools simultaneously served as justification to end what at that point was one of the only substantial Black professional pathways to the middle class: teaching (Tillman, 2004b).

In addition to decimating what had been growing Black economic stability, adding to the impoverishment of Black communities, white schools felt no pressure to hire the now huge pool of African American educators experienced with and dedicated to teaching Black children (Moore, 1977). As Black children were legally forced into the closed arms of schools designed by and for white educators, the systemic silencing of Black educators was strengthened. The *Brown* decision legally validated the closure of intentionally Black spaces, which limited educator capacity to foster Black thought, at least within schools. Instead, intelligence and success—already defined solely by the whiteness that all public education was designed to perpetuate—became even more entrenched in whiteness. In short, desegregation helped remove both Black educators and Black schools from existence (Hudson & Holmes, 1994; Tillman, 2004a, 2004b).

Derrick Bell (2004) challenged the prevailing mainstream, thinking about the desegregation effort as transforming apartheid-era schooling, and instead suggested that fundamentally, activists should have been arguing for equality of resources. His point was that in hindsight, white people, and the courts, never agreed to transform white schools into culturally responsive, affirming processes of educating Black children. Segregated schools, he argued—echoing W. E. B. Du Bois's arguments almost 70 years earlier—were not the problem; white racism, and the marriage of white supremacy with schools, *were* the problem (Bell, 2004). Indeed, writing while the US was denying the status of African Americans within its borders, and simultaneous with the growing wave of Nazi genocide in Germany, Du Bois (1935/2004) argued that "race prejudice in the United States today is such that most Negroes cannot receive proper education in white institutions" (p. 424). Twenty years before the *Brown v. Board of Education* decision, Du Bois predicted further: "If the public schools of Atlanta, Nashville, New Orleans and Jacksonville were thrown open to all races tomorrow, the education that colored children would get in them would be worse than pitiable" (p. 424). He concluded that such integrated schooling ". . . would not be education" (p. 424). Du Bois, and Bell after him, were not necessarily proponents of Black-only schools, but instead, argued that white schools—and the white educators who ran them—would not have the interests of Black learning, and certainly not Black-affirming learning, at heart (Watkins, 2001).

Despite these historic calls to deepen the battles for educational equity beyond access to white schooling and white-educators, and despite ongoing battles to overthrow standardized assessments and their racist foundation and contemporary racist biases, school systems still largely adhere to standardized assessments developed and maintained by global for-profit industries (Au, 2009; Darling-Hammond, 2010). This adherence maintains the historic purpose of schools as whiteness, ensuring intellectual adherence to white thought and the ongoing dismissal of Black children, Black thought, and Blackness. Without desegregation efforts, Black-affirming educational spaces might have persisted, yet instead, schools have become even more entrenched as the *de facto* method of educating for white supremacy. As Richard Wright (1953/1995) clarified in the years leading up to *Brown v. Board of Education*, this widespread global imposition of whiteness as education ultimately incubated "frog perspectives."

> This "frog perspective" which causes Asians, Africans, American or West Indian Negroes to feel their situation in terms of an "above" and a "below" reveals another facet of the white world, that is, its "whiteness" as seen and felt by those who are looking from below upwards.
>
> *(p. 8)*

Wright's thinking here can be applied directly to the success of whiteness as schools, wherein those in opposition to the violence of whiteness ultimately are taught to internalize the very negativity fueled by the schools they were legally obligated to attend. Schools have continued the purpose of defining whiteness as education, and thus maintain a silencing purpose for most African American children, whose educational success continues to be defined by tools that measure adherence to whiteness and presumed white standards. This intentional silencing is thus referred to as "ideological lynching," where Black people are forced to ingest the many racist images, messages, and interactions that constitute schooling, causing incredible psychological, emotional, cognitive, and physical harm (Garrett-Walker, in press).

Our point here is that schools intend to serve as a tool for colonization and a method for enforced assimilation, teaching as if there is only one form of English, eradicating accents, culture, and ways of being that exist independently, or simply differently, from the binaries of whiteness. Since schools have been violently thrust upon communities of color, however, people have resisted and done what was needed to navigate an oppressive capitalistic society, nodding silently while turning the other cheek, plotting systemic overthrows, or at the least, learning to read on their own. Blackness has survived in all manners of expression, including music, dance, food, poetry, spoken word, plays, films, clothing, ways of speaking. Blackness has thrived as conversations over the centuries, engaging in global analyses while rooting in local resistances. Black people, en masse, have never capitulated to the intents of schooling as colonization, just as many educators, teachers, school leaders have never agreed with the intent of their jobs. Resistance is precisely what has enabled us as co-authors to write and extend arguments made by many who came before us, who we walk with now. And because of the resistances of others, the intentional recording of critical thoughts that map out resistance strategies, we turn attention towards clarifying what we know about Black leadership within racially hostile school systems.

What We Know About Becoming and Being Black Educators

Much has been written about Black teachers and Black school leaders (Foster, 2005; Foster & Tillman, 2009; Moore, 1977; Murtadha & Watts, 2005; Tillman, 2007). Despite this depth of literature, what is framed as mainstream writing on leadership centers white perspectives, with Black voices funneled into silos about diversity, social justice, or dismissively framed as research studies (Khalifa et al., 2013; Lopez, 2003). As Brooks (2019) argues, ". . . the knowledge base of the field of educational leadership has been shaped by whiteness—and a noticeable absence or marginalization of the voices of scholars of color" (pp. 35–36). Neither literature on Black school leaders, nor a focus on preparing Black school leaders, are common in principal preparation programs, which largely continue a white-dominated approach to leadership preparation (Echols, 2006; Foster, 2005). Rather, ". . . the emphasis of programs in departments of educational leadership, indicate a privileging of voice that often excludes the historical, theoretical, intellectual, and practical knowledge of African American school leaders" (Foster & Tillman, 2009, p. 2). This privileging of white voice is reinforced by mainstream school leadership literature that continues to deny the "unique history, leadership, constructs, and present-day circumstances that contribute to effective leadership in schools where students of color enjoy academic engagement and achievement" (p. 1). "Since everyday racism involved a socialization process," Dantley (2009) argues, "purpose-driven school leaders then understand that not only the policies and procedures on which educational leadership behavior is grounded, but also the curriculum and pedagogical methods traditionally used in schools are stepped in racist and socially marginalizing discursive practices" (p. 46). The intentional result of "This standardization of educational leadership behaviors suggests that there is essentially one way to lead schools that all leaders should exhibit for all students" (Khalifa et al., 2013, p. 490), and that this one way promotes anti-Black school structures while proclaiming a false non-racial approach (Epstein, 2008).

Given this pervasive race-neutral presumption that all children, and indeed, all school leaders, should approach education the same way reinforces ". . . educational leadership practice . . . [as] . . . primarily to reproduce these conditions rather than challenge them" (Khalifa et al., 2013, p. 500). Even leadership models and practices framed as social justice or transformative-oriented "are mostly colorblind, and are measured almost exclusively within the discourse of high-stakes tests" (p. 497). This avoidance of engaging in the history and contemporary context of Blackness, both in terms of Black students and in terms of Black school leaders, reinforces a silencing that "limits our ability to develop ways to improve schools and communities for children who live in poverty and children of color who are becoming the majority in this nation's schools" (Murtadha & Watts, 2005, p. 591). This silencing further reinforces the whiteness of the teacher workforce, as well as the realities that many teachers simply do not live in, and are not familiar with, the geographic, cultural, and racial realities of students of color (Epstein, 2008; Rogers-Ard, Knaus, Epstein, & Mayfield, 2012). In the same vein, "Many school leaders do not see urban communities, in part because they drive into them from their homes in the suburbs without ever engaging in or with the community" (Khalifa et al., 2013, p. 506). The impact of this distance is that, as Kalifa et al., argue, "Ideologically, culturally, and educationally, these spaces are invisible to many school leaders" (p. 506).

While the denial of critical voices, historical legacies, and contemporary realities of African American educational leaders has been challenged extensively over the past 150 years, there has been a failure of white-framed educational spaces to validate and integrate African American leadership theory into practice or praxis (Echols, 2006; Foster, 2005). Indeed, Foster and Tillman (2009) urge that "African American school leadership is an under researched, under-developed, and undervalued topic in the discourse on school administration and leadership" (p. 1). As Randolph (2009) argues, current research fails "to account for cultural models of leadership, and do not take into account structural impediments facing African American school leaders in the form of racism and sexism" (p. 23). Brooks (2019) contends that even while many academic disciplines began to engage in race analyses, educational administration chose to essentially ignore race, and has largely maintained this white-centric stance. This failure frames the entire field of educational leadership as white-centric, further contributing to a narrative of white theories as the preferred knowledge to guide school leadership practice (Brooks, 2019; Theoharis, 2019). Yet, "By studying African American educational leadership, researchers find that mainstream theories are increasingly deficient in understanding leadership from the perspectives of diverse cultural groups who fight for equity in this society" (Murtadha & Watts, 2005, p. 606). We want to note that despite the more recent trends around Black female school leaders (Garrett-Walker, in press; Mullen & Robertson, 2014; Reed, 2012), research about Black women's authentic voices in educational leadership remains extremely limited.

This deficit framing not only reinforces the historic exclusion of Black educators and school leaders but also requires an anti-racist approach by Black school leaders. Randolph (2009) urges that ". . . leaders in predominantly African American schools today need to acknowledge the context of racism existent in American society and fully prepare African American youth to advance within the racist structure of society . . ." (p. 22). And while certainly school leaders of all races have supported and encouraged Black-affirming educational approaches, African American leadership has modeled resistance to mainstream status quo education. Indeed, Dantley (2009) asserts, "African American leaders have had to spend time in surveying the status quo and strategizing ways to overthrow it in order to construct a fairer and more democratic new order" (p. 40). As we have attempted to highlight, however, there are too few opportunities to learn about, much less practice, strategies for interrupting systemic white supremacy in schools and school leadership preparation programs.

Black School Leadership Pathways

Prior to becoming a school leader, Black educators must journey through racist, inadequately funded schools, through a college curriculum rarely attuned to cultural responsiveness, and ultimately across a litany of racialized barriers that shape the teacher education pathway (Rogers-Ard et al., 2012). This was not always the case, as early slave communities were committed to teaching each other literacy and acquiring and sharing books, despite the risks of violent retribution from whites (Williams, 2005). Black communities ultimately began organizing well before the common school became normalized in the late 1800s and early 1900s, with African American teachers leading and teaching in freedom schools. White educators often soon wrestled control of such schools, however, demoting teachers and school leaders in an early pattern of removing Black expertise from classrooms and schools filled with Black learners (Watkins, 2001; Williams, 2005). Thus, since the beginning of early systems of schooling in the US, a deeply rooted anti-Black educator ethic has insidiously led to the cyclical removal of Black teachers and school leaders (Epstein, 2008).

This anti-Black educator ethic has continued through a range of institutionalized barriers intended to impede African American student success, precisely while excluding African Americans from serving as teachers, school leaders, or any educator with substantive control over classrooms or schools. Many of these barriers are well-documented, particularly around the systemic exclusions along the pathway to becoming a certified teacher (Epstein, 2008; Rogers-Ard et al., 2012). Once a person might consider becoming a teacher in a public school, regardless of whether they consider the impact of being a teacher within a racist system or not, they face structural barriers that reflect intentional exclusions. These barriers begin with limited numbers of low-income students, students with disabilities, students raised by single parents, and students who attend less-resourced schools (all of which are disproportionality Black), graduating from high school (Rogers-Ard et al., 2012). Many students of color who do graduate high school do so with cumulatively negative experiences, further discouraging interest in teaching within school systems that appear racially hostile (Rogers-Ard & Knaus, 2013; Rogers-Ard et al., 2012).

In addition to these contextual limitations to the sheer number of Black people interested in and educationally prepared to become teachers (in part due to lower high school and college graduation rates), a range of additional structural barriers have been placed to limit those interested in becoming teachers of color. One of the primary structural exclusions is in the method of teacher certification pathways, most of which remain despite recent interest in circumnavigating traditionalized university-based teacher preparation programs (Gist, 2017). The traditional route to become a teacher entails either a bachelor's, post-baccalaureate, or master's certification program. Most require a year of full-time, or nearly full-time, unpaid classroom teaching. While this supervised teaching experience might seem to be helpful, the experience requires the financial capacity to not have an income for the duration of a year (Epstein, 2008). These barriers add to racialized disparities in income and wealth: "In addition to tuition and difficulties balancing a full-time job while earning a credential, test fees, test study guide fees, tutoring fees, college application fees, fingerprinting fees, and other required fees become financial barriers that extend the wealth gap" (Rogers-Ard et al., 2012, p. 455). Indeed, as Madda and Schultz (2009) report, "the lack of adequate financial, academic, and social support mechanisms has served as a major roadblock in ability to pursue higher education" (p. 4).

Partly due to these economic barriers, traditional university teacher education programs remain predominantly white and female (Gist, 2019). This monocultural framing reinforces additional academic barriers, including a predominantly white university faculty, as well as a white-centric university curriculum and teaching approaches that further exclude students of color (Epstein, 2008; Gist, 2017; Rogers-Ard et al., 2012). Relatedly, "Because teacher education is largely delivered by a majority-white group of educators who haven't taught in an actual urban classroom for years, even decades, new teachers find themselves lacking skills needed to engage a diverse group of children" (Knaus & Rogers-Ard, 2012, pp. 7–8). Since most teachers are white, teacher education programs often focus on developing preservice white teacher racial consciousness through multicultural education, and these efforts are often limited to one course in a teacher education program (Bell, 2002; Gay, 2000; Sleeter & Milner, 2011). These courses (and programs) also focus primarily on preparing white teachers, not teachers of color (Sleeter, 2001). This again reinforces a white-centric preparation process that ignores the unique needs students and teachers of color have within the classroom (Epstein, 2008; Evans-Winters & Twyman Hoff, 2011; Foster, 1997). Additionally, these approaches ignore ethnic studies and teaching knowledge rooted in communities of color (Sleeter et al., 2019).

Despite the range of literature clarifying the racially disparate impacts of standardized testing, schools of education (and state certification boards) still largely require standardized assessments before, during, and at the conclusion of teacher certification programs (Au, 2009; Epstein, 2008; Petchauer, 2016). Maintaining this requirement reinforces a commitment to standardized testing that has been demonstrated to exclude students of color, those who speak English as a second (or third or fourth) language, people with disabilities, and low-income populations (Au, 2009; Epstein, 2008). This is despite substantive research on the effect of stereotype threat and the impacts that low self-efficacy can have on test score performance (Steele, 2011), as well as clear critiques of test validity, particularly in relation to perceptions of classroom teaching (Au, 2009; Bennett, McWhorter, & Kuykendall, 2006; Goldhaber & Hansen, 2010; Kohn, 2000). This barrage of standardized testing has been shown to serve as barriers that systematically exclude students of color on the pathway towards teaching (Rogers-Ard et al., 2012), yet their usage continues to be maintained at the national and state levels, and across teacher certification programs, often regardless of impact on measures of teacher quality (Angrist & Guryan, 2008).

Over the past 25 years, opportunities to circumnavigate the barriers associated with traditional teacher education programs have ironically increased opportunities for a "temporary teaching force that is predominantly white and often unexposed to cultural nuances, linguistic differences, local contexts, and racial struggles that shape classroom dynamics and out-of-school life" (Knaus & Rogers-Ard, 2012, p. 4). This growth of alternative routes to teaching and alternative certification processes (for more on the differences between the two, see Gist, 2017) were ostensibly to address teacher shortages. Many routes did lead to increases in para-professionals and career changers becoming teachers, and resulted in more racial and gender diversity in candidates (Gist, 2019). Yet not all of these programs were intentional about specifically supporting adults of color within local communities, nor did many of these programs focus on culturally responsive, race-conscious teacher development (Rogers-Ard, Knaus, Bianco, Brandehoff, & Gist, 2019).

Within the past 15 years, teachers of color-focused preparation efforts that have a specific commitment to being community-rooted are now often referred to as Grow Your Own (GYO) programs. While many argue for a diversification of the teacher workforce, "GYO additionally works to (re)construct this ideal by preparing teachers who are not only highly qualified but who are also best equipped to work with student populations represented in urban schools" (Madda & Schultz, 2009, p. 206). The focus of identifying that white teachers may not always be best equipped to become teachers for all student populations is unique to GYO programs, which still encompass a wide range of types. Many programs thus identify as GYO, including pre-college, college or university-based, school district-housed, and community-organized, and participants may start their pathways in middle school through to career changes with graduate degrees (Gist, 2019).

Recent work has applied a critical race theory approach, centering a race consciousness to specifically address barriers people of color face along the pathway (Rogers-Ard et al., 2012, 2019). In this way, GYO programs move beyond traditional and alternative route pathways to teaching through an explicit commitment to justice in relation to recognizing the many barriers teachers of color face across the pathway to and through classrooms (Gist, 2019). GYO programs thus remove "traditional barriers that stand between individuals from low-income communities and a career in teaching through provisions such as financial assistance, academic mentoring, and a comprehensive network of social support" (Madda & Schultz, 2009, p. 205).

Grow Your Own programs diversify the teacher workforce through increasing the placement of teachers of color in classrooms, and through increasing teacher retention (Gist, Bianco, & Lynn, 2019). Such efforts are based upon a more holistic approach to preparing and supporting professionals across their lifetime. Critical race theory-informed programs are thus defined by "highly collaborative, community-rooted, intensive supports for recruiting, preparing, placing, and retaining diverse classroom teachers who dismantle institutional racism and work toward educational equity" (Rogers-Ard et al., 2019, p. 27). Importantly, these efforts approach each of these four phases (recruit, prepare, place, and retain) as "addressing structural barriers and providing culturally responsive development along the lifetime trajectories of educators" (p. 27). Through ensuring additional support for pre-service and once-placed teachers, programs are able to continually center "concerns about racial and structural barriers aspiring TOC face within teacher education programs and schools" (Gist et al., 2019, p. 16). The important link here is that, while GYO programs proliferate, their success requires district partnerships with communities of color, and most directly, with school leaders who are prepared to transform the way they support incoming teachers to, in turn, transform their classrooms. This requirement pushes against the current school leadership field and would require centering the experiences of Black school leaders.

The range of barriers reinforcing a white teacher workforce are paralleled again, however, for Black teachers who leave the classroom for school and district leadership roles. As Tillman (2007) clarifies, "These barriers include ineffective recruiting efforts, hiring practices that are based on a White male standard, the lack of socialization and mentoring, and professional challenges that affect the retention of African American principals" (p. 59). Additional barriers include a lack of principal support while serving as a teacher and limited career pathways, reinforcing a racial isolation that is exacerbated as Black educators rise to higher leadership roles (Knaus, 2014). These barriers are expounded upon for Black women, who face increasing intersectional racism as they attempt to move into leadership roles (Knaus, 2014; Peters, 2011; Sanchez-Hucles & Davis, 2010). Indeed, "Although [B]lack women school administrators are usually elementary school principals assigned to the 'so-called tough, predominantly [B]lack school[s],' the expectations for their performance are extremely high" (Peters, 2011, p. 24). These differential expectations, despite being placed in more difficult to work within schools, are reinforced by a "triple jeopardy because of the multiple stereotypes associated with gender, race, and ethnicity that they trigger in others" (Sanchez-Hucles & Davis, 2010, p. 174).

Knaus (2014) conducted a study that clarified the lack of support along leadership pathways for three longtime African American women teachers who wanted to become school leaders. Despite sharing leadership aspirations with their white principals, each was ultimately dismissed as a culturally responsive classroom teacher that was not focused on standards-based approaches, despite principals having evidence that contradicted such stereotypical presumptions. As Knaus clarified, "The African American teachers saw their principals as antagonistic, unaware of what they were doing in their classrooms, and unaware of the cultural linkage to the larger Black community" (p. 436). In each of these cases, the principals withheld leadership opportunities from Black teachers, instead offering those opportunities to less experienced white teachers whose students had similar, or lower, test scores. These white leadership practices ultimately "justified a racially biased leadership development process that encouraged White leaders who do not have to demonstrate a commitment or connection to urban communities" (p. 439). Ultimately, this research reinforced the literature on school leadership preparation processes, clarifying that the entire pathway is wrought with structural exclusions limiting if and how African Americans can serve as culturally responsive leaders.

Despite these barriers, however, African American educators have maintained the historical arc of Black-affirming classrooms and schools, often intentionally pushing beyond traditionalized standards-based achievement in contemporary schools where they are punished for doing so (Knaus,

2014). "African American leadership in schools is rooted in historical and purposeful intellectual traditions that are collaborative in context and scope" (Foster & Tillman, 2009, p. 2). This collaboration, across classrooms, schools, and geographic communities, began historically as an effort by school leaders to empower newly freed slaves and has continued into contemporary classrooms that still struggle within white-framed constructs (Foster & Tillman, 2009). Because of the many barriers African American students must overcome to graduate intact from P-12 systems, because of the additional coping strategies required to navigate through higher education systems, and because of the contradictory role they are often placed in white-framed and often white-led schools, Black leaders exist on a foundation of resistance to white supremacy. Indeed, it is because of these dynamics and intentional commitments that suggests the burden of professional engagement, such that, "[African American principals] must reach out, work with, and listen to the communities around their schools . . . " (Randolph, 2009, p. 33). This commitment reinforces the complicated reality that Black school leaders' sheer persistence within the education system marks them as community leaders. Thus,

> . . . African American leadership in schools reinforces...advocacy that includes input and support from parents, teachers, and principals in planned and deliberate ways that fortify the unique historical and cultural context in which education and student achievement are honored and esteemed within the African American community.
>
> *(Foster & Tillman, 2009, p. 4)*

In summarizing Lomotey (1993), Davis and Madsen (2009) clarify two key roles for African American principals. "In the bureaucrat-administrator role," they argue, "the principal creates an organizational structure where African American children achieve academic success and facilitates a socialization function of the school" (p. 115). In the ethnohumanist role, however, "the principal is concerned with the individual life of students and the overall improvement of the status of African American people and the community" (p. 116). Davis and Madsen's study of African American school leaders concluded with a shared belief in "placing the school in the heart of the community" (p. 137). This ultimately required efforts to ensure a diverse teaching staff reflective of the community, as well as a "socialization process for teachers' entry and adjustment phase to work with students of color" (p. 138). These commitments to community reflect an intentionally oppositional approach to the whiteness of traditional school culture and of teacher and principal preparation programs that rely upon white supremacist frameworks of knowledge. It is this foundational commitment, to root the purpose of school within African American communities and to cultivate a school-wide climate that translates such a purpose within the classroom, that this book is based.

Applying Critical Race Theory as Method

To approach a range of differently raced Black school leaders in ways that centered authentic experience and honest reflection, we applied critical race theory as a research methodology, shaping who we invited to participate, the types of questions we asked, the ways we engaged participants (feeding most during interviews, creating comfortable environments to share personal experiences), and the ways we analyzed interview transcripts for details and quotes. While we both have applied critical race theory in previous writings as a framework to examine educator development and racism (Knaus, 2014; Rogers-Ard & Knaus, 2013), this research project began with the use of CRT to help us remain centered on our purpose: to cultivate safe spaces for Black educators to share their racialized experiences as school leaders in authentic voices.

Our understanding and approach to CRT begins with Derrick Bell, who is often credited as being one of the founders of the critical race theory movement in academia (Delgado & Stefancic, 2012; Taylor, 2009). What began as a discussion of legal scholars and practitioners around how to center the perspectives of people and communities of color in ways that challenge the whiteness of US law unequally applied, has since been adapted to a wide range of disciplinary fields (Ladson-Billings, 1999). Indeed, critical race theory extends its legal studies roots to engage scholarship across seemingly every field (education, ethnic studies, gender studies, queer studies, but also nursing, health care, economics, sociology, writing assessment, teaching), and across the academic enterprise (including its use as a theoretical model, informing research methods, and shaping academic programs; see Gillborn et al., 2018). CRT's widespread application reflects limited scholarship centered on narratives of those most oppressed by systemic racism, and the need for models that help inform how academics and educators conceptualize of transformative change processes (Khalifa et al., 2013; Taylor, 2009).

Ladson-Billings's (1999) seminal article frames CRT in relation to education and educational research. Over 20 years ago, she warned of CRT's eventual cooptation, where CRT may inform "scholarly papers and debate, and never penetrate the classrooms and daily experiences of students of color" (p. 26). Ladson-Billings correctly predicted CRT's proliferation into mainstream educational research; a Google Scholar search of articles that mention CRT resulted in over 17,000 hits in the past four years.[2] CRT is indeed mainstream, though its adaptation has inevitably led to misappropriations, misapplications, and articles that cite CRT but do not fully clarify which tenets guide which aspects of research methodology, scholarly inquiry, or practical applications (Donner & Ladson-Billings, 2018). Ladson-Billings's challenge remains: "Adopting and adapting CRT as a framework for educational equity means that we will have to expose racism in education *and* propose radical solutions for addressing it" (p. 27). All CRT-framed work, we assert, must propose, engage, model, and/ or wrestle with solutions to the many forms of racism. This book, then, is an attempt to apply a critical race theory lens to expose racism and propose solutions to address the very forms of racism Black educational leaders experience, at all levels.

Our purpose is not to clarify all tenets of CRT, nor to fully clarify the history, critiques, or use in a wide range of structural change efforts, as many other scholar-activists have previously clarified CRT tenets in much greater detail, including Delgado and Stefancic (2012), Gillborn (2008), Gillborn et al. (2018), Ladson-Billings (1999), and Solórzano and Yosso (2001). Rather, we identify four specific tenets to frame our approach to educational leadership. These tenets include the permanence of racism (under which we include tenets we see as related), intersectional oppression (often referred to as intersectionality), voice and storytelling, and interest convergence. These tenets guide our thinking of research processes, educational leadership practices, and challenge the way mainstream US educators conceptualize of education more broadly, and the way most schools and districts approach their very purpose.

Racism is Everywhere and All the Time

The first critical race theory tenet is often argued to be the recognition of racism as a permanent aspect of Western society, or as we like to say, racism is everywhere and all the time (Zamudio, Russell, Rios, & Bridgeman, 2011). Indeed, we argue that the purpose of schools is to normalize and justify racism through a white supremacist alignment of curricula, teaching, assessment infrastructures, the design of school buildings, and the structure of the school day (Knaus, 2018). We extend Mill's (1997) notion of the racial contract to the reality that schools were created to violently colonize indigenous people—not only in our US context but across the globe. Legally requiring students to attend school systems that continue their colonial mission reinforces the systemic nature of racism. While certainly progress has been made since the imposition of colonial schools in the US, the very structure of the school day and classroom designs eerily resemble those of schools 100 (or more) years old (Spring, 2018). The permanence of racism tenet argues that the history of oppression in schools directly shapes contemporary classroom and school district practices (Zamudio et al., 2011). CRT ultimately views schools as preparing children to navigate within the rigid ways of whiteness, in ways that reinforce white supremacy (Knaus, 2018).

CRT defines racism as much more than the violent imagery of past Ku Klux Klan members, or the quiet affirmation by many whites of acts of violence against people of color (Gillborn, 2008). As Bell (1992) argued almost 30 years ago,

> . . . beyond the ebb and flow of racial progress lies the still viable and widely accepted (though seldom expressed) belief that America is a white country and blacks, particularly blacks as a group, are not entitled to the concern, resources, or even empathy that would be extended to similarly situated whites.
>
> *(p. 7)*

Instead of a focus on overtly racist individuals, CRT highlights how this lack of concern for Black people and communities reflects white supremacy enacted through multiple forms of racism spanning macro, micro, and individual levels.[3]

Macro-level racism is enacted through systemic, structural level laws, federal funding priorities, and decisions often based upon past racially disparate practices. These include racialized inequities in school funding, racial segregation in schools, racially biased college admissions processes, and related systemic exclusions of people of color based upon the continued use of racially biased processes (Ladson-Billings, 1999; Taylor et al., 2009; Zamudio et al., 2011). Critical race practitioners thus examine and document how the majority of racial disparities—in housing, health, economics, education, and any other social indicator—are intentional outcomes of local, state, and national policies designed to maintain white supremacy (Delgado & Stefancic, 2012; Gillborn, 2008). Redlining, or the historic practice of excluding communities of color from living in specific white-zoned geographic neighborhoods, reflects this intentional racism, showing how geographic segregation has remained despite years of efforts to desegregate communities and schools (Delgado & Stefancic, 2012). These macro-level policies shape the value of homeownership and protect white property investments, while also directly limiting school enrollment block-by-block (Falck, 2012; Orfield & Joint Center for Political Studies, 1983). Thus, the very schools that Black educational leaders work within are framed by (a) systemic racism shaping the communities served by a school or district boundaries, (b) racially biased funding formulas, and (c) pathways to certification that reward white access to higher education (Knaus & Rogers-Ard, 2012). Calls to diversify the educator workforce without recognizing the macro-level racial barriers that exclude people of color from even entering into the teacher education pipeline are one example of how macro-level racism shapes the field of education.

CRT practitioners also highlight micro-level practices that make up the day-to-day of educational racism. Indeed, critical race theorists see "mainstream education as one of the many institutions that both historically and contemporarily serve to reproduce unequal power relations and academic outcomes" (Zamudio et al., 2011, p. 4). While macro-level racism shapes who lives in which communities, micro-level practices include the everyday operation of schools and districts, the structure of classrooms, required curriculum, teacher expectations and support, and localized school funding. Curriculum theorists help clarify how the US-based school system has maintained a commitment to teaching white-centric, English-only perspectives, even when integrating ethnic studies or more truthful histories (Au et al., 2016). Thus, the everyday English-only curriculum infuses through every subject, even those intending to promote multilinguality, prioritizing standardized English over all other Englishes, ignoring the vast linguistic range found in classrooms across the US (Barbian, Gonzales, & Mejia, 2017; Zamudio et al., 2011). CRT practitioners thus call out that what is taught in schools is often considered "politically neutral" (Zamudio et al., 2011, p. 95), hiding the historic white supremacist intent of mainstream US schooling (Au et al., 2016).

The reliance upon standardized assessments based in Eugenics to measure what children know created an anti-Black, anti-people of color way of thinking about knowledge (Au, 2009). Within the curriculum and assessment of white supremacy, the ways schools are organized, which children are offered which opportunities to learn what curriculum, and how teachers are allocated all contribute to the infrastructures of racism (Darling-Hammond, 2010). Classroom management and disproportionate punishment systems that specifically target Black youth create a slate of micro-level policing practices that prepare students for the school to prison pipeline, further limiting who can access what sorts of curriculum (Cartledge, Gibson, & Keyes, 2012; Gooden, 2013; Heitzeg, 2016). How the curriculum is taught (and by whom) has long been a CRT focus, with multicultural education, culturally responsive teaching, and ethnic studies serving as examples of how to diversify a white-centric curriculum and teaching approach (Banks, 2006). That all three are still seen as alternatives to mainstream education reflects the commitment to day-to-day racism by requiring students of color to learn whiteness without any critical foundation or challenge (Au et al., 2016).

A third type of racism is based on individual practice, though again, the focus is not on the stereotype of a white hooded racist, but instead, institutionally supported behaviors that center and normalize white supremacy. CRT practitioners often refer to these behaviors as microaggressions, a term that emanated from Chester Pierce's (1970) early research on documenting how racism is systematized through everyday offensive mechanisms. While "often innocuous," Pierce, Carew, Pierce-Gonzalez, and Willis (1978) describe microaggressions as "subtle, stunning, often automatic, and non-verbal exchanges which are 'put downs' of blacks by offenders" (p. 66). We note here that microaggressions were first framed in relation to anti-Blackness, though the term has since been applied to many anti-people sentiments that reinforce oppression. Allen (2010) demonstrated how middle-class Black males and families similarly experience systemic microaggressions, reinforcing that class is not a shield from the anti-Black racism of microaggressions.

Rollock (2012) clarifies how microaggressions include false affirmations and racist comments that, when compared to the myth of racists wearing white sheets, are more easily dismissed as minor offenses. Microaggressions, according to Rollock, "are 'missed' as being racist not just because of their subtlety but because of an inherent misconception that 'nice' people cannot be racist" (p. 519). This reframing of racist incidents as white supremacy normalized through everyday interactions demonstrates the systemic way in which Black people are targeted by racism (Pierce, 1970; Rollock, 2012; Solórzano, 1998), linking the individual practice of microaggressions to micro- and macro-level practices. Thus, the term racism, as used throughout this book, reflects these multiple levels operating at the same time and presumes that racism has informed the past, the present, and will continue to inform the future, at least until we transform all interconnected forms of oppression.

In the meantime, CRT's framing of the permanence of macro, micro, and individual level racisms provides a context to examine other commonly used tenets. One such tenet is the social construction of race, or the notion that race does not have fixed, legal meaning, particularly when considering skin tone, multiraciality, language diversity, and the myriad types of people that are classified as "Black" (Delgado & Stefancic, 2012). Race continues to be socially constructed in ways that reinforce one-drop rules and binary thinking, with monoracial assumptions that place people into one category of race (such as Black) instead of recognizing the vast array of multiraciality (Knaus, 2006). This binary thinking does not allow for consideration of intersectionality, nor does this allow for a more full recognition of the way people are raced as a violent construction of identity coercion (Collins & Bilge, 2016).

One example of the ways Black leaders are raced came from a recent districtwide leadership meeting. The superintendent of the 35,000 student district, a Black-identified woman, mentioned the need for increasing Black principals. After the session, two principals challenged that the district-provided numbers of Black principals did not include them. One identified as Black and white, while the other identified as Black and Latino. Defensively, the superintendent responded that she meant Black people that others would identify as Black, to which both principals erupted in rage. This was clearly not the first time they had been raced as non-Black, and they would not let up, arguing that the microaggressions they faced from their white teachers were real, as was the Blackness of their parents. They carefully pointed out how they had been publicly raced by the superintendent (as not Black), and their challenge crystalized the binary thinking that shaped their experience. Black educational leaders, multiracial and monoracial alike, operate within a context where they are constantly being raced—by the students and families they serve, by their peer leaders and teachers across the district—and this hypervigilance adds to the context of microaggressions they face.

CRT's commitment to naming the processes in which race is constructed to oppress people of color builds upon another commonly framed tenet, that of race neutrality or colorblindness. More than the denial of race as a social construction, race neutrality stems from the notion that racism will end if everyone treats everyone the same (Delgado & Stefancic, 2012). Zamudio et al. (2011) clarify how "the notion of colorblindness is a product of liberal ideology that equates political rights with social equality without interrogating the many ways that race and racism play out in contemporary society to reproduce ongoing social inequality" (p. 21). Law students, for example, learn how racism is a normalized foundation of "the tone, culture, factual analysis, and reasoning of the practice of law" (Jordan & Harris, 2006, p. 11). The very way law is taught reinforces the false notion of race neutrality by hiding behind language as falsely objective. Jordan and Harris continue: "In addition to internalizing the labels of 'relevant' and 'irrelevant' facts, students learn how to write objectively. The dominant perspective is described as neutral and objective . . ." (p. 11). Black educational leaders continually see how the false notion of objectivity is actually a white-supremacist foundation built into the assessment system (Au et al., 2016). Claims at colorblindness ultimately deny anything not-white, thus dismissing the need for culturally responsive approaches, ethnic studies, or student of color-centered learning approaches (Khalifa et al., 2013; Knaus, 2018).

Shonda, one of the principals and now district leader in this book, went through an interview process that precisely illustrates the false claims at colorblindness. During a districtwide public interview, Shonda was asked how she would be a leader for all children. As the only Black candidate, the implication was clear. Not only did other (white) leadership candidates not get asked that question, the question itself was a setup. Of course, her role would be to support all children. The implication, however, was that she would need to utilize a race-neutral approach, and the interview panel wanted to know how she, as a Black leader, would enact such an approach. Her answer challenged the panel's colorblindness—she asserted that culturally responsive approaches required educators to engage culturally with each child individually, and that meant understanding each child's many social identities. Her answer called into question the panel's notion of race neutrality, and she pushed deeper, arguing that resources needed to be divvied up to those with the most need as well. While she may have made the interview panel uncomfortable, Shonda was clear that their discomfort needed to be challenged, as did the false and outdated liberal notion of treating children as if they are all the same.

A third commonly used tenet is the property investment in whiteness or the notion that whiteness is a property that the state will protect. As Bell (1998) argued, "The law recognizes and protects this property right based on color, like any other property" (p. 9). In much of the previous history of the US, Black people were "constructed as property" (Ladson-Billings, 1999, p. 17). While white people historically sought legal resources to maintain their right to own people and land stolen from indigenous people, today, white people often resort to calling the police and weaponizing the state to remove Black people from using public areas (Austin, 1998; Jones, 2014). Every few months, an example of whiteness as property erupts on social media, with Barbeque Becky, Permit Patty, Cornerstone Caroline, Golfcart Gail, and Pool Patrol Paula all demonstrating how white women call the police on a Black person most often for sharing public space (Farzan, 2018; Herron, 2018; Hutchinson, 2018). The whiteness-as-property tenet clarifies how these white women are enacting a set of practices that have historical links and contemporary impacts. From disproportionate policing and sentencing to disparate interest rates, Black people are intentionally victimized by legal protections of whiteness (Austin, 1998; Bell, 1992).

This legal investment in whiteness directly shapes Black educational leadership as well. One example comes from the second author's experience teaching in a high school. A fight broke out during an afternoon break between classes, and students rushed in front of the school to watch. When the second author arrived outside the school building, the principal, an African American male, was surrounded by three police officers. As the chaotic scene continued, with a few officers restraining a handful of students, an officer continued to ask why the principal was in front of the school. Within seconds, students and staff encircled the police and principal, urging the police to let him go. Meanwhile, a white neighbor, who had not been seen outside at all, cut through the circle and pointed at the principal, claiming he had started the fight. The white neighbor continued to say how he always saw the principal out in front of the school. Without asking anything about the white neighbor, the principal's hands were soon handcuffed behind his back. It took the school resource officer to interrupt the pending arrest to clarify that the principal was indeed the principal. At the schoolwide townhall the following evening, the principal reminded the mostly Black audience that no matter how professional Black people may be, many white people will still see only their Blackness as a threat to be contained.

A conversation with a multiracial Black doctoral student highlighted another CRT tenet, academic interdisciplinarity. At a sushi restaurant in Honolulu, a few colleagues discussed the purpose of education while munching on grilled squid, hamachi, and roasted eggplant. The doctoral student repeatedly asked for scholarship by mothers of color, and in particular, Black mothers of color. Her status as a full-time student at one of the nation's preeminent universities, with quite a range of well-known professors of color, was not lost on the two faculty members who began offering a list of well-known mother-scholars (including Audre Lorde, Barbara Christian, and Alice Walker, to name but a few; see also Collins, 1987; Roberts, 1997). The doctoral student was extremely frustrated by the lack of access her own faculty had provided in comparison to these many examples, as indeed, most of her reading list consisted of white scholars, with a few sprinklings of academics of color whose work was largely relegated to traditionalized research studies. Those who center their identities and positionalities—Black, woman, mother—in the work were simply not seen as relevant to the canon of educational research and scholarship, reinforcing the very clear need for interdisciplinary approaches to address educational racism, including the centering of ethnic studies, gender studies, queer studies, disability studies, and related oppression studies as frameworks.

Derrick Bell's foundational scholarship is increasingly accessed through excerpts in compiled critical race theory readers or through short pieces assigned by undergraduate and graduate programs in education. Yet actually reading entire books or legal articles by Bell, however, appears increasingly rare within the field of education. The relegation of one of the core founders of critical race theory to the corners of formal study in education reinforces his very approaches: interdisciplinarity is key to race-informed academic activism. Far too often, Black educational leaders review literature determined by others to be relevant to school leaders, just as teachers too often review literature determined to be of use by education faculty. When faculty limit the critical engagement to only those allowed to write mainstream texts, a systemic exclusion of Black and people of color authors persists. CRT urges us to push against these boundaries and binaries to more fully engage in critical Black-centric studies.

For the purposes of this book, we include the social construction of race, the myth of race neutrality, the property investment in whiteness, and interdisciplinarity under the tenet of the permanence of racism as each adds contours to definitions of racism, clarifying how systems serve to promote white supremacy while specifically maintaining anti-Black practices. When applied to Western-based education systems, the permanence of racism tenets culminate in a societal agreement around the purpose of schools: to silence children of color (Knaus, 2011). The way to do this silencing is to convince educators—particularly educators of color—to speak *one* English, to teach *one* way, to all students (race neutrality), to construct racism as historical, and to acquiesce to standards. Those aiming to disrupt systems of racism, then, particularly from positional leadership roles, must begin with a recognition of the totality and permanent nature of racism and recognize schools as the societally agreed upon method of teaching that racism. Similarly, efforts to evaluate the effectiveness of teaching align with measuring acquiescence to whiteness. Black educational leaders, then, are intended to be head slaves guiding educational plantations, convincing teachers and students alike that all will be better, at least for the individual listening, if one just turns into their desks, and away from their culture(s), language(s), histories, and identities.

Intersectional Racism

One of the most effective ways to stifle critical thinking about racism is to frame racism as only about race, instead of also about the intersections of all identity-based oppressions. While we earlier defined racism within the context of macro, micro, and individual levels, intersectional racism links any engagement with racism to other parallel forms of oppression. Bell's (1992) early CRT thinking framed a race and class analysis: "It is now clear that racial equality will not be achieved without a continuing effort by blacks at every socioeconomic level" (p. 905). Bell was writing at the same time as Crenshaw (1989) and Harris (1990), both of whom argued for a centering of Black women narratives. Crenshaw and Harris, along with Patricia Hill Collins, Audre Lorde, June Jordan, Barbara Christian, Zora Neale Hurston, and many others, have carried on a tradition of applying intersectional lenses to race, gender, class, and sexualities. Zamudio et al. (2011) argue that

> . . . CRT feminists have made the concept of intersectionality a central feature of CRT analysis in order to capture the unique experiences that emerge when race intersects with gender and class structures as well as with sexuality and citizenship status.
>
> *(p. 37)*

Crenshaw (2009) distinguished between three categories of intersectionality, including structural, political, and representational. These distinctions are helpful to recognize how intersectional oppression operates within and across systems to maintain power imbalances in ways that reflect the dynamics of racism. For example, with structural intersectionality, Crenshaw explains how many responses to violence against women, for example, fail to recognize the dynamics of class and race, normalizing relatively privileged white women's experiences as impetus for crafting solutions to much more complicated problems. Within leadership conversations, a structural intersectional lens could clarify the limitations, for example, of recent efforts to support Black youth through the creation of men of color or Black men specific programs in schools. While these well-intended programs may proffer support for cis-gendered Black male youth, what they often fail to do is engage gender binaries, address sexualities, class, immigration, and intentionally exclude Black female youth. Structural inequalities abound within efforts to interrupt racism, often by strengthening other forms of oppression (such as sexism, classism, heterosexism, ableism, and so on).

Crenshaw (2009) clarifies political intersectionality as highlighting, "the fact that women of color are situated within at least two subordinated groups that frequently pursue conflicting political agendas" (p. 217). Using the prevalent example of rape and violence against women, Crenshaw argued that many justice-oriented lenses are single-issue focused, and thus inadequate to address "the compound marginalization of Black women victims, who, yet again, fall into the void between concerns about women's issues and concerns about racism" (p. 217). Within a leadership conversation, efforts to diversify leadership fields often focus on increasing numbers of women or on leaders of color, without engaging the specific barriers that women of color, and in particular, Black women, may face from white people and from men, including men of color. Crenshaw earlier highlighted how, as Black men and white women struggled for equality, they often left out Black women, essentially urging patience rather than intersectional coalition-building (Crenshaw, 1991; Delgado, 2011).

Representational intersectionality, the third category, engages in "the production of images of women of color" (Crenshaw, 2009, p. 236) while complicating the way those images are challenged as insufficient and problematic. Crenshaw provides an example of how mainstream hip hop has historically been challenged legally as presenting a "misogynistic assault on Black women by social degenerates" (p. 237). The representation of Black women, however, has long been misogynistic, and intersectional analyses might instead situate a history of white industries perpetuating (and making money off of) negative images that perpetuate violence against Black women (hooks, 1996). Only when Black male artists and performers also made money off of selling images and music that encouraged violence against Black women did a white critique against sexism begin, but this critique failed to address anti-Black male racism as well (Crenshaw, 2009). Representational intersectionality operates within Black leadership circles as well. Consider, for example, cases where Black men have been persecuted for being sexist or contributing to a climate of sexual assault, wherein previous white men in similar roles did not have to answer for maintaining that same anti-Black women climate and culture.

These three categories of intersectional lenses clarify some of the complexities in how oppression works to isolate aspects of identity, rather than engage in holistic analyses of how individuals are oppressed simultaneously by racism, sexism, classism, ableism, heterosexism, and related forms of oppression. But like most work centering complex systems of oppression, intersectionality has been used within progressive educational circles in ways that simplify and silence. Rather than using intersectionality as an approach to address the many ways oppressions interweave to create blankets to target specific hyper-oppressed communities (such as Black and queer trans women), intersectionality is frequently used as a catch-all phrase to mean multiple positionalities. At a statewide meeting for school principals and district leaders, a concurrent workshop labeled "Intersectionality" offered participants a chance to name their many positionalities, including parent, daughter, geographic location, positional leadership, and fan of particular sports teams. The next day, another keynote speaker described being intersectional, as both a person of color and an educator. A parallel convening in another state saw the same watering down of intersectionality into the many roles people in leadership play throughout the day. While all three examples were engaging in relevant work, they were also appropriating critical race theory and intersectionality, entirely missing the point of examining systems of oppression for the purpose of proposing solutions. Examples such as these abound across social media, as another CRT tenet becomes more mainstream, removing anti-Blackness from the definition of the term, further silencing those who identify oppression for the purpose of transformation.

Voice and Storytelling

Because whiteness will interpret and soften critical challenges to the status quo, CRT centers the specific voices and counter-narratives of those most directly targeted by intersectional racism. Thus, the third CRT tenet we center is voice and storytelling. As Delgado and Stefancic (2012) clarify, "Critical race theorists have built on everyday experiences with perspective, viewpoint, and the power of stories and persuasion to come to a better understanding of how Americans see race" (p. 38). "One premise . . . ," Delgado and Stefancic (2012) argue, "is that members of this country's dominant racial group cannot easily grasp what it is like to be nonwhite" (p. 39). While the purpose of storytelling is not only to educate white people about race and racism, "The 'voice' component of CRT provides a way to communicate the experience and realities of the oppressed…" (Ladson-Billings, 1999, p. 16). Storytelling has long been used as a way for Black and indigenous communities to share lessons, communicate values, and honor those who have come before. Thus, CRT builds upon these historic cultural traditions by centering narratives that clarify the nuances of intersectional racism. The focus on voice infuses through the research methods that guide this book, and parallel culturally responsive teaching and leadership, encouraging and committing to settings for Black educational leaders to authentically share their experiences.

CRT's framing of voice "is often characterized as counter-storytelling or counter-narrative because it resists and often tells an opposing reality to the 'official' legal system or version of events" (Khalifa et al., 2013, p. 494). CRT's use of voice has largely focused on legal storytelling to identify systemic abuses and qualitative research methods that center the perspectives of individuals of color (Delgado & Stefancic, 2012; Solórzano & Yosso, 2002). As Jordan and Harris (2006) argue, "Narratives, when subversive instead of hegemonic, use an individual story to reveal a collective wrong" (p. 11). Many people of color often "suffer in silence or blame themselves," for the structural racism they navigate professionally (Delgado & Stefancic, 2012, p. 43), and CRT helps provide space to recognize collective experience. The sharing of such stories and experiences also can have tangible benefits for participants of color: "Storytelling and counter-storytelling these [marginalized] experiences can help strengthen traditions of social, political, and cultural survival and resistance" (Solórzano & Yosso, 2002, p. 32).

We argue elsewhere that the purpose of schooling should be to foster voice, both in students and in educators (Knaus, 2011; Rogers-Ard & Knaus, 2013). This notion of voice reflects schools valuing the identities of those particularly oppressed for being those identities. Thus, Knaus argues, voice ". . . is a concise capturing of the author's reality, responding to the author's culture(s), language(s), race(s), gender(s), sexuality(ies), ability(ies), religion(s), spirituality(ies), and class-based experiences" (p. 75). Schools often misinterpret voice as offering perspective, such as when administrators ask for student or family input. Both authors are regularly asked to help facilitate feedback sessions with Black families or students, often under the guise of needing to tap into student or family voice. Yet CRT-informed analysis would push back against input, arguing that tapping into Black family voice might require creating welcoming, encouraging settings that decenter racism and instead privilege critical insight around intersectional racism. Knaus asserts, "Voice captures and exudes passion, moving audiences to feel a depth of emotion that reflects the speaker's life" (p. 75), and this work requires much more than a survey or question and answer session. We argue that voice and counter-storytelling require intentional efforts to help people feel comfortable sharing experiences that are often extremely uncomfortable, potentially violent, and recognize that sharing such experiences puts the speaker at considerable risk. Hence, for example, the participants in this book use pseudonyms so they could more fully examine the multiple forms of intersectional racism that shape their experiences.

Interest Convergence

The fourth CRT tenet we apply is interest convergence, which Bell (1998) defines as the racial reality that ". . . civil rights policies, including affirmative action, are implemented for blacks only when they further interests of whites" (p. 39). Bell (1998) explains how most of the civil rights policies heralded as benchmarks towards equality ended up benefitting white people and white interests more directly, including "the Emancipation Proclamation, the post-Civil War Amendments, the decision in *Brown v. Board of Education*, the Civil Rights Acts of 1964, the Voting Rights Act of 1965, and Affirmative Action" (p. 158). Each of these decisions or actions were initially seen as progress by African Americans (and across the globe), but soon thereafter, another set of racialized barriers were erected (or resurrected) to maintain white supremacy (Bell, 1998). Thus, laws, policies, and even micro-level practices are implemented only when tangible benefits to whiteness and white supremacy are maintained.

Bell's seminal example of interest convergence is spelled out in the way *Brown v. Board of Education* is still taught as the foundation of racial equality in schools, despite that public schools have not been racially desegregated, and racial disparities are just as profound as ever (Bell, 2004; Darling-Hammond, 2010). Deeper, in the aftermath of the *Brown* decisions, Black teachers and school leaders were fired, Black schools were closed, and Black children were forced to attend white schools and be taught by white teachers, many of whom protested having to teach Black children (Bell, 2004; Tillman, 2004b). The *Brown* decision was ultimately carried out in part as an answer to the world's increasing focus on, and judgment about, US civil rights issues, especially given US resistance to the rise of Communism (Bell, 2004; Tillman, 2004b). Thus, *Brown* helped the United States' global image on civil rights, even as it closed Black-led schools, decimated Black educators and middle-class pathways, and created the conditions for in-school tracking and the expansion of disproportionate special education to remove Black children from white schools (Delpit, 1997; Foster, 1997; Tillman, 2004a, 2004b).

Khalifa et al. (2013) clarify how the standardized assessment industry further reflects interest convergence. As the pressures for high test outcomes have increased, pushout rates for low-testing Black and Latino students have similarly increased, removing lower-testing students from the academic sphere of white students (Au, 2009, 2013). Additionally, each new iteration of federal policy requiring standardized testing ensures testing corporations continue their access to the schooling marketplace (Au, 2009). Khalifa et al. (2013) argue that "even if small or moderate testing gains were experienced by Black and Latino students, it seems that White students and businessmen benefited so much more" (p. 494). Indeed, as global corporations and foundations continue their hold upon the curriculum, assessment, and teaching approaches used in public schools across the globe (Au, 2016; Knaus, 2018; Zeichner & Pena-Sandoval, 2015), achievement and opportunity gaps remain stable (Darling-Hammond, 2010; Madaus & Clarke, 2001). The benefits to global corporations have reached billions of dollars, while public schools that serve children of color continue to struggle with low funding, all while relying upon corporate curriculum and assessment packages that further reinforce measurements of inequality falsely defined as achievement gaps (Au, 2013; Au & Ferrare, 2015).

Applying interest convergence to CRT research, Stovall (2016) offers an important caveat around storytelling, suggesting that, "while a key component to CRT, it cannot exist as the primary contribution to the construct in education" (p. 277). Stovall challenges that CRT work cannot exist in "archived contributions in journals, book manuscripts, and edited volumes" (p. 281). Stovall's caution extends the notion of interest convergence, as CRT publications ultimately can be used to justify that racism is not limiting race-centered work. Bell argued just this point across his writings, ultimately highlighting that work in the service of anti-racism can just as equally be used to support racism. "The courage to confront racism," Bell (1998) asserts, ". . . should not obscure the fact that the powerful can employ our confrontative statements to serve their ends as effectively as they can those deplorable self-blaming comments by blacks" (xiii). Bell's reminder of interest convergence highlights the notion that CRT scholars are allowed to research and publish specifically because such work can still serve the interests of whiteness.

Returning to the permanence of racism tenet, continued efforts to exert control over Black bodies, minds, and expression reflects interest convergence. Voice alone is necessary but insufficient to challenge intersectional racism, and Stovall's (2016) reminder is essential here: "I cannot remove myself from the realities that are taking place in the communities like the ones from which I come" (p. 281). Who Black educational leaders are, where they come from, the communities they operate within are central to understanding what authentic, anti-racist Black leadership is and can be. The work of educational leaders committed to transforming schools—towards an affirming process that voices the many positionalities of Blackness—requires that ". . . we also need to consider the idea of rising against the state in a process beyond the page"

(p. 281). Thus, CRT serves as a hands-on guide, operationalized through the HEART model to foster self-awareness, collectivity, self-care, and the capacity to combat the continual effort to colonize Blackness and silence Black children, families, and educators. And as we began this chapter, rising against the state also requires that, like Rosie, we know when to remove ourselves from the everyday battles of positional leadership so we can survive, recuperate, re-energize, and renew the struggle.

Conclusion

As professional colleagues, we know that schools will work to teach the foundations of hate to all children, demonstrated equally effectively through pushout rates and repeated school shootings by white, suburban children. We know that schools will work to teach academic and social competitiveness in ways that reinforce capitalistic greed and global inequalities, just as schools will teach children to internalize systemic failure. Schools will continue to exclude and isolate, churning out students who doubt themselves, doubt their communities, and strive primarily for economic improvement even at the cost of maintaining systemic inequities. Yet we also know that life *must* be different. Education must also be affirming, loving, full of laughter, safety, linguistic diversity, and a full embrace of each of our individual parts, our many contradictory and complementary identities. The choice to struggle against schooling is ours so that we build upon the foundations that have long since been set by those who came before, who resisted and left many blueprints for our survival. Few of our ancestors' blueprints look anything like contemporary classrooms or schools.

Alicia Garza, co-founder of #BlackLivesMatter and the Movement for Black Lives, clarified our foundation: "When we say Black Lives Matter, we are talking about the ways in which Black people are deprived of our basic human rights and dignity . . ." (Garza, as cited in Watson, Hagopian, & Au, 2018, p. 20). Our goal is to not only achieve a dignified meeting of basic human rights, however. We aim to build systems of education that empower youth to be who they are, how they are, with a core foundation in knowledge of how to transform systems, everywhere across the globe, into soul-affirming processes, where we all leave work better prepared to love our families, communities, neighbors, land. Our focus and hope through this book is to center local, regional, and national conversation about school and school leadership on Black voices to strengthen our foundation in what Love (2019) refers to as abolitionist teaching. As equity efforts ebb and flow, we simply cannot imagine a way forward without the expertise of Black educational leaders, whose experiences highlight structural barriers while simultaneously illustrating a tapestry of dignified hope and renewal.

Notes

1 We use African American throughout this book as a term inclusive of the full Diasporic range of Black people, recognizing intersectional oppression, forced migration, recent immigration, multiraciality, and colorism all shape experience, identity, and power. We understand that Black is more inclusive of the Diaspora outside the United States, yet use African American and Black interchangeably throughout, following the everyday usage of most participants in this book.
2 Google Scholar search of "critical race theory" (including quotations) on December 3, 2019. Search was for articles published since 2015.
3 For more on definitions of racism, see Derman-Sparks and Phillips (1997).

2

THIS IS WHO WE ARE

Trey walks into the office with confidence, not arrogance; with intelligence and a touch of humility, lest a white person feel intimidated. Today, Trey wears black slacks, dress shoes, a button-up, long-sleeved shirt underneath a gray V-neck sweater vest and bow tie. He walks with his hands in his pockets or behind his back, as if he knows white folks fear Black men's hands. He has a ready smile, even though it's clear he is stressed. When asked how he is doing by a friend, he replies, "How much time you got?" As Trey shares some of his work-related challenges, his entire demeanor shifts from professional to angry and back within a short time frame. When he entered the office he was a model of professional cool, but as he felt safe, his body language shifted from his ramrod straight posture to a relaxed lean in his chair.

Trey is a tall, black, 45-year-old man with dreads. Several years ago, Trey, a native of Los Angeles, moved to the Bay Area with a dream of opening his own charter school; after working with African American men in an educational outreach program, he became a program manager at a private charter school. He then spent three years as one of two African American site administrators in a predominantly white school district. The pressures he faced there made him purposefully seek out leadership opportunities where he could have more impact on students of color. Always professionally attired, Trey began growing dreads when he became an Assistant Principal at one of the city's lowest-performing schools; after being in the predominantly white school system, he felt reborn as he worked within an entirely student of color population.

Yet today, he is feeling every bit of the shift. While the site staff is somewhat diverse, he is having communication difficulties with the Vietnamese principal who doesn't see him as an equal. One of Trey's main challenges is being seen as an instructional leader; even though he manages the testing process and other managerial tasks, he is seen mainly as a disciplinarian and therefore, the overseer of the largely African American student body. As the only African American person in leadership at the school site, another main challenge is being seen and acknowledged for what he brings to the table. Trey often has to remind his colleagues of how he grew up:

> Hold up. You don't know my background. I grew up in LA. I grew up Crips and Bloods all day. I grew up not owning a red shirt until I was in college because I grew up in a Crip territory. I grew up with Mansfield Gangster Crip all up on the walls. I grew up burying friends. I grew up with friends right now in prison.

Trey's background is an important part of how he moves as an African American educational leader, father, and community-builder. So, when other people, particularly other educators of color, do not see him in his multi-layered totality, he grows frustrated. If they cannot see him, he wonders, how will they be able to see their students?

Trey manages master scheduling, all discipline problems, special education resources, legal concerns, is the testing coordinator, and sees his role as being the glue to hold together the entire site. His principal, however, sees Trey as an outsider with different ideas about discipline: "Instead of addressing the teachers and what's going on in the class, it's putting an add-on or another program or whatever to fix the kids." Trey shares that between managing teachers who do not understand their students and dealing with a principal who is not invested in his growth and development, he became unsure about how long he could sustain in this toxic context: "You can come in and say, 'I'm a principal. I'm going to do this. I'm going to do that.' Teachers say, 'He's saying that, but I'm going to go to my classroom, and do something different.'" The disjoint between Trey and his principal reflects Trey's belief in growing students and teachers, versus a larger district approach to managing students and teachers.

Recently, Trey was invited to a two-day, district-sponsored Implicit Bias training. When he told his principal he would be at the training for two days, though, his principal did not approve: "I was like, 'Aren't we saying we're trying to do things better? Aren't we up here trying to make a change in these kids' lives? So why I can't go to a free training at the district?'" The principal relented and allowed Trey to attend, albeit for one day. At the training, Trey met a board member who told him his school would be closing at the end of the school year. "I was like, does [the principal] know? She was like, 'Yeah.' I couldn't believe it . . . but then I could, you know what I'm saying? Because that's how [the principal] does; keeping his stuff secret." Eventually, Trey was invited to a lunch meeting where the principal announced the school closure.

He was like, "The school is closing," but didn't have any other things to share. Like, no plan, no "This is the way it's going to go," nothing! That's when I knew . . . you know what I'm saying . . . I knew he had a plan.

Trey eventually found out his principal took a leadership position at the central office. Trey walked away from that experience thinking that being a principal may not be his path after all; his negative experiences at a charter school, in predominantly white school systems, and finally, as a leader in a predominantly African American school made him reflect on other ways he could support students and communities of color.

Studying Black Leaders

We begin this chapter where we introduce each participant and share details about their personal and professional lives to help readers contextualize their voices with Trey's leadership journey. When Trey is with people he trusts, he code-switches comfortably, peppering his words with euphemisms from his background. In writing this book, we also code-switch, writing for multiple audiences in ways that hide identifying information. Given the importance most participants attributed to masking their identities for fear of retribution, however, we have altered details to maintain participant confidentiality. Thus, while fundamental details regarding racial identity, years of experience, school level, and other markers have not been changed, locations and references to other identifying geographic, social, and educational indicators have been slightly altered. These alterations were made essential by the reality that many participants expressed concern for job safety if their real thoughts and experiences were found out. This is particularly disconcerting, as educators sharing experiences about racism and sexism, a systemic toleration for negative treatment of students of color, and other serious critiques that echo extensive literature about public schooling in the US should not be at risk for retribution. In the persistent racially hostile climate of schools and districts, moreover, the lack of tolerance for critical honesty that names racial hostility parallels the lack of respect given to students, families, and employees of color. This racial hostility is precisely what drove these Black educators into leadership roles, and understanding their commitments to navigating hostile racial climates requires listening to their experiences and professional pathways.

In applying critical race theory, we intentionally identified Black school leaders that we knew would be willing to talk about racism and their specific struggles navigating and transforming school systems as Black-identified professionals. We rested upon the notion of voice and counterstorytelling as a solution to the silencing impact of schools on students of color and administrators of color (Knaus & Rogers-Ard, 2012; Solórzano & Yosso, 2002; Zamudio et al., 2010). Thus, we encouraged participants to pick settings in which they felt most comfortable sharing their truths in raw language, and for many, that meant focus group settings with other Black administrators with whom they could connect, break bread, laugh, rage, and cry together. As researchers, we created safe spaces for these educators to rage against the system, knowing their words and voices would remain true. For others, that meant individual conversations with one or both researchers, and we honored individual requests to participate in groups or for one-on-one discussions.

For all participating leaders, we discussed the purpose of schooling in the United States as a silencing mechanism to ensure African American acquiescence and maintain white dominance. All participants paralleled critical race theory tenets at the outset, including a recognition that schools are defined and operationalized to justify the continued criminalization of African Americans who differ from the intended status quo of whiteness. They spoke about how their social, emotional, and physical well-being was a contradiction to serving as administrators, encouraging self-analysis of how to be a professional educator within a system that silences and justifies the killing of Black children around the world. They knew national dropout rates, and because of their proximity and dedication to Black students, knew children who were killed by police, by other children, and felt the impact of global anti-Black violence. Whether they had been denied the opportunity to teach, were impacted by a career of being silenced within the school and district office, or ultimately were forced out of the profession, they knew, well before we engaged in such discussions, that the educational infrastructure they were committed to unraveling is both unjust and unkind to African American teachers and administrators. Our point here is to remind readers that Black school leaders' professional lives reflect the pulse of anti-Black educational genocide, and any engagement in researching voices and perspectives of such must begin with the recognition of how opposition is experienced. Thus, our purpose was to create the conditions for discussion, to serve as facilitators, and our commitment here is to report back what we learned in honor of the voices of those we are dedicated to serving.

This book is based upon individual and focus group interviews with 13 school and district leaders. Eight participants joined in at least three of five focus group interviews, with four participants engaging in all five sessions. The remaining five participants were interviewed individually, at participants' requests. This added an additional layer of confidentiality and protection of participants concerned about linking their identity to their critical perspectives, due to potential backlash from colleagues and administrators. Each interview and focus group was audio-recorded, transcribed, and analyzed using grounded theory methodology and thematic coding. Both researchers reviewed all transcripts and co-generated themes, engaging in several reflective discussions to ensure the identification of all major themes and to recognize and engage with any contradictory information or perspectives. This process enabled themes to emerge within and across individual participant data sets, to allow for comparisons across job positions, genders, sexualities, school types (elementary, middle, and secondary), and years of experience. All names, identifying details, geographic indicators, and other revealing information have been omitted and/or altered through pseudonyms and other confidentiality measures designed to maintain the integrity and authenticity of participant experience and voice. Thus, details have been changed to obfuscate individual identities and limit reader capacity to identify schools and districts. While we have kept identity markers (racial identities, sexuality, gender) the same, additional information (e.g., children, family size, school type, positional role, geographic area, years of experience, and other pertinent details) has been altered across the sample to further hide the identities of participants.

Focus group discussions were facilitated by both researchers, and began with general questions about participant experiences within educator preparation programs, as classroom teachers, and then chronologically as participants progressed through to current leadership roles. During focus groups, participants became a close professional community, with participants increasingly engaging with each other outside of formal research activities. Indeed, focus group participants continue to support each other, offering space to discuss and reflect on current issues within their positions, as well as opportunities to strengthen each other's practices. These relationships coalesced around the focus groups, in part because the conversations were often cathartic, wherein participants built a shared language and community around the intense isolation and hostile racial climates that shape the context of their schools and districts.

Participating Educators

The sample (as clarified in Table 2.1) included six participants who identified as men and seven participants who identified as women,[1] all of whom identified as African American and/or Black. Years of combined experience as teachers and administrators ranged from 8 to 24, and all participants have served in formal positional leadership roles, from assistant principal to assistant superintendent. Six participants were currently in assistant principal roles, four were serving as principals, and three were in district leadership roles. Three educators had over ten years of school building and/or district leadership experience, and three participants had three years of leadership experience. Participants ranged in age from 34 to 51 years young. Several participants had young adult children, and several had newborns within the past two years.

We begin with snapshots of each participant in the hopes that future efforts can publicly identify individuals within a context of protected critical honesty. Indeed, we argue that future efforts at promoting critical Black educational leadership voices must be able to honor and respect these leaders as public intellectuals known for their critical awareness of, and action against, systemic oppression in schools. For now, however, the political, social, and professional backlash against

TABLE 2.1 Participants

Name	Age[1]	Degrees	K-12 Experience (years)	Current Role
Byron	43	Master's	18	Assistant Principal
Raine	36	Enrolled in Ed.D.	8	Principal
Dawn	34	Enrolled in Ed.D.	9	Principal
Jayson	30	Enrolled in Master's	10	Assistant Principal
Mason	51	Master's	16	Principal
Trey	45	Master's	16	Assistant Principal
Nicole	40	Enrolled in Ed.D.	18	Assistant Principal
André	44	Enrolled in Ed.D.	24	Principal
Shonda	42	Ed.D.	22	District Administrator
Alicia	47	Master's	12	Principal
Rosie	48	Master's	12	Assistant Principal
Ricardo	51	Master's	17	District Administrator
Jill	52	Ed.D.	23	District Administrator

1 Data were current at the time of study. Updates are found at the end of the book, in the *Where Are They Now* section

those who speak out about racism is tangible, and for these reasons, our current goal is to honor participant voices along the pathway towards transforming schools into processes of transparent trust, love, respect, and growth.

Rosie

Born in upstate New York, Rosie identifies strongly as a "New Yorker." While she has lived in the Bay Area for ten years, her New York accent and impatience at the slower pace of the Bay Area come across immediately. A tall, "thick" Black woman who often shaves her head, Rosie carries a powerful presence, which she attributes partly to her time in the US Army. A proud veteran, Rosie's muscular arms and wardrobe of hip athletic apparel suggest that she spends a lot of time in a gym. Rosie also carries her sexuality publicly, self-identifying as a "dyke, lesbian, queer Black woman." The Bay Area was initially a draw because of its reputation for leftist politics and queer-friendly orientations. Upon relocation, however, she soon realized that the openness to queer identities was largely limited to queer white men and women who fit within narrow confines of cis-gendered heteronormativity: "Shit, man," she clarifies, "Ain't no good to be really queer here, like trans or a Black woman lesbian. These muthafuckas ain't ready for us." Throughout her life, the notion of not being "ready for us" has been a guiding principle for Rosie. In all our conversations, moreover, Rosie continually states that in education environments, any time someone mentions equity, "they don't mean us." When pressed to define "us," she expands, "Anyone with fucking melanin or sexuality or, shit, anyone kinda different, poor, abused, anyone who can't hide that we are dealin' with real shit."

Since she can remember, Rosie has always spoken directly, in what she attributes to growing up in New York and being in the military. Rosie also developed an early social justice orientation, as her adoptive parents were devout members of the Bahá'í Faith, and firmly believed that growing up experiences should revolve around learning to advocate for those around us. Rosie specifically attributed her racial awareness to her father, whom she spoke of with great regard: "He is just present, you know, like he's hella confident in who he is." This confidence led him to raise Rosie within a multiracial family, with a household that included adoptees of color and white birth children in a way that challenged the family structures she saw around her. "Most of the families around us were single-race families," she remembered, "but our family had race conversations from an early age. Everything was on the table, all the time, and usually, in a good way." This focus on being able to talk about intersectional oppressions that shaped race, gender, and sexuality-based identities, in addition to adoptive influences, helped shape a deep commitment to social justice. "There's no other way," she argued, "social justice was the only way in my family."

In part because she was raised in a race-forward, multiracial, openly transracially adoptive, and queer-friendly family, Rosie developed an early focus on leading with who she is, knowing that others may not be ready to accept her regardless of how she presents herself. This orientation made her first years as a professional within customer service fields difficult, as the focus on being polite and superficially friendly was never her strong suit. Perhaps more deeply, Rosie just did not believe in being fake or in being nice to people who she saw as offensive to her or to other people. Rosie's abrupt approach, fast-talking demeanor, and social justice commitment made her work in education a continual tension, as she has remained student and family-centric, even as she pushes against her peers at every level, advocating for every social identity she comes across.

Rosie's professional pathway as an educator began when she decided she had had enough of customer service. She always had in the back of her mind that she'd be an educator, but remained reluctant, in part because she had negative experiences in schools while growing up. After spending a few years volunteering in an afterschool program, though, Rosie eventually became an adult education teacher. Five years later, she became the director of an afterschool program so that she could focus on programming and not be bound to the narrow curriculum her school required. After five years in that role, she transitioned to an assistant principal, where she has been for the past two years.

Trey

Trey, who introduced this chapter, identifies as an African American male and is in his late 40s. Born and raised in Los Angeles, Trey relocated to the Bay Area

15 years ago. He is a well-dressed, married father of four. In previous leadership roles, Trey wore his hair in a close-cropped fade, with sweater vests and bowties accentuating his six-foot-tall, athletic frame. Recently, Trey started growing dreads, relaxing his professional attire, transitioning to look more like the communities he works and lives within. This transition has reinforced his attention to detail, and his intentional focus on appearance helps him seem more accessible to teachers, students, and families. After years of working in afterschool programs and then adult education, Trey obtained his teaching credential and became a middle school teacher. After two years, he transitioned to a continuation high school, where he soon transitioned from the classroom to an outreach consultancy role, working directly with truant youth navigating back into schools or adult education programs. Trey's first administrative position was as an assistant principal at a charter school serving low-income children. After two years, he shifted to an affluent school district, again serving as assistant principal, enjoying the resource-laden experience for two years.

Serving as only one of two African American administrators throughout the entire district, however, took its toll, as did focusing his energies on primarily affluent children, mainly because of the many assumptions he faced as a Black male administrator:

> My principal was like—I guess he thought he was kind of giving me credit or a positive or whatever type of thing in a meeting but talking about me being there and how great that is. "We had an individual who had a prison background and everything, and he's able to relate to Trey . . . ." What? I've never been arrested, don't have a record. What are you talking about? And that's how he can relate to me, so that's your assumption about me and my experience? Both of my parents went to college, you know what I mean? Father was in an advanced degree program. College was always spoken about—period. Whatever I wanted to do, you're going to college. So that was always the expectation. Graduating from high school was a joke. There was no "Yay, I did it." It was like, "Okay, next thing. It's cool we're done with this, but I've got to go bounce to do something better."
>
> And even more so, walking around a campus, "You must have played ball, right? You're kind of tall. Basketball, right? Or you're kind of lean, track and field? Because you don't really look like a football player." Hold up, no, none of that. I played recreationally just to have fun. But that's not how I got through school. So, why is it that because I'm Black—now, when these white teachers walk through here, you automatically assume they got a PhD, and they got it on their own merit. But when I'm walking through the halls, "Come on, let's play basketball." And, at the same time, unfortunately, the same expectations presented to our students, as my minority students talk to me, it must be, "Why are you talking white? You're not from where I'm from. You don't understand my experience."

While he was having a positive impact on students, Trey ultimately realized his purpose was to support students of color, and specifically, African American children. He thus sought a leadership position where he could serve African American children and is in his third school, serving as an assistant principal. This current position reflects his desire to serve children of color, and is situated in the heart of urban decay; across the street from low-income housing, the school is on a main thoroughfare with liquor stores, fast-food chains, nail shops, and a funeral home surrounding the campus. Trey's current school has had a revolving door of administrators over the past six years, and although he enjoys this challenge, he is actively applying to principal roles to build up a sustainable leadership core.

Byron

Born in Texas, and raised in the urban bay area, Byron identifies himself proudly as being "hella Bay." With matching sweatpants and baseball cap representing a local community college, Byron presents a friendly demeanor. His late-40s age belies his clear athleticism, and his in-shape physique suggests a regular presence at a gym: upon discussion, it becomes clear that his gym of choice is often the school gym, where he can connect with young men and women beyond his role as assistant principal. Byron is an ardent sports fan, following the A's, Raiders, and Warriors, as well as local community college and high school teams. His fanaticism (he has season tickets to the Raiders and Warriors) was born from his own athleticism; he excelled in football during high school, resulting in heavy recruitment by several Division I colleges. Prior to graduating high school, however, his first daughter was born. Unable to pay for child care while finishing their senior year, he and his then girlfriend (and now wife) were forced to quit high school so he could work and she could raise their baby at home. He eventually worked his way through community college, and then a bachelor's degree, never able to take advantage of his athletic promise.

After a few years as a substitute teacher, Byron earned his teaching credential and taught for nine years before taking on administrative roles. As a classroom teacher, Byron taught math, and increasingly sought applied topics, eventually teaching business, economics, and politics. Byron's leadership trajectory began as a teacher on special assignment, mentoring new teachers in the school he taught at for his entire teaching career. He then left that school to become a dean of students at a rival high school in the district. He returned to his old school, where he serves as an assistant principal. While he formally left classroom teaching, he continues teaching a business incubation class every year, allowing him to mentor new teachers and stay connected to students. This class also requires students to partner with local businesses, helping Byron to maintain his community-wide presence. He is aware of the way in which he presents to the staff:

> I'm a unicorn. I'm the only one like me anywhere near this school: A Black man who can handle the work and still love my students. I'm constantly under attack, with all this white teacher insubordination. Even though we have the highest graduation rates in the district, they are hating on me, causing drama, bullying, harassing, because I am following policy. But when the white administrators do the same thing, they don't trip. I've learned to be consistent in inconsistent places, especially where teachers push against anything. Even when you do what they ask for, they push against that.

Byron is currently in his second year of service as an assistant principal at South High, a high school that shares its sprawling campus and range of services with a credit recovery program and an adult education program. The leadership team consists of a principal (the fourth in five years), two assistant principals, a dean of students, and a teacher on special assignment responsible for creating a learning community for ninth-graders.

Though only in his second year at the school, Byron is seen as the most experienced leader on campus, partly because of the context of principal turnover and lack of sustained presence, and because he has been in neighborhood schools for the duration of his 18-year career. He is thus sought out for any emergency first, before the principal, and regularly meets with teacher's union representatives, head teachers, and department heads, and is responsible for hiring new teachers and administrators. Additionally, Byron coordinates a team of five security personnel, which he refers to as the outcome of an "uncomfortable compromise that at least got police officers off campus." I asked several students and teachers who led the school, and they all agreed: Byron was the *de facto* principal, even as the district maintained the positional authority of the (mostly absent) principal.

André

Born and raised in urban Southern California, André has a large, quiet presence. Standing at 6'1", he leads with a warm, engaging smile, and when not wearing slacks, he wears baggy clothes and baseball hats as comfortable attire. His thick graying goatee and short, cropped graying hair frame his face, and with wrinkles leaving large imprints around his eyes, André looks like he has seen and been through a lot. A quick conversation confirms his appearance: André waits patiently to talk, often giving space first, encouraging others to share their voices and insights before he speaks. When he does interject, he speaks with a soft, confident authority that evokes wisdom and compassion developed along his 50 years of life. He asks questions, gives pause to answers, and his presence conveys experience with those who have been deeply traumatized.

To let off steam, and perhaps to balance his compassionate presence and calm demeanor, André is an avid sports fan, and his energy transforms from healer to voracious sideline coach when watching his favorite NBA team. In schools, André lets students know he is a fan, hinting at his personal life just enough to let students see him as similar to people they know in their own lives. André has been in schools for over 25 years, first as an Upward Bound teacher, then a middle school teacher for five years, and then a long series of leadership roles. André has been passed over for the head of school position throughout his career, despite having decades of experience—he was a vice principal, a dean of students at two schools, a vice principal again, and then eventually a principal.

As focused as he is on his leadership orientation, strengthening his school, and developing teachers, André is a caring, hands-on father. His youngest daughter is "four going on 15." He describes her as "trying to run the house," and laughingly recognizes that this is his new "struggle." During one focus group, his daughter was running across the room, and André paused in the middle of making a point about the importance of educators "listening to our babies," and as if to demonstrate the point, leans back and asks what she is doing. She continues running about, and he gets up, scoops her into his arms, sits back down, and continues: "These children are our babies, and we need teachers who know this, who live this." Another participant rejoices in what she just witnessed, and states, matter-of-factly, "Black dads rock." The moment is a powerful reflection of how André balances many roles, including the very stereotypes he faces as someone who looks like he was one of the young Black boys and girls targeted by local police and many of the teachers he supervises.

André recently enrolled in a doctoral program, eager to learn more about systems, and spends increasing amounts of time reflecting on leadership strategies to transform schools. Part of the rationale for earning his doctorate was also rooted in what André regarded as the privileging of white educators with doctorates, because "them white folks are going to remind you all of the time that they're doctors." Black educators with doctorates, however, continue to be referred to by their first name, and André noted that Black superintendents are referred to by their first name by teachers, principals, and district staff. This dismissal of Black educators, coupled with a claiming of doctoral titles and expertise, frames André's experience as continually being passed over and denied the vast experience he represents.

Raine

Born and raised in the Bay Area, Raine brings a unique sense of self and hip style to school. She is known for wearing flowing skirts, a jean jacket, and for always sporting Chuck Taylors or some other bright, hip shoes that students continually get excited over. One immediately gets the sense that Raine is passionate about young people and their education through her always blunt comments, and her consistent awareness of what is needed to "move these babies forward." Raine attended Bay Area schools and describes that experience as "horrible," though she uses her memories of these negative experiences as positive energy towards transforming schools. Being labeled and misunderstood throughout her early education impacted her trajectory and self-esteem growing up, yet Raine identifies her need to "prove they were wrong" as a driving force for her later academic and professional success.

After working several years as a marketing analyst after college, Raine decided to transition to a certified teacher role while in her mid-30s. She joined a diversity-focused urban teacher education program and was placed as a teacher while earning her teacher credential, taking evening classes after a full day of teaching. She taught at three elementary schools over six years, continually shifting schools at the district's behest. Raine completed her administrative credential in her fifth year of teaching, completed an additional leadership program in her sixth year, and has been an administrator for the past two years. Now as the head of an elementary school, Raine has been transforming the school culture while nurturing new teachers.

Self-described as "sold out for kids," the teachers Raine leads acknowledge that she pushes them to deliver their absolute best for "our babies," but some of these teachers also mention how difficult it is to work for a such a perfectionist:

> My responsibility is to coach and teach. And this is the school where we're not going to sugar coat it. And your grievances and all of that, I ain't afraid of that. I'm not afraid to be fired. I don't even care. If you fire me, I still can get a teaching job. I got a credential for the rest of my life.

Never content with the status quo of those around her and of herself, in addition to being a school leader, Raine is also pursuing her doctorate in educational leadership and aspires to further transform educational systems from the superintendent role.

Shonda

Born and raised in Southern California, Shonda, a single mother of one son, is all about blending the glitz of Hollywood with the multiculturalism of the Bay Area. From hot pink Chuck Taylors that match the highlights streaking through her hair, to warm lavender socks that complement an anime sweater, Shonda reflects current youthful trends. She wears hip clothes that women 20 years younger would have a difficult time pulling off without awkward stares, yet because she coordinates every outfit with shades of pink and sparkles, and because she blends a friendly, relaxed demeanor with no-nonsense professionalism, her presence conveys diverse urban elementary student-centeredness. The children who attend Rainbow Academy mirror the bubbling positive energy that evokes from her early-40s frame, and within five minutes, visitors cannot escape the reality that Shonda evokes a child-friendly California swag that embodies Disney, anime, and African American historical contexts in ways that encourage students to talk to her. Bathed in every shade of pink, her office is adorned with posters, lunchboxes, cards, toys, and assorted promotional items from Pokémon to Marvel to Christie (the one African American Barbie doll)—students enter her office reminded that they are children first. Their comfort is immediately clear, and they ask if they can touch items as they stare in awe at the abundance of toys, knowing their principal is hip beyond belief. Shonda's office and the way she presents herself is deeply intentional, reflecting both her knowledge of what children care about and demonstrating a way of modeling how to integrate children-centered concepts with adult-friendly ways.

Shonda moved to the Bay Area as a young adult and started in education as a substitute teacher. She immediately fell in love with elementary-aged students. "I love the babies," she clarified, "mostly because I can resonate with how they see the world and how they talk about what they need." She continued, "I see them and encourage them to be who they are." She believes staunchly in living and working within the local communities of a school, and earned her teaching and administrative credential, as well as a doctorate, at the same university, just a few miles away from where she has lived and taught for 15 years. The shift to principal was a difficult one for her, not because of any administrative responsibilities, but because the school was in a community that would be new to Shonda.

Shonda had taught third and fourth grades, gifted and talented populations, and courses specific to newcomer immigrant communities at two different schools in the same neighborhood. Her students have always reflected her own personal context growing up, including predominantly African American and Latino, but also Asian, Pacific Islander, and an occasional handful of white students. This urban diversity essentially drove her to continue teaching, despite facing negative treatment from principals and having severe disagreements with district policies. Her focus on empowering children to be who they are, to speak their first (and second, third, and fourth) languages, and to dress however they wish kept her classroom a warm and welcoming space, despite the deplorable conditions of the schools she has worked in. At the time of the study, Shonda had just completed her first year in an executive leadership role at the district office.

Jayson

Jayson is a well-built African American male with long dreads in his mid-30s. Born and raised in the Bay Area, Jayson went to a local state university. Jayson's father is a surgeon and his mother remains an active leader in local educational policy issues. The youngest of an African American family that grew up middle-class, Jayson is well-aware of his class privilege, which he continually juxtaposes with how society at large views him negatively as a Black male. Jayson recently married and had his first child two years ago; he regularly brings his toddler with him as he heads to district meetings and other gatherings, arguing that educational spaces should be welcoming for all children, and particularly babies.

While he had moved out of the Bay Area after college, his mother was a catalyst for bringing him back home to enroll in a teacher transition program to become a math teacher. In his first year of teaching, which he describes as fraught with the usual problems associated with novice teachers, Jayson found himself uniquely able to relate to students in ways other teachers could not; his youthful-looking appearance and understanding of the local context made him a favorite with students and the principal, but he experienced challenges with colleagues who revealed their own problematic presumptions of his background:

> How people perceive of me is silenced by my perceived exceptionalism, how I was raised, and guilt of other people. And what I mean by that is my staff knows I went to college; my parents went to college; "He's not a regular Black man." And so when I come in, I'm like "Kids learn their math, need to know their science. It needs to be difficult. It needs to be rigorous. Let's work on that." And people are like "Well, Jayson, not everybody goes to college." So in staff meetings, I'm a quiet person. I'm just quiet, and I watch, and I observe, and I observe, and I just watch the conversation go to like, "How do we lower expectations more?" And then I say some things, and they're like, "Jayson with the doctor dad and teacher mom, he doesn't know what he's talking about, about struggle and things like that." It's like my grandfather was a principal in Louisiana. My mom's house was shot up by KKK members that were police and mailmen and preachers. For them, it's like you can learn wherever the hell you're at.

Jayson's high school classroom is always bubbling with youthful energy, and he attributes his love of students with his leadership trajectory. After having taught for eight years at the same school, Jayson transitioned to a teacher on special assignment, helping to support new teachers and participate in district leadership development projects, while continuing to work at his school. At the time of the study, Jayson was completing a master's degree in educational leadership and had enrolled in a district administrator placement program.

Dawn

Dawn is a dark-skinned, heavy-set African American woman in her mid-30s, who was born and raised in the East Bay. Dawn graduated from high school and has never lived outside the community she considers home. Well-known across the city due to her extensive efforts as a youth advocate, community activist, and church leader, Dawn conveys a powerful presence, reinforced by her capacity to cite scripture as often as she does the historic activists and hip hop artists that helped shape her community. Dawn changes hairstyles frequently and wears clothing that complements her curves, part of her intentional orientation to claim who she is and love her African American body.

Dawn owns the many contradictions she presents, claiming a distinct Bay Area-proud approach to how she looks, talks, and moves in the world:

> I actually don't have—aside from the people at this table I actually don't talk to other administrators. I just don't. I don't engage with them. I don't talk to them because a lot of the time that I hear them talking or I'm in a room with them I find them to be very not concerned with what's happening with children. We want to talk about how can we move this money or we're talking about [results-based budgeting] or we're talking about master schedule, but we are not talking about how this connects to or is going to affect families and how our kids are going to be successful. And so I just don't have time for it. My face tells it all and I'm going to be like, "I think you're an idiot." So I just don't engage with them.

A continual stream of students and neighborhood children wish to spend more time with Dawn. Indeed, Dawn's rapport with students is legendary across the district, as is her work ethic, as evidenced by her current enrollment in a doctoral program at a university 50 miles away. Dawn started as a middle-school teacher, and after six years, left the classroom to take on a school-wide leadership role as a teacher on special assignment. After a year, she was promoted to an assistant principal role, which she held for two years. She is in her first year as principal of a local charter school, serving the same students she had in the district school after having jumped into the more highly politicized world of charter schools.

Mason

Mason is an African American male in his early 50s. A well-built former football player of average height, Mason is in a long-term marriage and the father of two grown young women. Mason started a career in law enforcement, and eventually shifted to teaching so he could work more directly with youth. Teaching and mentoring children before they interacted with the criminal justice system compelled him to transition careers to become a much lower-paid teacher. Mason entered teaching in middle school, ultimately serving as a physical education teacher for 12 years. During this time, he was a founding teacher of a new school and then began his positional leadership trajectory by becoming a teacher on special assignment. He then served (with Dawn) as an assistant principal for two years, and then became a principal, where he has been for the past two years.

Mason's school campus is an oasis in the middle of the urban jungle. Situated in the hills above deep urban decay, Tradeway Academy boasts several portables tucked between huge trees and rolling, grassy knolls. While the portables are old, they are well-maintained and recently painted; several beautiful murals adorn each building, with local icons, basketball players, and historic community activists emblazoned upon them. The beautiful grounds combine with the murals to suggest a welcoming, cared-for campus. Class size is small and the staff operates like family, as visitors to the campus are greeted warmly, guided to the appropriate building with smiles and laughter. Mason elaborated:

> The minute I stop enjoying something, it's time to get out and do something else. I've always believed that, and I've always done that. I started in law enforcement. And it was great for the first five years. And then, the sixth year, it was the worst job I've ever had. So I got out. That's what got me into education in the schools, and that's where I've been ever since. My support group has been my family and just meeting like-minded people within education and coming to groups like this; if I wasn't motivated before, there's no way I couldn't be motivated now.
>
> When my girls were young education gave me, as a Black man, the opportunity, because of scheduling to be there when my kids needed me and to be there when they didn't need me. I was the dad that picked them up; I was the dad that was at all the meetings. I was the dad that when you called, this brother came. And I loved that. So, I think now that my kids are in college getting ready to graduate, I just get joy out of sharing this experience with kids that I feel wouldn't get that and really need it regardless of what they know.

Away from his own school, however, Mason is experiencing dissatisfaction with district leadership, in part because his focus on transformation does not always align with the district orientation and his personal core values. Mason's dedication to his craft, his leadership, his staff, and his students makes him feel like it is necessary to remain under the radar while managing his school site, to keep his students safe and his staff away from the politics with which he is becoming increasingly frustrated.

Jill

Jill is a 52-year-old divorcee born and raised in the Bay. Jill is a dark-skinned curvy woman who is often under-valued even as she challenges others' perceptions and biases. Behind Jill's nurturing character lies a sharp wit shaped by the realities of the many identities and roles Jill plays; her day is fueled by people sharing rumors, feelings, and fears, so much so that she often is not given time to truly process changes before the next challenge is presented. Jill's current work analyzes major gaps in workflow processes, as well as racial, gender, and hierarchical biases she sees at the most senior level.

> What you have to do is decide; it goes back to authentic leadership, you have to decide is this the hoop that I'm going to jump? I'm not going to cry today, but I just want you to know being in the district is hella isolating. . .

She clarifies, "and thank God I have folks that I can call on because this stuff is no joke! These hoops are high. The higher up you go, the more isolated you become, and the less of a joke it is. The work is really hard. It's really hard." Jill's greatest strengths are her longevity within the district, personal relationships, and genuine warmth and caring she demonstrates for colleagues.

Ricardo

Ricardo's leadership pathway opens Chapter 3, though additional details offer further his context. Born in Seattle to an African American mother and a Spanish-speaking Black and Latino Colombian father, Ricardo's parents grew up in Los Angeles, and he has family ties to Oakland, Seattle, and throughout Colombia. While his father primarily spoke Spanish at home, his mother never learned Spanish and always thought Ricardo should speak English only. This tension shaped Ricardo's life as a child, with his mother wanting him to be Black first (which, according to Ricardo, meant speaking only English), while his father had a far more global orientation to Blackness. His mother's association of speaking Spanish as "a White Latino thing, instead of a nuanced language" led to increasing fights at home, and his parents divorced by the time he was in middle school. As a child, he had a difficult time thinking through racial identity, as he always considered himself Black and Latino and Colombian—just like his father had—and grew up trying to learn Spanish every chance he could get. His mother's rejection of his father's influence, his Spanish-speaking development, and ultimately many of the neighborhood Latinos, however, led to what Ricardo framed as "a complicated negative Black identity, where I started to question, maybe I was more Latino than Black." This self-doubt drove Ricardo to embrace his more complex racial and linguistic identities as a teacher, so that students would not perpetuate a Black/Latino divide.

Ricardo came to education after a six-year career as a mechanical engineer, where he was "grinding day in and day out," as part of what he framed as "the corporate hustle." He realized early on that he had been preparing for work that did not motivate him, though he fully appreciated the paycheck, as he was able to pay off his student loans (from his bachelor's and master's degrees), help a younger sibling attend college, and support his single mother, at one point paying her mortgage on top of his own. But by 30, he knew corporate engineering was not for him, and he began a transition to teaching. "I wanted to do something tangibly meaningful," he clarified, "as here I was making money—a lot of money—but it had no meaning. I felt like I was just working to work." After enrolling in a program designed for mid-career adults transitioning to teaching, Ricardo knew he was finally in the right career. "Listen," he said in his still-demanding classroom teacher voice, "I needed something compelling, and teaching was hard enough to capture my attention, but rewarding enough to keep me motivated to be better." The transition was difficult, especially the salary drop of over $100,000 per year, but Ricardo felt that he could model being someone who "had made it and then walked away from corporate America" and into schools.

Alicia

Born and raised in Martinique, Alicia's West Indian family is from Trinidad and Jamaica, yet resettled in Martinique, where they remain today. Alicia identifies as racially "mixed," and her family includes a range of Black and multiracial identified individuals from several countries across the Caribbean. Alicia's vaguely West Indian accent is barely an undercurrent during conversations, and most people presume she is from the US. Extended conversation, however, gives her occasion to annunciate some words with a stronger accent, belying her Caribbean roots. After graduating from an independent high school on Martinique, Alicia matriculated to an elite private university in New York, earned her bachelor's in sociology, then her master's degree in humanities. When she and her then husband relocated to the Bay Area, she had already decided she wanted to work with younger students. She was hired as an administrator in the central office at an independent high school and is the sole participant in this book who did not first serve as a teacher.

Eager to take on more leadership roles so that she could address some of the barriers she saw students of color facing in the independent school context, and in alignment with the school reorganization plan, Alicia was hired as the dean of students. After her first year in that role, she enrolled in a principal certificate program to "learn about some of the systems everyone sort of seemed to presume I already had knowledge of." She also began classroom teaching to augment her administrative role, in part because she felt a bit like an imposter because she had never been a teacher before being in a leadership role. Despite her imposter syndrome, Alicia began to notice some very specific gaps in teacher effectiveness within the school.

That's why I don't want to be here anymore. That's why I said it's not my school anymore. It's like I can't fix it because I have no say. I can't do anything. And I feel like if I'm in a context where I am the one who is going into that classroom and saying to that teacher, "You are not serving these children, let's figure out how you could serve these children." If I am that person, if I have that say, if I have that voice, which I did once kind of, then I don't care about, I mean I care, I'll have to figure out how to deal, but I'll be dealing from a different position. I'll be dealing from a position of power. It's like either I'm empowered to do what I know is the right thing or a good thing to do, or a productive thing to do, or to try even. Because I don't have all the answers, nobody has all the answers. But if I was empowered to go into that classroom and work directly with that teacher, I would go do that. In fact, you know what, I might probably replace him. Because that dude clearly does not know what he's doing.

These tensions of not having institutional power to make the "right decision" led Alicia to continue her leadership trajectory, and within a few years, Alicia was promoted to principal of the high school, a position she ultimately designed with the then executive director of the school. Alicia has been in administrative leadership roles for 11 years at independent schools, and at the conclusion of the study, had just completed her first year as an elementary school principal.

Nicole

Nicole is an African American woman in her early 40s, married without children of her own. Born and raised in the Bay Area, Nicole wears her hair in a ponytail or braids and is always dressed casually, often in a tracksuit or other athletic apparel that reflects her deep passion for sports. Nicole went to college on a basketball scholarship and has been an advocate for youth athletics as a pathway out of poverty ever since. She is well-known locally as an advocate for youth, particularly African American girls, and has a regional presence as someone to help students begin to take their athletic journeys more seriously.

I think I'm silenced in a way where being a collegiate athlete, being African American and being a woman, and then, being lesbian. It's a lot that goes into that. But when I look at the teachers who I'm serving, the teachers who are serving our kids, a lot of times, when I say what I say, I feel like they think that I just got there because I could play basketball. Or I only focus on fun and the sports and the athletes. And all the time, I always want to make that statement like, "Just so you know, I was an honor roll student all the way K through 12." I received a basketball scholarship gratefully. And then, I was a scholar athlete at Division I institution. I've also been in education for 17 years, where I've taught, I've coached, I've been a counselor, and now, I'm an administrator. There is no way in the world that you can say that I don't value education and don't feel like our students need to be educated and academics need to be at the forefront. There's no way you could say that. But I also understand, for myself and what happens for many of our kids, is that, if it wasn't for leadership, if it wasn't for basketball, if it wasn't for having PE, if it wasn't for those things, I wouldn't be where I am today and being able to give that to the kids.

Nicole began teaching shortly after graduating from college and served as a classroom teacher in a local high school for six years.

She increasingly became involved with athletics at the school, working with students to focus and develop their athleticism, and coupling that inner drive with academic support. Nicole eventually transitioned to the school's Activities Director, allowing her to focus more fully on athletic development, coaching, and more individualized supports for students, again particularly for African American girls. After 16 years, Nicole shifted to become an assistant principal, a position she held for three years. Within the past year, Nicole has gotten married, been admitted to a doctoral program, and completed her first year as principal of a middle school.

Leadership Pathways

Participants took various pathways towards school leadership, even as most were initially resistant to ever becoming an administrator (see Table 2.2). Yet all modeled an intentionally affirming Blackness, in addition to a specific focus on supporting Black children, as core to their educational purpose. Each attributed their leadership commitment to elevating Black students so that those students could, in turn, elevate Black communities. While each participant ultimately took on school leadership roles, most did so reluctantly, or at least with trepidation, knowing that schools were not designed to support the children they were dedicated to, nor their own trajectory.

Indeed, all but Alicia began in traditionalized pathways, where they first served as classroom teachers in elementary, middle, or high schools or adult education. Most kept teaching when they took on their first administrative post, and indeed, many continue to teach one class so they can remain connected with students. Trey was the only participant with four years of teaching before leaving the classroom; the rest had five years or more, with Jill having 10, Mason 12, and Shonda 15. Thus, the range of years—from 4 to 15—demonstrates significant classroom experience. Additionally, none of the participants went from the classroom directly to serving as a principal. Indeed, most served as a teacher on special assignment or program administrator before serving as an assistant or vice principal, and this is an important recognition. In addition to being paid less than principals, teachers on special assignment

TABLE 2.2 School Leadership Pathways

Name	Years Full-Time Teaching	Years Admin	Leadership Trajectory
Byron	9	10	Teacher → TSA → Dean → AP
Raine	6	3	Teacher → AP → Principal
Dawn	6	4	Teacher → TSA → AP → Principal
Jayson	8	4	Teacher → TSA → AP
Mason	12	7	Teacher → TSA → AP → Principal
Trey	4	13	Teacher → PA → AP
Nicole	6	14	Teacher → PA → AP
André	7	16	Teacher → Dean → AP → Principal
Shonda	15	8	Teacher → TSA → Principal → DA
Alicia	0	12	Dean → Principal → AP
Rosie	5	7	Teacher → ASD → AP
Ricardo	8	13	Teacher → AP → Principal → DA
Jill	10	11	Teacher → DA

Notes: TSA = school-based teacher on special assignment; ASD = after school director; PA = school-based program administrator; Dean = dean of students; AP = assistant or vice principal; DA = district administrator

and program administrators are typically not given the same levels of salary or district support. Throughout these interviews, participants were clear that they were given additional steps that their younger, white peers did not need to take. That these steps were paid at lower rates reflect the continual context of racist barriers that made these leadership pathways longer than those often attributed to white leaders.

In the next three chapters, we share these African American educational leaders' stories in an attempt to allow district and other stakeholders to listen, learn, and have an unprecedented glimpse of critical, authentic Black leaders' experiences, perceptions, and aspirations.

Note

1 We use "women" and "men" throughout this study to reflect the terminology used by participants, in recognition that gender is a socially constructed category that differs from sex. Thus, while some participants used gender and sex referents interchangeably, we recognize that this language does not fully address the non-binary realities of many communities and individuals.

3

BUT I DON'T WANT TO BE A PRINCIPAL

Intersectional Racism and Black Leadership Pathways

> "I never, ever, ever thought that I was going to be an administrator."
>
> – Nicole

Ricardo lives between worlds. Throughout school, he was told he was too Black and too Mexican, and that he had too much of an accent when he spoke English or Spanish. His growing up years, he recalls, were filled with rejection by peers for never being what they wanted him to be. "As a kid," he clarifies, "the world just wasn't ready for a Black and Colombian multiracial kid – everyone liked our music and dance, but no one was really ready to imagine us in the flesh." His teachers echoed this racial binary, considering him Black for much of his schooling experiences, going so far as to ridicule him for speaking in Spanish, and placing him in introductory Spanish classes in middle school, despite his fluency. This continual rejection for always being too much something else ironically developed a deep sense of multicultural pride in Ricardo early on, and he eventually turned these slights into sources of strength.

Ricardo attributes this rejection of his dualistic identities to his quick navigation through what he framed as "racist as hell school systems." He was thus on a professional pathway early on, earning a large corporate salary from his job as a mechanical engineer by the time he was 25 years old. Always the only person of color within his professional roles, he followed his parents' strategies at work, learning to embrace the way his peers and supervisors never saw him for who he was, nor his tireless work ethic. He did not correct people when someone referred to him as José, Luis, or shortened his name to Rick, never interrupted when he was presumed to be a custodian instead of in executive leadership, and never showed his frustration at being hypervisible yet treated as if he was entirely invisible. By the time he transitioned from corporate jobs to public school classrooms, he shed this invisibility, recognizing that he now needed to be a model for other children of color. Transforming from invisibility led him to challenge white supervisors, who always had "less of everything relevant in leadership, less experience, less education, less patience, less respect of others, and less dignity."

Ricardo retells the following stories repeatedly, as he continually reminds "district colleagues that the leadership pathways that worked for them worked because they were designed by and for white men just like them." He argues that different approaches "that challenge the norms of district and school politics" are needed to support people of color and women of color who might want to become school leaders and uses his own experience as a guide. His foundation as a school district leader is based on being in leadership roles at a young age, of having a father and a mother who worked in powerless roles in schools, and of his experiences of having white people often presume his white supervisees are his boss:

> I was the first in my family to graduate from college, but my family is a family of educators. My father was a high school custodian who became a labor leader later in life, and my Mom was a secretary at a community college. So I was around schools and colleges since birth. Plus, my older cousins went to Mom's college, so there were always family gatherings, and we'd talk about this sociology professor or this math teacher or this shady vice president and just go on and on. And there was always this tone of, "these white folk just don't see us," to every story being told.
>
> Moms would tell this story of her first boss, who would be hitting on every other woman who worked in the office. But Moms was Black, so he wouldn't hit on her. She was like, "Ricardo, sometimes not being seen is a blessing, remember that." She rose as her first boss rose, he always took her with him, as he went from department chair to dean to VP. She got a salary increase every step, and he was never bad to her, even though she was very aware of how he was to white women. And those white women hated on her, treated her like she was the one who was bad to them. She just didn't react, was always like, "Yeah, y'all ain't my people or supervisor so whatevs." It wasn't that she didn't care, she just knew the nuances of leadership. Her boss' racism protected her from his sexist ways. Leadership to her was always going to have some negative, and so you just rode with it in the way you could.
>
> Papa, though, had a totally opposite stance. He was never seen either, not as a custodian. I mean, a Latino-looking janitor in a mostly Black high school? And he mostly had white principals, too, and they never knew his name, mixed him up with the other Latino. That always pissed him off cause his colleagues were always Mexican or Salvadoran, and he

had a little Colombian chip on his shoulder, cause he was also Black and Latino, but looked more like what Americans think of as Latino. And then he had a Black principal, and he was the same, called all of them José. Papa was like, "They can't see me so I don't have to talk to them."

This is what these White admin never seem to get, and sometimes the Black ones, too, it kills me to say. When Papa got the opportunity to take on a leadership role in the union, he changed it all up. He was no longer invisible. He made a middle-class salary for the first time, made as much as Moms finally. He started challenging these white guys, and man they weren't ready for him. He knew all these administrators, and none of them knew he had worked for them for decades. He knew their children, he knew where they lived, yet they didn't even know his name. They kept calling him José. But Papa was a calculated man. He took that invisibility and used it to fight for salaries, for health care, for other benefits. He would say "Don't you pay attention to these white people. Be invisible to them so you can watch them, move around them, and then push them when they are not expecting it."

Both my parents knew how to navigate white leaders, kinda by being invisible, until it was their time to shine, then they pushed. Papa would say "let them think you [are a] custodian, but make sure you know the custodians first." [My parents] really had an impact on my leadership pathway, because I was already thinking of these issues and already had managerial experience before I even started teaching.

Ricardo clarified how his leadership trajectory began before he had even committed to become a teacher. "I already knew about the importance of seeing everyone in the hierarchy," he elaborated, "and I knew leadership would never see me, so I used to think I'd be the perfect leader."

When Ricardo joined a transition to teaching program, the program planted the seeds for his eventual leadership transition. "The program had its issues, especially around race," he clarified, "but one thing I credit them with was they always had us thinking beyond just our classroom." Program participants were eligible for grants to support enrollment in a national leadership preparation program after their second year of teaching. At the time, Ricardo wanted to strengthen his classroom teaching before jumping to administration, so he rebuked their offers. A few years later, however, after teaching in his third middle school in six years, Ricardo was growing frustrated by what he called "culturally offensive school leaders." As a classroom teacher, Ricardo always wanted to make sure he could reach every child, and that included "children who spoke other languages, who came from different religious backgrounds, whose home life just looked totally different from mine." His focus on growing as a teacher, combined with his continual critique of the majority white teachers around him who could not relate to students in the way he felt he was, kept him moving from school to school in search of more inclusive, culturally responsive school leaders.

He was eventually recruited to a new middle school by a Black principal well-known for his cultural presence and leadership within Black and Latino communities. Within his first year at the school, the principal asked him to consider joining a local urban-focused principal preparation program, Ricardo agreed, appreciative of the rare mentorship, and after one year of courses and a brief internship, he ultimately replaced one of the assistant principals he had worked under at Burton Middle School Academy. Two years later, he was promoted by the district to principal, a role in which he served for five years. He then left the district to serve as a new principal coach in a nearby district and was promoted to districtwide principal supervisor two years after that. Ricardo has been in his current district role for three years, during which time he has supervised dozens of principal interns, assistant principals, and principals, always with a self-avowed focus on culturally responsive instructional leadership.

Becoming School Leaders

We begin this chapter with Ricardo specifically because his experiences are unique from most participants in this book, from his family of educators who were never seen for who they were despite working with and around positional leaders for decades, to his previous experience as a corporate executive, and to his relatively early leadership trajectory. While many teachers and educators aspire to school administration as the pinnacle of success, most participants in this book share a racialized framing: their invisibility as leaders, the lack of culturally responsive leadership, and negative experiences with school and district leaders instilled an oppositional stance to formal leadership. Indeed, a shared experience across these Black leaders was a passing over by and for white administrators, and a related invisibility around being seen as leadership material, despite that these leaders were seen as exemplary teachers.

For most participants, school leadership was, as Rosie succinctly argued, "for the sell-outs, the ones who need that affirmation, and if they ain't one of those, well they better appeal to white teachers, and that means being light-skinned cute." This critical dismissal was shared by all participants, including Ricardo, but while Ricardo saw this context of racism as an opportunity, most instead echoed Nicole's opening quote about never thinking they would become administrators. This resistance to seeing themselves as formal leaders, even when taking on some of those roles prior to having the title, reflects a set of racist barriers that keep Black leaders from taking on, and being recognized for, formal leadership roles.

For some participants, the principalship was viewed as negative based on a white-centered notion of school leadership. Before accepting positional leadership roles, ideas around administrators were based largely on their observation of former leaders, most of whom were white. Because the leaders in this book considered themselves social justice advocates, they had concerns that becoming a principal would shift their identity into something they dismissed. Some found themselves suddenly thrust into an assistant principal position; this leadership through the attrition of white leaders before them was difficult because they were not prepared to make the identity shift towards school leadership. For others, the notion of how they authentically fit into the role of leader was daunting, especially with the multidimensionality of race and gender painting an institutionalized racist educational back-drop. How to be authentic within a context of anti-Blackness when school leadership was viewed as white- and male-centric was a continuing concern, in part because there were few examples of Black-centric leaders.

The other exception to reluctant school leadership trajectories was André, who knew before he even became a teacher that he was going to eventually become a school administrator. "I remember at black graduation, everyone had to say what they wanted to be," he recalled, "and I said I wanted to be a high school principal." André already knew he was going to be a teacher, that was the easy part. But when he looked at the pay scale, he "mapped everything out and re-thought just being a teacher." As soon as he calculated the difference in pay, André had a pre-professional revelation: "I just thought, 'Oh, I can be an administrator,' so at the Black graduation, I just said something very elite. 'I'll be a principal.' I just knew then." The irony is that André faced the same continual barriers to his leadership trajectory as the others, despite having already decided he would become a school principal in high school. In this way, for even the two male administrators who were already leadership-oriented, racism created a series of barriers to professional navigation and then shaped a hostile racial climate regardless of their positional title or leadership aspirations.

While each participant was recognized as outstanding teachers because they engaged students of color within their classrooms, they also lamented a lack of leadership exemplars across school districts and colleges, including a lack of leadership development to help them deepen instructional skills. This lack of positional leaders who could effectively teach children of color created a vacuum that they ultimately felt called on to fill. This calling led to classroom-to-school leadership transitions that were often filled with frustration, pain, and more intersectional racism, where these educators were discounted because they used culturally responsive approaches and strengths-based orientations to Black children and communities. Including Ricardo and André, each participant expressed resistance to seeing themselves as formal leaders in part because they were told along the pathway that they were insufficient. Most were repeatedly passed over for less-qualified white and/or male administrators, and all were systematically ignored and dismissed, even while being acknowledged for teaching expertise.

If Not Us, Then Who?

The largest concern about moving from teaching to administration was the notion of leaving what most participants referred to as "our babies." Leaving the classroom meant leaving what André had called the "nurturing safety" of classrooms they had taken years of struggle to create. The shift to administration would mean walking out of effective classrooms that would further the opportunity gap they fought against, and the weight of further endangering students was felt as a personal burden. There was a huge concern prior to becoming a principal that these responsive educators would not be allowed to focus on children and students. Instead, their experience working with administrators led them to believe that their focus would be on more trivial matters such as punitive staff management, district paperwork, and budgetary issues they might not have control over. Principal work, they were initially clear, was not as important as teacher work. Because of their daily experience with administrators who did not model culturally responsive approaches, did not know local communities, and did not model engaging teaching, these educators dismissed administrative work as often in opposition to what Mason called "the real work of classroom teaching." Each participant became a teacher specifically so they could provide protection for children, while conceptualizing of teaching as an advocating role for children of color; becoming an administrator was seen as moving away from that commitment.

The lingering frustration of having to witness, interact with, and circumnavigate ineffective, culturally non-responsive administrators kept urging these educators to re-think leaving their classrooms. André clarified this tension: "I just kept wondering to myself, 'who will teach "our" kids?' I mean seriously, if not us, who? And yet, I still knew I had to leave the classroom to get a systems view." He continued, "I'm sitting here thinking I don't know if I want to be too far away from the kids. Dealing with adults in the principal's seat is more than a notion. That's where the action is, right?" André continued with this tension:

> I love teaching. But I only have so many kids. But there are thousands dealing with wack ass teachers, and then my thought was, "Okay, maybe I can impact change in the classroom *and* cover them, so they can have an advocate." Because a lot of the teachers don't look like us, and they're just treating [our babies] wrong, not understanding their trauma, disrespecting and being racist to them, so they need an advocate in our seat.

André's entry into administration was a balancing act as he was a founding teacher of a school in his fifth year of teaching.

André explained how he ultimately used the same skill sets he had developed as a teacher to translate into leadership roles, even as his entry into leadership was shaped by white stereotypes of Black leaders.

I ended up moving here to help start a school. And, by default, I got put into a position of leadership because these folks [starting the school] were getting affluent people from the east coast, with these novel ideas of no bells, while we're sitting right in the middle of the hood. We had just demolished some building and there are prostitutes on the other side of the street. And they didn't know what to do. It was a culture shock for them. So, as they were having these issues and with the disconnect with the kids, I was forced to have to be the disciplinarian. And I wasn't. It was just my ability to relate to kids, my ability to communicate with parents, my ability to go to other teachers and say, "You just can't be up there talking all day and not engage them on anything."

And part of me felt bad for the teachers I had to deal with, and sometimes the kids. Because [the kids] heard me, I hate to say it, cussing people out with the door closed. Because they were hurting kids. And we had maybe six principals in four years. And understand, this is a family school from day one. So, I was a consistent leader throughout all of that. So, I had never gotten to [an administration preparation] program until after about six years. And, I got into [the urban-focused admin program]. I needed the admin credential because I needed to know how to be successful at this school to make kids trust each other, to look out for each other, to take the elder role when new freshmen would come in, and show them the ropes.

André raised a number of important clarifications in re-telling his pathway into leadership. The first is that he felt compelled to take on responsibilities because of the dramatic lack of culturally familiar leadership. Indeed, he soon realized most of the leadership had no idea how to move within the impoverished, nowhere near gentrified urban community they had decided to open a school within. Most teachers and administrators were white and not from the local community, much less even the state. Their previous experiences in schools were limited to affluent areas, areas that André later pointed out were also where they had attended schools, so they had no prior training to address their lack of lived experience and commitment to the specific communities they were now serving.

A second clarification is the dramatic turnover in leadership, due in part to naïveté in white educators thinking they could lead a school within a community they had no cultural familiarity with. Adding to this turnover was a context of André's growing frustration with racist teachers and administrators who treated children negatively. In short, the lack of adequate preparation and knowledge of peer teachers and administrators drove André into school leadership, and ultimately, into an administrative certificate program. Despite his lived experience and cultural familiarity with the community, as a life-long learner and career educator, he had the humility to recognize that he could learn more about leadership to help strengthen his approaches. Underlying his pathway was a recurring commitment to make schools better places for children of color, and the recognition that most teachers and administrators were not going to do that.

Jayson had a similar justification for transitioning from the classroom to administrative roles. While he felt "pulled into the administrator direction" to address the same tensions André identified, unlike André, Jayson always intended to remain in the classroom. "I was like, 'I'll never be a principal,'" he clarified, "and then it became, 'I'll think about it once I can move my kids how I want to move my kids.'" In his seventh year of teaching, Jayson indicated that "it feels like it's going to be my last year in the classroom." He then paralleled André's concerns with teachers and administrators that ultimately led him to consider leaving the classroom:

> I've always thought of teaching as the way I reach the kids easiest, and to really realize that, at least for me here, it's not the kids that are really the issue. There's nothing really wrong with the kids at all. It's just the adults that they interact with, what they hear, and what they believe. I've been spending this whole year kind of opening kids' eyes and retraining them to trust themselves. And, I just feel like I can do more higher up at times. And so, as I've been here longer, I outlast, and outlast, and outlast the next person.

Jayson continued to clarify how a pathway to leadership never seemed appropriate, despite being a senior teacher at his school by his third year of teaching. The continual teacher and principal turnover led him to recognize that most principals did not remain in the classroom long enough to excel in teaching or leadership. "I've always been really uncomfortable with the principal that was a teacher for a day," he argued, "because now they're a principal, so that's why I was always like, 'I don't want to be a principal until I've been teaching for 35 years.'"

Yet after seven years in the same school, watching principals with minimal teaching experience lead in ways that did not feel authentic or relevant to children of color, Jayson's frustration grew. This frustration aligned with a new principal who had an immediate negative impact on the school community, but who supported Jayson's leadership trajectory. This experience, of being supported by someone whom he did not see prioritizing children of color, "really shifted how I thought about leadership" and propelled him towards administration particularly because he continually saw programs fail children of color yet continue to receive district support, while programs that appeared successful were being cut. The leadership team kept saying "'These kids can't' a little too much for me, and that's when things started shifting in my head." Jayson finally had enough of teacher and administrator support for efforts that did not show results, and the lack of willingness to consider evidence based on students was increasingly frustrating:

> It's just cultural issues happening. Because so-and-so's suspended, this person is about to leave, we're about to expel them and all their grades are terrible. And all of our Black kids that are doing well [are not the focus either]. When I see enough of that, how I feel and how I think, my default is I feel like I could do that better.

Mason similarly echoed André and Jayson's experiences, directly aligning with Jayson's initial commitment to be a classroom teacher for life. "I got into education 15 years ago thinking I was going to be a career teacher," Mason clarified, "I was like, 'I just want to teach. I don't want to go into all the politics.'"

After over a decade of classroom teaching, Mason's focus was on perfecting the craft of teaching, and he spent years improving his approaches, ways of engaging, and reflecting on his practice. "I want to do what I do, that I know that I do well," he reflected, "within a small framework in the classroom because I know that I can help kids that way." Despite his commitment to stay in the classroom, Mason continued his educational trajectory, in part because of his personal dedication to continual learning. He clarified his pathway into administration as a growing frustration with leadership coupled with his interest in proving the naysayers wrong, echoing André and Jayson's recognition that they could do better.

> I was in the admin program, but just doing it because it was a life goal of mine. And after completing it, and then going back to my school and seeing other folks do what they thought was right, what I knew was just ass-backwards, and then having to work for them was really a drain for me. They say that the school that I was at is a great school. I think it is, but that one particular person just did nothing for kids of color, period. They went back to, "Let's just give them all to Mason because he knows how to deal with them, and we won't have to see or hear from them because Mason's dealing with them."
>
> So, I was fortunate enough to hook up with mentor who's no longer here, which is a damned shame, but we shared similar mentalities, similar things that we had gone through. He actually pushed me, and helped me get an AP job. I went from a school of 400 to a school of 2,000 as a brand new administrator, not really knowing what I was getting into, not really receiving any of what I thought was the training necessary to fill that role. You couldn't even talk to me about becoming an administrator, prior to that one individual. Administration was something where I said I was just going to do so I would have that credential. I never really thought it would really take this and roll with it. I just wanted the credential because there were some folks that said I couldn't do it.

Mason's pathway reflected both a drive to address the deficit-enforcers who told him he could not navigate educationally, as well as the commitment to address systems that he saw negatively impacting the children he was most dedicated to teaching. And in the same ironic way as most participants, Mason ended up joining a leadership pathway to address the many leaders who seemed to not know what they were doing.

Trey's experience further echoed this simmering frustration with teachers and leaders not being committed to the students they were being paid to teach. But Trey also recognized he was essentially doing the work of an administrator already, which further helped him start his pathway.

> [Students] come to our program so they can finish up. And when they have a supportive environment, they're going on to finish their high school diploma and applying for college. We're working out family issues where it's like, "I didn't go to school because I was taking care of my older sister's baby. It's not because I couldn't do the work. It's because I had familial obligations." Or, "I had this little situation I got into with some people trying to jump me. Got into a fight, and I got put out. But, I still have aspirations for certain things." And, they're going through our program because it's a nurturing environment. And I'm like, these students have the aptitude.
>
> But it's other stuff that's getting in the way. When the adults are giving up on them or when the adults are saying, "I can't teach you," or whatever. I'm sitting here thinking to myself, "Wait a second. I'm in this classroom with these throw-away children where everybody else has just given up, tossed them out, because we can't deal with you. But they're still succeeding. And so, if I have the ability to do that with them, what could I do with a school of individuals who want to learn?"
>
> So, I started looking into, "How do I have my own program?" And in my position, at that time, I was considered an outreach consultant. So, I had a caseload of students. I'm looking at what I'm doing. I'm working with social workers, I'm dealing with probation officers, I'm dealing with foster care agencies, and everything else. I'm like, "Wait a second. This is an administrative role." I have a classroom. I've got two Tas who are technically more like teachers and dealing with teaching to the students specifically, as well as administrating, all this other stuff, coordinating different efforts for them, holding SST meetings, all the stuff I need to do to make sure the student is successful, except for it's in a smaller setting. I might as well go ahead and get this credential.

Once Trey realized he was already operating as an administrator, he joined an administrative credential program. His foundation, however, began when he started seeing how other adults dismissed the students he was having a positive impact on.

Trey's experience aligned directly with André, Jayson, and Mason, who each recognized how unique they were as the rare Black men at their schools, despite that most students were African American. They were the only Black men and often the only Black teachers, and seemingly some of the very few that were dedicated to teaching children of color well. Mason, Jayson, and Trey were driven into roles that they had previously discounted because the people who had previously occupied these roles were often uncritical, unaware, and culturally non-responsive. Ricardo and André, who had more leadership interests when they went into teaching, were still driven by the same leadership void. This lack of engaged, culturally responsive leadership was echoed by all participants, even if they had mentors who supported them. The daily experiences in schools that served almost entirely children of color continually reflected an isolation, a lack of structural commitment to their own development as educators, and a simmering frustration at the treatment of children and families of color. This accumulation led them to leave the classroom and transition towards leadership that required the development of a leadership identity.

Intersectionality: Racism, Sexism, and Leadership Identity

While the pathway to school site leadership may have been similar for André, Jayson, Mason, Trey, and Ricardo, for Black women leaders, the path was fraught with intersectional racism and sexism. Almost all of the women in this study were adamant they did not want to become site administrators; they regularly shared their distaste of what they knew about administration in entirely dismissive ways. Yet, just like the men, they were propelled forward, despite frustrations with administrators and a lack of mentors who would support their development of leadership identities. For Raine, who was insistent in her desire to advocate for children, the notion of being able to finally answer "What happens after me?" as a classroom teacher was a primary factor. Her fierce personality, however, so integral to her instructional expertise, was seen by friends within her professional community as a deterrent to leadership.

> All of my mentors were like, "This is not for you. You know you can't do it. You're going to get fired. You talk too much. You've always got an opinion. You're going to get fired." I was just kind of like, "I'm going to do it." There's this team that I've built, and students are happy and parents are happy, and it's pretty new. And so now, I'm at this place where I'm trying to think because I made this school my classroom. But I don't know if I can be an admin much longer. I was looking for teaching jobs last week! I don't want to leave my team, but I don't want to do this work and not be me.
>
> I really hate administration. I hate it. But, every day, I go back to my school, and I'm in love. I'm in love with my team and I'm in love with my babies. And if I could hide there like I did in my classroom, that's

what I want to do. And my fear is that it's so great that they're coming. They're coming. When I say them, I mean the district. They're coming. And they're going to take this joy, this moment that our kids are having and our families are having and ruin it. And I don't want to see that. And I could be overthinking it. And I just don't feel like I am. And it's scary. I'm scared. I'm over afraid.

There was a clear notion among the African American women administrators that in order to be a principal, they had to change, or in some cases, hide, their professional identity. While the Black men also faced rejection and dismissals by white colleagues and supervisors, the difference was that along the pathway, Black women were specifically told that who they were was not appropriate or would not last as leadership. Raine's insistence on hiding or not being seen as who she is mirrors the invisibility that African American women have felt as a part of the racist, oppressive educational system.

Now, when Raine is seeing success at her school, she welcomes that cloak to protect and maintain that success, in part so that she can be under the radar of the district. Because successful principals are often taken from their context and placed elsewhere, asked to replicate something they were able to build as if all communities need the same approaches, Raine was afraid of being the next. As soon as she started becoming successful in shifting the school climate and culture, she realized she lost her invisibility. African American women have been socialized to operate in the dark, under the radar, as part of this systemic, intersectional silencing Raine names here. Raine's vulnerability in admitting fear is not about the district coming for her, but instead about the district taking away the wonderful team and positive culture that she spent years fostering at her site, often in spite of district teacher placement practices. Like African mothers during US chattel slavery, Raine fears the snatching of her babies in a very tangible way. As soon as she was able to create a nurturing environment at the school level, the district, as typically occurs in her experience, begins to remove key elements, distributing educators across the district in ways that maintain professional isolation. Visibility, Raine learned early in her years as site administrator, came at a huge professional cost.

Nicole initially also never wanted to become a school leader, preferring to focus on teaching and engaging students. Unlike the rest of the participants, however, Nicole was actually supported and encouraged by white leaders to begin her pathway. Once she reluctantly started her leadership preparation work, she saw her capacity to maintain authenticity as a requirement to develop a leadership identity.

For a long time I thought that I would never be an administrator because I don't want to beat to somebody else's drum. So, I felt like being in the classroom, that was the only place that I could be able to do my own thing and give the kids what I felt like they needed. I had one principal who told me – this was like 12 years ago, "You are going to be a principal one day." And I said, "Like hell I am. No I'm not." She said, "You feel that way now, but I'm going to put you on some committees that I know you don't want to participate in that makes you go to the district office because you need to learn the politics." Then I met another principal. Now, both of these are white ladies. Another one who told me, "You're going to be a principal one day." And I'm like, "Yeah, right. No." The stuff that you all gotta do, and what I learned from them is you gotta take what the district tells you, and you've got to know what your school needs, and you've got to find a happy medium in between, and that sometimes is very challenging to do, no matter who you are, what color you are. That's challenging.

So, I got into the administration program. First day of class I get there and we had to put up on the board words that we thought we needed to be to be an administrator. And there were words like, "Authentic, genuine, compassionate, love, humor." It was all these things, and I'm like, "Wait a minute. That's me. Okay, that's me. Okay, that's me. Okay, that's me. Okay, so this might work." And so now I'm in the role and I'm able to be who I am. Because, I never, ever, ever thought I was going to be an administrator.

I'm able to be who I am. And, I think my background in sports and activities, which are two things that we all know nobody really cares about in district offices; nobody cares about that stuff. So, when I came into this role, my boss said, "I need you to do what you did [before]" when I was the activities director. "This place needs to be alive. The kids need to have fun here. That's what I want you to do. That's what I want you to focus on." I was like, "Bam, I can be who I am."

The reality of Nicole's situation was that she found white administrators who were willing to play to her strengths so she could be authentically present.

Even her first administrative credential professor had taught from a leadership approach that spoke to Nicole's main fear of having to change her very identity to be an administrator. Nicole's experience differed from the rest of the participants—she demonstrated the potential easing of the barriers if white administrators took on supportive roles. Nicole's context of support, as detailed in later chapters, changed dramatically after her initial administrative placement, but her supportive pathway helped her transition. Nicole's experience of being supported in an academic program and in her first administrative role, suggests the importance of systems of support, particularly for isolated African American educators.

Raine echoed the importance of such mentorship along the way, though her support came from Black women administrators.

> I said that I didn't have support coming into admin. But that's not true. What I do recognize is, in education, every administrator that I've had has been an African American woman. They've been magical, even the [teacher mentor] that I first had [Shonda] was magical in that there was never a point where I didn't have someone that I could talk to that understood my context, my history as a student, and just my life, and understood why I did and moved the way that I moved.

This caveat for Raine came after listing frustration after frustration with district practices and teacher resistance to culturally responsive approaches. What Raine saw before she started her leadership pathway reflected the same anti-student of color context, even though she had access to Black women administrators who were culturally responsive; in short, their limited presence, often isolated within the school or district, was powerful, but not enough to disrupt the systemic racism and sexism Raine felt.

For Raine, along with many other African American women principals, having another African American administrator to support was crucial to create safety, to understand the way these women move, and to seek solace when decisions were made. Raine further clarified how essential these supports are to Black women, but also how when these supports were not there, she had to take significant risks to challenge a supervisor. These experiences directly shaped her frustrations along the pathway towards leadership:

> I've never had to think about what kinds of support I needed. This white woman was like, "How can I support you?" I think if I had a Black boss, she would have been able to know what I needed. This was the first year I felt empty and not able to be authentically me because it was also the first year I didn't have a Black woman mentor. I had to ask the white woman, "Do you know what the clap-back is?" So she would know what was going to happen when I needed to clap back. [Shaking her head] I had to teach her that. Also, I had to tell her, "What you're getting from me when I'm being fake is the veil to keep *you* safe."

Raine's need to protect her white supervisor, to coach her in how to engage Black educators, and her need to wear a different mask while leading counters the more positive experiences that Nicole had. Whereas Nicole had largely seen administrators as supportive and encouraging, Raine's experience was highly racialized. Where her Black mentors and supervisors were "magical," but also unable to entirely provide protection from anti-student of color contexts, her white supervisor required coaching and code-switching, suggesting the need for differential approaches depending on the race of the supervisor.

Jill's transition from teaching to leadership was different; she was tapped by her principal after five years of teaching to attend a new district-based program that would allow her to be a site-based coach. Jill later learned that her principal asked her to attend not because she was most qualified, but because Jill was the only one who said yes. Jill later left the district to manage a local non-profit; her first supervisory leadership role outside the district allowed her to see different structures and set the stage for her return to the district several years later.

While leading the non-profit, however, Jill reported to two white women who had issues managing her. The tensions working with white women supervisors became an institutional norm for Jill, and she found the exact same situation when she returned to the district. "White women always want to *manage* me like they did in the big house," Jill clarified, "if they would just *lead* and let me work, we could both grow and be great." Jill's transition to leadership came with a needed patience at coaching up her white women supervisors, helping her learn the value of being authentic within slippery race and gendered contexts when others have institutional and societal race-based power over her. Her ability to remain grounded helped contribute to her sustainability while also developing a notion of coaching everyone around her, regardless of their roles or racial context.

In part because she worked at a more creatively structured school, Alicia was appointed into a leadership role prior to enrolling in an administrative credential program. While this pathway was less traditional, she still had to navigate a top-down white male leader, which often put her in uncomfortable spaces, particularly as one of the only people of color and women of color in the school.

> Even though I was principal, the superintendent would make decisions that didn't feel good to me. And I would have to run with it because he was the leader. And if students, parents, teachers came to me and didn't like what they got from me they had somewhere else to go and he didn't always have my back. Sometimes he did but not always. And that is not a cool position to be in either. But I mean every principal's in that position right, everybody has a boss.
>
> And another person who stepped into a principal role was a solid instructional leader. But she left for a year and this dude stepped into her role to hold on for her for a year because she was coming back. And so he just landed in the role and now he's the high school principal. Which is bizarre to me because he's not qualified to be principal. Neither is the middle school principal. And the difference between me and them is when I became school principal, I immediately went back to school. Because I was like, "I don't know how to run a school." I mean I know how to run a school, I've been running a school, but let me go find out how, let me go read a little bit. Let me learn some more. The two of them, though, not even, not even. They're just like "Oh, I know how to do this, I was a middle school teacher. I know how to run a high school. I know how to provide instructional leadership. I know how to frame education in a way that serves kids, sure."

Alicia's frustration grew as she increasingly noticed others being appointed to leadership roles without having experience, but also without having a drive or the humility to learn, echoing the trend André saw.

While Alicia identified the importance of improving her own skill set, she recognized that for the white males who stepped into leadership roles, they did not share her sense of humility. Even as she named that "everyone has a boss," in reference to the (white male) superintendent's top-down leadership strategies, she couched that recognition with her personal drive to learn more, to "go read a little bit." The over-inflated sense of ego and self-attributed skill sets that her white male colleagues exhibited reflected their racial and gender-based privileges, but also demonstrated the flipside of that privilege: her internalized lack of skills for a role she had already been in.

Rosie's transition into an administrative role similarly isolated her and took her away from more direct engagement with children, which she lamented immediately. She also realized that she could not trust white colleagues, especially as many were on a leadership trajectory, using teaching roles and partial administrative roles as stepping stones to more power. Observing how her white colleagues rotated between leadership roles, jumping to the next available higher position led her to question their commitment to their personal trajectory versus to students. Rosie echoed Alicia's experience with white male egos: "Administration was, you know, stereotypical white guy, 32 years old, white guy with no administrative experience or credentials or advanced degree in education saying, 'Oh, I can do this,' whatever." As the only Black woman, the only out lesbian, the elder in the room with more teaching and administrative experience, she faced multiple levels of oppression: "There was a lot of ostracization, saying you're the other quote unquote administrator," she clarified, frustrated, "Sometimes I didn't even get the full respect of the title."

Rosie's frustration highlights the shared experience that Alicia and Raine identified, further paralleling the observations from Trey, André, Jayson, and Mason, in that all worked within contexts with white leaders who often believed they did not need additional training. Further, these aspirational white leaders, most often men, with barely the minimum of classroom teaching, continually attempted to climb leadership hierarchies, essentially climbing over these isolated Black leaders. While all participants were overlooked in favor of white men and women with less experience and greater egos in relation to leadership skill sets, the Black women identified additional intersectional racism and silencing, including a lack of being seen as a positional leader, needing to change personal and professional identities as part of their leadership trajectories, which sometimes came through lingering self-doubt.

Part of the impact of intersectional racism and sexism is a silencing of African American women's voices, as leadership trajectories increasingly are aligned with limiting authenticity. Thus, while Black women also experience similar barriers, such as being passed over by and for less-experienced and less-culturally responsive educators, they also must navigate increasing threats to their authenticity as part of their transition to leadership. Rosie and Alicia not being seen by similarly positioned white administrators juxtaposes with Raine's efforts to maintain the safety of white administrators. This dance, especially along the pathway towards administration, ultimately requires energy focused on taking care of supervisors and peers while starting positional leadership roles, thus stunting the development of leadership identities that align with and advocate for authenticity.

Leadership as Whiteness: Am I Not Enough?

All research participants shifted towards administration to help provide an example of culturally responsive leadership within larger district contexts of whiteness. The proliferation of white teachers promoted to leadership positions without having developed skill sets in culturally responsive approaches reflects a systemic denial of the relevance of the science of teaching. Indeed, white teachers promoted into teaching after less than three years of classroom experience suggests an interest in fostering leadership that specifically does not reflect or engage students of color. Each participant shared stories of white teachers scaling leadership ladders within urban school districts, being rewarded with promotional opportunities without demonstrating excellence with students. While these promotions of whiteness ultimately became justifications for taking on administrative leadership roles, they also demonstrate the systemic prioritization of bad teaching, coupled with an intentional devaluing of instructional leadership. These racist values, contrary to adding anything positive to student of color learning, were apparent to these Black leaders while they were teachers, and they had to face the fallout of this commitment to whiteness as soon as they joined leadership pathways.

White administrators with few teaching skills and even fewer demonstrated leadership skills were thus a structural barrier for Black leaders, particularly as they had to challenge these administrators within their first days on the job (and often before, while still serving as teachers). Working to improve outcomes for students began to take on less of a focus in comparison to managing colleagues and supervisors whose whiteness shaped negative interactions with students, teachers, and families. Shonda's pathway illustrates these tensions and compounded intersectional oppression based on racism, sexism, classism, elitism, and anti-single parenthood:

> So, I went for my admin and my masters. And then I was told by the district that if I wanted to stay here, I'd need to go to a different program. Now, I started in that district, and my heart is there, and I live there, down the street from the school that I spent most of my tenure at, where I was basically doing a lot of the admin work, all the work with parents and all of that. And parents were asking me, "Why aren't you the principal? When are you going to become the principal?" And I applied,

and [the administrator], who tells my child that I inspire her but then shoots me down when I try to become an administrator in her district, told me I needed to apply for this out-of-state administrative credential program, and you need to go back east at their residency. But I'm a single parent, and so I can't just leave my child for however long. And also, *I already have that credential.* And her little perky self just told me she had her husband. I was like, "Yeah, so, I'm a single mom."

But the message was clear: If I want to ever be a principal in this district, I'd have to go through this one specific private program. And, I talked to some of my mentors, and they told me that the program would kill my soul. So I figured maybe someone who had been at the same school, in the same neighborhood would be desirable, but not only was I not, they wanted me to go to school on the east coast to learn about my neighborhood children? Going to a corporate model leadership prep program will hurt your heart. But what were my options? So, I did apply, and I got all the way to the last day of the process, and then I didn't get in. And, well, they were right, that killed my soul by itself. What do you mean I'm not worthy of your little program that I already knew would kill my soul if I got in?

And then, after saying no, the district called me and asked if I'd interview for this principal job. And, it was right after I had literally gotten on my knees and prayed because my school was gonna get a new administrator that didn't look like the kids in the school, and that wasn't from that neighborhood, and that looked a little crackish. But the administrator told me that because I was a Teacher on Special Assignment, that she couldn't trust me until I proved myself. So I got on my knees and prayed and said, "God, I can't do that." I can't run a school for somebody and watch them get paid for me to run the school.

Shonda ultimately was hired as principal of a similarly enrolled, predominantly Black and Latino school in a neighboring district, but this shift began a ten years-and-counting commute to other cities to lead schools (and now districts).

Shonda passes dozens of schools along the way to her current job, continually being reminded that her local urban district preferred leaders who were not local and not from a local certification program.

And, I live right down the street from the school, so I'm not going nowhere. But clearly the district thought I wasn't worthy. So, I've still got some school hurts. Some school district hurts going on. So, I decided to apply to other districts.

In addition to various white district leaders fueling Shonda's imposter syndrome, ultimately, the district preference for white leadership with no local ties was clear.

Echoing the experiences with whiteness that Raine, Alicia, and Jill identified, Shonda also clarified how the administrator who clearly knew her child, who knew she was a single mother, doubled down on an anti-women, anti-single mother leadership pathway. When a district administrator requires a 3,000 mile-from-home private college as the unofficially sanctioned pathway towards leadership, the district ultimately reinforces structural classism, sexism, elitism, and a privileging of those who have the social, economic, and familial context to leave their communities for a year. This stated requirement reflects the same biased process of teacher education programs requiring a year of volunteer teaching in order to earn a teaching credential (Rogers-Ard et al., 2012), reinforcing a predominantly white, privileged teacher and leadership workforce. In addition to dismissing all local colleges (including elite universities throughout the bay area), the requirement to essentially have unlimited resources and capacities to go away from a local community in order to come back to lead that community ignores all local community knowledge and experience. This is precisely the type of district-encouraged pathway that leads to teacher and leadership turnover, as those who move from out-of-state are encouraged over locally grown and developed educational leaders.

When Shonda talked about her soul being killed, all of the other participants hummed and nodded, mirroring a black church congregation affirming the pastor. The notion of whiteness that pervaded Shonda's experience was rooted in the very basic feeling of not being good enough. For many years, African American people have told their children a rule to live by: "It's not good enough to be good enough; you've got to be better than." For Shonda, the end of her pathway within the city schools she grew up in and taught in for over a decade was soul-crushing because she had done all of the right things already. She had all of the necessary credentials, was local, and had a legendary reputation at her school site and across the district, leading culturally responsive teaching workshops across the region. Yet, she wasn't *quite* right. None of her supervisors or district leaders were initially transparent about their elitist preferences; she learned these along the way, after she navigated traditional leadership pathways (which also cost her considerable resources, since she had already paid for two years of a master's program). When Shonda indicated she had school and district hurts, other participants supported her verbally and non-verbally; constantly being overlooked and dismissed by white district leaders was a shared experience for every person in the room and for every Black leader in this book.

Ricardo, who was not in the focus group, echoed the frustration at being overlooked by white colleagues as part of the leadership pathway. This frustration of whiteness silencing students of color led him to leave the classroom, even as he had already considered leadership.

I definitely never thought I'd be a principal. But the frustration of having these little know-nothing white dudes come and boss me around like I was the janitor . . . and they didn't even know the janitor's name. I never wanted to be them, but I knew my ego couldn't take 30 years of working under a revolving slate of white dudes who sucked as teachers and who wanted me to suck as bad as them. So I guess I didn't have a choice but to leave the classroom and make sure I made one school have one less of them. I definitely questioned myself a lot though, especially as a new administrator. I mean, they come at you from every direction, living under a microscope, while you're just learning the basics of how do I supervise and mentor, how does my budget work, who actually has power in the district. I started second guessing myself initially, partially because the messages were always negative.

All the training, from instruction, classroom management, special education, all of it felt like I was being told to quiet these kids down. And that shit got worse when it was leadership. Then it was like, if you have any of these hot shot Latino or Black or Asian teachers, you gotta get them to act right. All of it was like, a good leader is effective, and effective means test scores. And test scores mean job security and resources. Anything else is nice, but you better be white if you aren't going to have good test scores. If you are Black though, man, you better have high test scores or high increases or you'll last two years, at best. They'll put you in some horrible district job 'til you quit, or at least 'til they can overwhelm you with the lack of resources, basically.

Even as Ricardo was on a leadership trajectory early on, he still never thought he would be a principal. Just like every other participant, Ricardo got into teaching because he wanted to work directly with children of color. Both his credential programs prioritized whiteness, attempting to acculturate him into thinking like a white educator, complete with a deficit, anti-Black, and anti-people of color orientation. The transition to leadership exacerbated that whiteness, to the point where he began to question his own approaches, second-guessing himself because he was so isolated, and he had very few others who thought and looked like him, especially during his transition to leadership.

Participants were clear that, except for André, none wanted to be a principal when they began as educators. Once committed to the leadership pathway, however, they all shared in the experience that leadership pathways were driven in part by a need to transform schools from the racist, white-centric leadership they continued to navigate as teachers. All participants saw leadership as a negative endeavor, and not the best way to gain influence over the ways in which schools were operating as anti-Black. They all worried about what would happen to their students after they left their classrooms, and were concerned that their peer teachers did not know how to reach or teach "our babies." Leadership ultimately meant actively confronting systemic racism and leading the transformation of conditions of school, staff treatment, student engagement, and culturally responsive approaches throughout, and this was clear before leadership pathways began. But the notion of leaving children without an engaging, loving teacher was a stressor that each Black leader carries with them today.

These leadership trajectories aligned with hierarchical navigation, increasing racial isolation and proximity to whiteness, leading to a lingering concern about the capacity to do the type of work they wanted to do as leaders surrounded by white administrators. This was worsened by the presence of administrators of color who seemed long-ago silenced by the whiteness around them; their acquiescence added an additional burden and isolating impact for each participant. Unable to simply close their classroom door and create the conditions of care for students, participants learned that they were no longer invisible, and this increased visibility came with resource perks that were tempered by power struggles and increased barriers to continued leadership progression. Despite these struggles, these Black school leaders were extremely clear that being an administrator was a choice they made after years of teaching within frustratingly white-centric leadership spaces, and that their leadership trajectories, and navigational strategies within whiteness, were just beginning.

Jill's experience as a district leader who spends time with school leaders helps provide a transition to the next chapter, in which we focus on ways Black educational leadership engages within an anti-Black student context. Jill recalled a workshop she led on culturally responsive school leadership filled with a range of site-based educational leaders, including deans of students, community engagement specialists, assistant principals, and principals, all of color. She reflected after the workshop:

> What I've heard from almost everyone was "I didn't want to be an administrator because I've seen examples of folks who are not leading from their core or who are putting their masks on so that they can assimilate and get along as opposed to doing what they need to do." What's really funny is, I remember having the same conversation with many of them when they first started out as teachers. And after they got frustrated after a few years, I was like—the only way to change the way principals are viewed is if those of you who think differently start becoming principals and model how different it can be.

Jill's workshop participants echoed the transition to leadership these Black administrators took, identifying the same barriers and ongoing frustrations regardless of their role as a teacher or school leader. Yet Jill also left the workshop in a space of positivity, helping the participants re-engage with their purpose, moving from identifying frustrations to also considering what keeps Black educators in leadership roles, even if just temporarily.

Jill concluded that workshop by sharing with participants, "Now, you're all administrators, and three to five years from now, what's your thought process?" Jill reanimated her point:

> The only way to shift change is to be in it. You've got to be in the belly of the beast. You've got to be thinking about how you can stay, because the reality is that's the only way you're going to shift change on an even larger level. Yes, it's highly isolating, but if we continue leaving, we will never change the system.

In the next chapter, we shift to operating as Black educational leaders working specifically to create cultures and climates that promote positive senses of Blackness for our students, applying Bettina Love's (2019) call for abolitionist teaching to school leadership efforts.

4

THEY DON'T SEE OUR BABIES

"I really need my teachers to not diminish my students' intelligence."

—Trey

"We can break behaviors, but we're not breaking babies."

—Raine

Angelica, a junior in high school, wants to talk about violence against Black women. On a chilly winter day, we chat over black sesame bubble tea, her purple t-shirt proudly proclaiming "Fuck tha PoPo." Her backpack is adorned with assorted buttons, including "Radical Black Feminist," "I Voted," "Vegan(ish)," "No Means Oh Hell Nah," and "Hella Berzerkeley." Her thin braids intermingle her natural hair with strands of pink, purple, and red, reaching down past her shoulders, and she wears matching Converse All-Stars, alternating each day with pink, purple, or red pairs. Angelica lives with her adoptive parents in Berkeley, California, yet attends school 30 minutes from home, having been expelled from local school districts for repeatedly smoking weed.

We meet Angelica in a café near her current school, and she relays this story:

> My favorite teacher at my old school was Ms. Smith. She was young, hella dope, had pink braids, kinda like mine, but hers was all natural, like she'd been growing her hair out since she was born. She was like the prettiest teacher ever, and she had hella #BlackGirlMagic. She would run up on us like she was my older sister, snap me outta some stupid shit I was doing, always made me get serious and shit. Like I was ready to slip off campus,

and she come outta nowhere and was like, "Come on, girl, no matter what is going on, leaving ain't gonna solve it." Then she take me to her room, feed us, make sure we was drinking enough water, and we just chill, a bunch of other Black girls all just chillin to old school MC Lyte or Lauren Hill or early Beyoncé.

But one day that all change. She was cold, snapped at us, like something had happened. We kept asking, but she was like, "Y'all mind yo damn bisness." And we were like her posse – we just followed her everywhere, always hung in her classroom, and shit, like my mom would call her to check in on me. And one day we came to class and we had this sub. She was gone. Ms. Smith was out. No goodbye, nothing. No notice from anyone or anything. No one told us shit—everyone just tight-lipped. My homegirl, who graduated like two years before, say she saw Ms. Smith a few weeks after that and broke it down: the principal, Mr. Martín, had been fuckin' with her for years. Like trynna talk to her nonstop and shit. Never taking "no," just disrespecting her, but like we never saw any of that. So I guess like after a few years, she finally break down and say something, and he sexually assaulted her. She called the police and everything. And I guess the district didn't do shit, cause Mr. Martín is still there, but ain't no one see where Ms. Smith is.

And I mean, we all hated that principal. All of us. Cause he would always say to us, "don't be a bitch, be a mujer," and would always be like looking us up and down all nasty like—like mujer means street walker or something. Ms. Smith was the one who taught us to see that, to stand up for our shit, especially to watch out for older men, and then to know she was being fucked with by the principal, who we all thought was nasty, it's like we kinda knew—or shoulda knew—it was happening. But I mean, we was like 15, 16. We only saw it in hindsight though. It wasn't real til my homegirl say something, but then like everything kinda hit me hard, like all the men in my life who was nasty to me, the two times I was raped, how school be like hella not caring, and then it was like, shit, school protecting this nasty man? And my mom was treated all nasty by brothas, by the principal, too—he disrespected her too once. Like everyone treats Black women nasty, like we they sex objects or just in they way.

I can't imagine being a teacher—the amount of shit Ms. Smith had to deal with. Teachers are like in the middle of all this anti-Black women shit. What we 'posed to learn from when everyone we look up to treated like this? And she was the one who had to quit? Ain't that some shit? All this school stuff just protects men, and protects the nasty men the most. So I'm like, why go to school? Why put up with that? And they want us to invest ourselves in that? Fuck that shit. The people who lead, they always seem to be the ones who the most nasty. And sometimes it's our people who the worst.

Throughout these interviews, participants repeatedly centered on the importance of supporting students like Angelica, of being culturally responsive and caring, and of pushing against teachers who simply did not care enough about "our babies." Angelica went to schools within the extended community that most of the participants in this book taught at, led, or were at least extremely familiar with, and several participants also knew Mr. Martín, a principal well-known as a social justice advocate, and in smaller circles, as a sexual predator the district tolerates. Angelica's frustration with the "most nasty" school leaders was bigger than Mr. Martín, however, as she was frustrated by the systemic protection of his sexualized, anti-Black women violence. Angelica saw schools as enabling those who cause harm to her mother, her friends, and her favorite teacher, and recognized that this protection aligned with a national context of anti-Blackness. Angelica also recognized that she needed protection herself, and struggled with remaining in schools designed to cause her, and people like her, structural harm.

The notion of instructors and leaders of color being on-site as more than just role models but also as advocates for children of color has been mentioned elsewhere (Ellis & Epstein, 2015; Knaus & Rogers-Ard, 2012; Rogers-Ard et al., 2012; Sleeter, 2001); however, these educators were called towards leadership roles because they needed to do something not just about the condition of schools, but about the dramatic anti-Black violence against their "babies." Indeed, these educational leaders saw many district teachers, most of whom were white, as core parts of the schooling mission to colonize and silence children of color. But they also saw school leaders and teachers—many of whom were people of color—perpetuate the same silencing, and in some cases, the same violence. Thus, their absolute certainty that leadership was always about more than individual gain rested on their commitment to cultivating educational spaces where Black children could grow.

Part of the necessity of advocating for children of color at school sites is based on leaders' clarity around education being a necessity for all children, especially children of color, to successfully navigate the United States' continued reliance upon oppressive systems. Because white supremacy is the underlying thought and practice for US educational systems (hooks, 2013; Love, 2019), it is critically important that African American leaders are grounded in the importance of being site leaders to provide educational safe passage for our children. While Mason reiterated that "I love every single one of my kids," he also was intimately aware that he needed to support students experiencing the anti-Black racism of schools. Listening to culturally rooted site leaders yielded three themes around the silencing of students: (a) fucking with our babies or the compilation of intersectional racism facing Black students; (b) removing Black children from classrooms and schools; and (c) student-centered vs. adult-centered learning systems, in which adult interests continuously compete with—and take priority over—student interests.

Fucking with Our Babies

All of the Black leaders in this book became teachers so they could have a positive impact on children of color, and more specifically to support African American children. And all of these leaders were extremely frustrated by the ways they saw children of color being treated by teachers, by school and district policies and practices, and by larger societal forces. In the same way that André's earlier quote named the war for the souls of our children, these leaders knew the intense anti-Blackness their babies faced because they also faced this, as children and students in the same (or similar) schools, as teachers and leaders in the same schools, and also as parents of children in the same (or similar schools). Thus they had firsthand knowledge from at least four vantage points, firmly distinguishing them from the vast majority white teacher population that did not attend urban schools, did not live in the local community, and rarely taught at the same school they later led.

Shonda provided a powerful example of the multiple roles Black educational leaders often play, ensuring lived knowledge of the impacts of racism on her children and students, and keeping her in cycles of racist trauma. Her son "had a teacher that sat him in a corner for the whole year." Not only was her child made to sit in isolation, missing out on much of the instruction, no one responsible told her, and deeper, "nobody cared." While she was a principal in a nearby district at the time, this experience reminded Shonda of the systemic nature of racist exclusions of Black children across all schools. The only reason she even knew about the treatment of her child by a teacher was because another administrator she was friends with told her, and then she started realizing there were a number of problematic educator behaviors intentionally hidden from her. Shonda clarified:

> I'm like, you just let my kid sit in a corner? Or the other administrator he had gave my son a search and seizure? My kid is probably the sweetest child in the universe. And they searched his backpack. And I'm like that you know that's against the law. I did the mama thing: I sat in the meeting, and I said, "So you searched my kid's backpack. And, in fact, you implicated yourself in an email telling me that you did." I said, "So that's against Ed Code." And [the administrator] says, "Miss Shonda, you need to leave." And I said, "It's against Ed Code. I'm his mom. I need to know why are you searching my . . . . Well, I saw his piece of homework hanging out, so I went through the—." That's against Ed Code. Did you have a reason? Did you think he had drugs or what? So watching my own kid go through that and then as a principal I have teachers who don't do anything or do the same thing.

This experience reminded Shonda that interrupting school practices that isolate and harm Black children like her son is not systemic; there will always be another racist teacher or administrator. Indeed, she would not have even known her son was being mistreated and isolated without having the cultural capital to be friends with district administrators. Shonda realized that while her relative privilege helped protect her son, she was unable to always be in the room, unable to interrupt the onslaught of efforts to silence him.

The cumulative nature of lived intersectional racism from multiple perspectives further sharpened Black educational leader focus on systemic racism. Mason summarized the frustration they all shared: "These kids are getting fucked and they don't even know it. Their parents don't even know it." That Shonda was a parent and only knew because of her professional colleagues reinforced this collective frustration. The realities that many Black children are being systematically abused by their teachers, schools, and districts was normalized across each participant, even as they realized that most white teachers and administrators would cringe at that accusation. Indeed, most white teachers and leaders had created senses of self that built upon saving Black children. The white savior mentality infused across every school and district, with white educators blissfully unaware of the damage to children of color they were actively tolerating, engaging in, and fostering.

Raine argued that part of the problem is that "[white people] have to serve these Black and Brown kids here because that's who we have, but they don't really believe that they can be academically successful." This disbelief in Black children was a common frustration with Black school leaders focused on improving teacher behavior. Dawn would often ask students about their teachers as a way to better understand what was happening when she wasn't in the room:

> I asked the kids who are in the class, "What do you guys do?" And one kid was like, "Well, we learned in our class about not to call kids niggas." I'm like, "Well that's good," and then he's like, "And we put a quarter in the jar when we don't cuss." When they don't cuss! They're teaching them if you cuss it's wrong, so if you cuss you put a quarter in the jar. My question is, where is the data, right? Where is the data that's saying that this is successful?

Dawn's frustration at a classroom management strategy that forces children to literally pay for cussing reinforces the low expectations this particular teacher had for her students. And on a deeper level, in an age where seemingly everyone claims to be data-driven, Dawn questioned this teacher's use of a strategy that had no way to measure impact. Allowing stereotypes of how a student should talk within a classroom and a pay-to-speak scheme suggests minimal care for the students in the classroom, but also has little to do with academic learning.

Shonda echoed this frustration at teacher and administrator apathy around many of the issues facing children of color. "The week before," Shonda recalled, "A girl tried to kill herself because her grades weren't high enough." In talking with students and families, Shonda realized there was a severe lack of trust, "We don't trust any of these admin, we can't trust them. They'll put us on blast." While Shonda relayed that she would not tell other educators anything unless there was a safety issue, she lamented that "I have to figure out which adult to tell." Trying to maintain a safe environment for children and their families that feels antagonistically anti-Black was a continual struggle for Shonda, often putting her in between the district and the families she was committed to supporting:

> I've been at two middle, two high, and two elementary schools. Everybody is saying they don't trust the teachers. The teachers are here for a paycheck. [The Black kids] actually say, "We are a paycheck to them." There's ability issues: They make fun of all of the kids with special needs. Sexual orientation issues, a lot of that. People hiding in the bathroom. People not going to the bathroom because the bathroom they are dressed for is not the bathroom they're allowed to go into. People are leaving the school to go to the bathroom—ditching, just to go to the bathroom outside of the building. So, I'm also taking on gender spectrum, because that's what's needed.

Shonda named ableism and anti-gender fluidity as ways that children mess with each other. As students were making fun of each other, teachers often looked the other way, ignoring the peer ableism their silence was complicit in. Similarly, school policy around bathroom use based on socially constructed gender ideas, rather than gender identities, normalized transphobic, gender binaries that further enabled student harm. While Shonda was operating at a district level, trying to align school policy and practice with affirming student identities, most teachers were ignoring the bullying students were negotiating, and, as Shonda earlier pointed out, not all students were surviving. Noting that student suicide and self-harm appeared on the rise, Shonda was concerned about school climate, demanding that teachers create welcoming spaces for all by interrupting peer violence and harmful school policies.

While wrestling with structures at the district level, Shonda was increasingly frustrated with having to deal with teachers who continually cause harm to Black children. "I don't really care about the teachers right now," she argued, "because they're the ones messing up shit." She went on to describe a number of instances where teachers demonstrated their lack of care for children, and were ultimately supported by the district, union, or school board for doing such, echoing Angelica's point about how nasty educators are often protected:

> I have some teachers that are just nasty. And I can say what I want to say. I can write them up. But once they get to the board, nothing happens.

Some of the board members have been fired as teachers too. So it's because I've been fired, I'm not going to let you ever fire anybody, even if they're terrible and hurting children.

Shonda's frustrations at the systemic support for harmful teachers were billowing over. Continual barriers to her confronting, much less addressing, teacher lack of care were held in place by a school board election process that enabled those with resources, often one-issue candidates, to win their elections.

At one point, more than half the board were formerly fired teachers, and their without question protection of harmful teachers came at a systemic cost to children of color, particularly given some of the more obvious grievances. Shonda clarified:

> I have a PE teacher who doesn't like Black and Brown kids, but he works at a Black and Brown school. And so my little Black boys have to sit out of PE because they misbehave or [say something]. One time, one of my little boys got [kicked out of class] class, and I was like, "If class just started. How are you here?" He said, "I can't be in his class." And I was like, "Well, what did you do?" "I really don't know." So I'm like, "Let's hang out because, if I send you back, you're just going to get more torture." So what do I do with that?
>
> [Another example was] this teacher went to a family's house, drove down the street, saw the kid he was mad at from [earlier] that day, gets out of his car, and proceeds to scream and berate the child in the community right on the street. And the mom comes out. His mom barely speaks English and he says, "Tell her what you did. Tell her what you did," screaming at the top of his lungs at the mom, at the kid. And I wasn't allowed to do anything about it.
>
> I took it to HR. I made the families write letters of complaint to the district. I did all of that. And even with that, my families and I were silenced like you can't really do that. The only person that listened to me was our superintendent. And he was like, "Well, [that teacher] needs to go." But all of these things are in place, so there's nothing I can do. And he's been here forever. And I'm like, "I don't want you on my site." I can't even speak to him without [union] representation. He's like, "I don't trust you." But I'm going to call you out every time you hurt a kid, even if the district won't do anything. And so every year, we're fighting.
>
> I've got another teacher that won't teach to save his life. He just stands there, and he complains that kids in Africa, they do this. And in Africa, they do this. Well, you're in America, babe. You need to figure out what's going out with these kids and teach these kids because they're in front of you. And you're in a fifth-grade class, you can't handle them. I put you in a second grade class, you can't handle them. And my kinders will come

and tell me what the teacher is doing wrong. When my sixth graders will say, "This person is screaming at us telling us we're stupid," I'm like, "Why again can I not fire these teachers?" And one of the Black teachers, he'll be like, "You can't write me up, I'm Black." So what happens is I just make him uncomfortable until he leaves my site. But then, he just goes to another school. And so what's right for our children?

Shonda's repeated examples highlight the number of teachers that harm children, in and outside their classrooms, and the protection these teachers are afforded, by the teacher's union and through district practice.

The one Black teacher compared their children to a supposedly more colonially rigid structure that stereotypically presumed all 56 African countries employ, chastising children for how he wished they were, rather than teaching the children he had. One teacher violently confronted a student and their mother at their house, outside of school time, without regard for the image that might convey to the school or district. Yet the district human resources office disregarded both series of incidents, ultimately supporting the teachers who were overtly displaying anti-student and anti-family biases. The third teacher (and first story here) reflects extensive research on predominantly white teachers removing Black children from their classrooms, often without cause. Each of these examples was common across Shonda's district, and in every case, the adult teachers were always supported in continually, as Shonda sighed, "fucking with our children."

Removing Black Children

Shonda's example of the PE teacher who regularly removed Black children before class parallels the extensive literature on the school-to-prison pipeline. In this section, Black educational leaders share daily and cumulative experiences with the removal of Black children from classrooms, schools, and ultimately, gentrifying communities. While there were examples of educators of color aligning their approaches to the white supremacist practice of removing children from classroom-based educational opportunities, the majority of the exclusion of Black learning was facilitated by white teachers and district administrators.

Rosie clarified a systems-wide practice of educators removing Black children from their classrooms, highlighting a dismissal of the conditions that many Black children struggled through outside of school.

Most of the kids that came to my office were Black. They came to my office pissed off. They came to my office because they got kicked out of class. Sometimes it was a setup from the teacher. Sometimes the kid was acting out but the teacher didn't really wanna figure out why or what happened to the kid before they even made it to school. You know if they're hungry or if they saw something, or if dad didn't come home, or they got kicked out of, you know whatever. No one did basic social emotional investigation to get at the level of where this kid is coming from.

Rosie further clarified that there was an operational climate at the school that enabled teachers to remove children they had difficulty teaching. Rather than cultivate a climate of support, where teachers would ask for help when needed, or where leadership would provide instructional support or outside-the-classroom support in the form of counseling or basic assessments of child readiness to learn, teachers were expected to show test score results on their own. The building blocks for academic engagement were simply not part of the school culture, and aside from one or two other teachers, most of the white teachers were disengaged and culturally non-responsive.

The easiest approach for them, Rosie highlighted, was to remove children who were not learning, and the office and principal supported those actions because they also did care enough to learn what to do.

> The same kids were getting thrown out of classrooms with no support really from teachers. The school was unhealthy; the culture was unhealthy. It was divided amongst Black and Latinos, and Latino families had more power and more say. Teachers were culturally adrift or inept. The curriculum was piss poor, it didn't teach kids about themselves, it didn't teach them how to be young students of color or adults of color in this world. It didn't teach them their history.

Rosie's frustration further suggests a prioritization of Latinx students, in part because, as she reflected later, the school had a larger middle-class Latinx population and a predominantly working-class Black population. Thus, the additional support for Latinx students was missing for Black students, and none of the students were learning *who* and *how* they were within a deeper context of ethnic studies to keep them academically engaged.

The notion of a school teaching Black children their history, teaching how to be adults of color in a hyper-racist world, was largely dismissed by these leaders as a great idea that most white teachers were neither interested nor prepared to engage. While they all agreed that ethnic studies and related student-centered, culturally responsive curricula should be required, their daily struggles with offensive curricula taught by offensive teachers were more pressing battles. These anti-Black school contexts were reinforced by normalized school and district practices that ignored student needs. While these leaders knew exactly what their students needed, though, their central office leaders, teachers, and teacher advocates treated students in ways that always led to the removal of Black children.

All participants shared stories about how the white teacher problematization of Black students was reinforced by district practice. Shonda further clarified how teachers exclude Black students, and how she is ultimately unable to challenge the causes of teacher removal:

> It's [two Black kids] that are in trouble. And those are probably the sweetest kids. But they're always in my office. And I'm like, "What happened? He talked? Put him back in your classroom. Maybe you should talk to him. Maybe you should give him opportunities to express himself." And so the fact that I can't even go and address those things without all of these different [political] pieces coming . . . is hard.

Similarly, Alicia argued how a deeper problem is that, particularly in high school, Black children are significantly aware of how their teachers, and district practice, frame them as problems. "We can get them to come," she argued, summarizing school recruitment strategies, "but if we can't figure out how to teach them, they're not gonna stay." Alicia further suggested "that is the experience that kids of color are having," where ultimately, children of color require advocates at the classroom and school levels in order to simply remain within the classroom.

Seeing their babies being targeted had a strong impact on participants, as their roles were to advocate, and as they progressed into leadership, their roles became increasingly limited to advocating for students they felt had done nothing wrong. Alicia's frustrations illustrate the interest convergence of white teachers diversifying schools after white families push out families of color in cycles of gentrification. She succinctly clarified:

> How dare you put all of these kids here that you're supposedly here for, but it's all for show. The district says we need to get more diverse kids: "Let's get more diverse kids!" We're on this thing about how it's all about diversity. And it just makes me mad. It makes me angry, it makes me sad. And I want to jump back in sometimes and say, "What are you all doing?" But mostly I'm just like whatever. Because they're just gonna do whatever they're gonna do anyway.

Alicia clarified how the barriers placed in front of students of color enable teachers to not have to teach someone who may require more effort on their part.

Thus, pushing children out of classrooms, and potentially schools, while complicating diversity recruitment efforts, ultimately enables teachers to teach using less effort:

And I'm watching them do this disservice. This student wants to come back [to the school] and he asked me if he could come back. I was like, "Dude, he wants to go to college." But, I was also like, "If you come back, you may not graduate." If he stays where he is at least he will get educated because [that school] understands how to teach him. And if he comes back, the director wants him back because of his athletic potential. But it's like, fuck that! He wants to be so many things, a lawyer, a surgeon—this kid can do and be anything. But ya'll don't know how to teach him! How dare you tell him he can come back here.

Teachers get frustrated, which I understand. But you have a bunch of kids who you don't even have to think outside of your box to communicate with, and they're doing alright. And then you have this one kid in your classroom who's not. And the parent is like, "You all fix it." And then the teachers are like, "This kid must need an IEP." But it is so fricking clear. And it's not just race, it's class . . . . You have African American, Latino kids from middle and upper middle-class families, they're good, they're golden. Because they have cultural capital.

Watching a school recruit a student they already kicked out for not learning from the way they are dedicated to teaching was extremely frustrating for Alicia. While she was tasked with recruiting a more diverse population at the magnet school, she increasingly saw children of color leaving because they were not doing well, exacerbated by her school's lack of willingness to learn and adopt culturally responsive approaches. The dismissal of children she knew would be strong students under the right conditions—first through falsely identifying them as special education, then by removing from the school—was infuriating.

Yet Alicia highlighted an important caveat: not all children of color, even within the same schools, are treated similarly. Indeed, echoing Rosie's experiences, Alicia identified how families of color with more wealth and cultural capital were seen as an important constituent across districts and school sites. Families with fewer means and resources, however, were often ignored or dismissed, and due to having to work more jobs and longer hours, and due to past negative experiences often within the same schools as their children, were less willing to participate and communicate with educators that seemed antagonistic to begin with.

Alicia further clarified how students at the magnet school were watching community and school gentrification happen during their high school years. Thus, they entered a racially diverse school, but four years later, saw the school enrollment whiten dramatically. "They watched it happen," Alicia clarified, "And for them, it was uncomfortable. The students felt the school changing." Because these students faced new barriers that were not in place earlier in their schooling, they increasingly felt "isolated." Alicia highlighted that because of this isolation, "they don't stay." She indicated:

> I had this one kid. I'm so in love with this little boy. He's 16 now, he came to us in the ninth grade. He became like the poster child in my head for the kid that we just have no clue how to serve. Born here, lives in a Latino community in Oakland. Spanish at home, Spanish in his community, Spanish immersion in elementary school. Mom got a light-bulb moment when he was in the fourth grade that Spanish immersion, probably not the best idea, let me switch him. Moved him to a school where everybody is Latino. And so he completely functioned in Spanish, he knows conversational English. Wicked smart kid, completely functioning in Spanish until he landed here.
>
> And all of a sudden, he was expected by everybody to function in English. And the disaster that was this boy's ninth grade year. I mean there were days he would sit at my desk, and I would be trying to help him with an algebra problem. And he knew the math but could not decipher the question. He would be sitting at my desk, his head on my shoulder, and he'd be like, "I don't know what that means, what does that word mean?" He left because he was failing everything. He's super talented. But we can't fucking teach him. We have a handful of African American and Latino [students] who teachers have no idea what to do with. Because the reality is, there are a bunch of skills gaps, but teachers did not come to this school to teach to those gaps.
>
> And the principal claims to be all down, but here they are, 20 students of color in one class. And then whatever they didn't get in the ninth grade, they're not getting in the tenth grade, and next year, and the year after, if they stay—if they stay, I will be saying, "You all need to be going to a different school if you wanna get a High School diploma." And it's not okay.

Alicia wanted to be clear that while the context of removing children from the school ostensibly focused on lower-income Black and Latinx students, the underlying issue was an unwillingness to learn to teach all students. Working within schools that celebrate diversity while hypocritically fueling teacher apathy to teach a diverse range of learners, angered Alicia and the rest of these leaders.

Jayson echoed what was seen as a systemic alignment against children of color by white teachers, suggesting this limited willingness to teach was linked to a fear of challenging students of color: "There's almost this fear of like [white people] don't want to say all kids can go to college because [they're] uncomfortable with pushing a kid who doesn't look like them." This discomfort was shared by the predominantly white teaching staff at his school, who aligned around low expectations. "And when you have a school full of people like that," Jayson continued, "they think they're doing kids right by graduating them; [the kids] can't count change, but they can graduate. It's really difficult."

The limited willingness to engage the racially diverse students every school and district celebrated on their websites was exacerbated by the anger and violence Shonda earlier highlighted, where a teacher screamed at a parent and child. While many students of color did not directly witness such white rage from teachers, they did witness the withdrawal of resources as their peers of color slowly dropped out or moved. Meanwhile, they tried to learn from teachers whose own low expectations manifested in their insincere interest in teaching. These leaders recognized that school and district practice supported white teacher rage, just as removing Black (and Latinx) children from the classroom or school was deemed to be in the teacher's interest. Yet the child's interests were rarely considered. While these Black educational leaders identified how teachers often cause problems for students within their classrooms and schools, through ignoring peer bullying, upholding gender binaries, isolating Black children, and low expectations, these were all seen as steps towards the systematic removal of Black children. For the children who are allowed to remain in the classroom, many struggle through teacher apathy towards their learning, reflecting Jayson's point about teachers' fears of academically challenging Black students.

Trey echoed these frustrations, identifying how when teachers cause intellectual harm to Black students, they are often supported by school practice. Thus, teachers who remove children from the classroom expect some behavioral magic to solve the child, when most often, the behavioral problem is a set of reactions to disengaged teaching:

> Teachers send the children out to get fixed and then we're supposed to send them back. Here's my issue; I really need my teachers or the adults in the room to not diminish my students' intelligence because they're trying to avoid work because the students cannot read. They're trying to avoid a situation in which the room is chaotic and they don't want to be in there. That's why we have these students who have an issue come down to the think tank and finish the entire day's work in 30 minutes, so it's not the student. It's what you're *not* doing in the classroom.

While Trey was able to create work-around opportunities for students to learn after being removed from the classroom, his point is that such work-arounds should not be needed. Indeed, work-arounds to educate Black children outside the classroom ironically enable teachers to continue ineffective teaching, while encouraging removal of those whom the teacher had deemed to be more difficult to teach. Interest convergence aligns with the creation of programs and opportunities to educate Black children removed from classrooms because ultimately, teachers that remove such children instead focus on those more able to take advantage of the ways those teachers teach. Benefiting from smaller operational class sizes, teachers are perversely incentivized to remove children.

Many programs are created to educate the children who are removed, who, these Black educational leaders were clear, are most often Black, Latinx, and Indigenous. These programs often reinforce deficit approaches to children of color because the focus is often fixing behavior to just send children back into toxic classrooms. Raine extended Trey and Jayson's point about the interest convergence of removing children to avoid engaging in intellectual development:

> When they have those conferences [during the school day] the focus is really about what do we do for our young boys; mentoring, drum circles, how do we get our young boys lots of drum circles, lots of rapping, lots of spoken word. How do we get our young men to basically be able to sit still better so that teachers can teach them? But it's not about how do we measure achievement and not about how do we move and break down silos in our classrooms. Because right now the whole going to whatever the other room is, this other pipeline to prison that they've created is depressing.

Raine was referring to a districtwide program focused on Black males. This widely praised program took Black males out of their regular classrooms and placed them into Black male-specific spaces. As Raine indicated, these included drumming, spoken word, and other Afrocentric and culturally responsive ways of helping those identified develop a positive sense of self. The issue, as Raine and Trey asserted, is that such programs do not develop the academic skills that these students will be measured on, that they need to graduate. Deeper, while the content may be relevant for some Black males, gender binaries and ways of being Black and male are reinforced through such programming. This well-intended removal rewards teachers who want Black children removed from their responsibility.

Shonda clarified how the interest convergence of Black removal from classrooms to benefit teachers' limited willingness to teach Black students operates across districts:

> We have these blue ribbon schools, but what's happening with Black and Brown kids? Shit is happening with them, and we're transferring them out of school, moving them into continuation schools. They are not given Algebra so they can't go to college. They're pushed out. And no one wants to talk about it. That's the problem. And it seems like everybody from the board to the union to everybody else is like, "Who cares about what's happening with kids? We want to make sure adults are okay." And I go in there every day, and I think about my kid. And I'm like would I want this for my kid? What if every day, my kid came in, and he's got to go from the class before he even gets inside?

Shonda identified the larger context of removal of Black students in a way that helps clarify Raine's critique of a program that, in theory, adds value to a white-centric curriculum.

While these administrators advocate for ethnic studies-related curriculum, they do so in alignment with helping prepare Black children to navigate and transform the world they live. Removing Black students from classrooms simply aligns with the larger context of removing Black people from schools. School practices, including the creation of continuation schools, enabling teachers to exclude children they do not want in their classrooms and schools, perfectly echoing the effects of *Brown v. Board of Education*. Since the vast majority of teachers remain white, the effect looks like white teachers removing Black children from "integrated" classrooms and schools. Districts then create alternative spaces to educate Black children, often with fewer resources and less opportunity for academic success.

While the focus on removing Black children existed, Dawn pointed out how the corollary also existed: schools tried to recruit white children to replace students of color. And with the increase in white children—enhanced by the simultaneous regional gentrification and pushout of families of color—came increased resources for programs specifically targeting families with wealth. With this changing demographic, the narrative within Dawn's school shifted from remediating children to now "we just say that all these kids are smart and we can do it." Dawn's point was that such an affirming approach took root only with the shift in student population.

> So I sit in a space at a school where I serve 1,800 kids and maybe 12 of them are white, but we have so many resources at North High because we are about to change. They are going to get all of those kids from private schools and all them kids back at North High in that community because parents are tired of paying and [another school] is having some issues going on and they are about to flip North High. So I sit at a table with people who I have to be like, "Help me understand how this is going to serve all kids. Help me understand how this is going to serve 800 kids that come to North that should be at flatland schools, who don't feel safe?"

As schools prepared for an increasingly white student base, ushering resources to bolster what was previously framed by the district as a limited resource community, Black and Latinx-focused programs were being cut.

Meanwhile, schools that were projected to remain almost entirely of color continued to implement programs to remove Black children from classrooms. Shonda highlighted how one school in her district had a practice of removing Black children who were considered behavior problems from their normal class and placing them into "African-American history," echoing the practice Raine identified. The message this removal sent to Black children was that if "you're misbehaving, you're in trouble, so you have to learn about your people." Rather than have African American history as an elective that fulfills graduation requirements, that particular school set up an ethnic studies-focused class to punish Black children. Shonda clarified how ethnic studies "should be something you elect to do, something you want to do, something you get to do." Instead, however, she argued it was framed as "something that you do because [teachers] can't control you." This example reinforced how, even Black-initiated ideas that may make sense intellectually for Black children, are often used in ways that, as Shonda said, "control Black kids."

Shonda's point about controlling Black children sparked a longer focus group conversation about removing Black children, and every interview with each participant at some point highlighted that schools were trying to control Black behavior. Ricardo and Byron both had created programs specifically designed to support Black and Latino boys in developing business plans; these courses combined math, English, and/or economics and increased academic engagement and achievement data. Yet these programs were also resource intensive, and, as both Ricardo and Byron pointed out, focused only on boys in ways they were uncomfortable with. As they both (separately, in different schools) tried to expand enrollment to girls of color, they were forced to open enrollment to all students, thereby weakening the impact. Byron argued that this opening was "designed to make it so we could not be too effective with men of color" while Ricardo dismissed the effort as "trying to get one teacher to teach all students, instead of trying to get *all* teachers to teach all students." Shonda further clarified how another program that had been successful in "moving achievement data" was subsequently canceled "because we can't actually let these kids learn because then they're dangerous."

The fear of Black children being seen as dangerous was echoed by each leader, specifically as an outcome of having a predominantly white teacher and administrator workforce. Black learning, then, was seen as contrary to white teachers and administrators, who often retaliated against programs, teachers, and administrators who were successful with Black children. The white removal of Black children from classrooms and schools parallels contemporary Black removal from the communities that surround urban schools. The impact of gentrification goes deeper than housing and new cafes; the impact of having white, middle-class teachers for predominantly Black and Brown students sustains an instructor gap. It is not enough to speak the language and read books about culturally responsive teaching; teachers must create deep relationships with people in the same communities as their students to reach those who are still being pushed out of classrooms and schools. The notion of having to both lead and support educators who have not committed themselves to develop skill sets to teach all students created a frustrating dissonance for these community-centered leaders, presenting management challenges for those supervising and being supervised by white educators.

Student-Centered versus Adult-Centered Education

Another theme that emerged from the research was leadership awareness of how adult-centered schools are. Participants were clear that students come first as a core value, requiring a shift in the way decisions are made, how curriculum is purchased, and how content is delivered within classrooms. While most districts claimed to be "Students First," the implementation of that directive involved many adult-centered decisions. The focus on adults first added even more frustrating dissonance around efforts to create a safe, healthy learning environment where students are at the center of every decision and resource. All participants saw the general context of targeting children of color, the lack of willingness to learn the skills needed to teach the children within each teacher's classroom, and the removal of Black children as reflective of a larger commitment to adult-centered school systems.

Part of the duality of being African American site administrators centers on being an effective leader while also providing safety for Black children chronically seen as problematic by teachers. This systematic dismissal of African American students was extended to the site-based leaders who intentionally position themselves as advocates, making leadership work take on additional struggles, especially when site leaders have to grapple within structural whiteness. André reflected on how his own survival skills helped build awareness to support children, but that the real battles are against the systemic intersectional racism targeting children of color across the educational system, through to college.

> That helped me survive the streets of LA and learn how to navigate stuff so I can live. But how do I bring that to the kids so they can be far ahead? So when they get to college, and they deal with these white racist motherfuckers who really feel empowered at college, and there's still not enough of us because there's only one of us in the college classroom, how do you even survive that piece?

André's point was that part of the work of being a Black administrator is to prepare children to survive their current contexts, so they can continue the struggle beyond, potentially in college. The same battles with "white racist motherfuckers" exist in whatever comes next. André's background helped prepare him to see the long struggle, and to approach preparing children of color for a life of conscious struggle, but most teachers, particularly white ones, were not committed to educating children to survive unfamiliar-to-them contexts. This lack of preparation was often seen as a white educator focus on reducing their workload. This represented the largest frustration raised by participants: white teacher inability and/or unwillingness to reach and teach "our babies."

The huge amount of head nodding and other non-verbal agreements in focus groups indicated a shared level of frustration with ineffective white teachers. Nicole assessed, "I don't really think these people feel like these kids, the Black and Brown kids, can learn." Rosie, in a separate interview, added, "I saw an upset kid that wasn't heard. And maybe the way that they were trying to be heard wasn't the right way or wasn't the best way, but the kid's 6 years old." Rosie's anger at adults not recognizing the socio-emotional limitations most 6-year-old children have in expressing why they might be angry added to her daily frustration at children simply being ignored: "They had these adult expectations on these little people which just wasn't fair and it wasn't right and it just added to stress." Raine further clarified the split between teachers who care and those who just want order in their classrooms: "There are two types of teachers: the ones who're like, 'Can you come get them? Can you come get them?' And the other ones are like, 'Man, stop taking my kids out of class. They're failing.'" The teachers who fight to keep students in their classrooms, Raine clarified, are rare and need support. The teachers who fight to remove children, however, are supported by systems within schools and across districts.

André was particularly frustrated by teachers uncommitted to children, particularly given the extensive trauma that children grow up with. In part because he grew up around the same trauma, and because he has always taught in schools that serve high concentrations of traumatized children, his expectation is that adults would invest in their own skill sets, in learning what they need in order to best prepare and support children of color.

> Just really focusing on hitting the kids' heart before we can hit them with academics. A lot of the kids I've dealt with, they all come through a lot of trauma. And, before you can try to get them on a college track, you have to get them to trust you and deal with the issues that they're coming in with. I'm just watching all of these people file in that don't look like us. All these white folks coming in, these white women, and a couple of Black men, and a few of us here and there. I'm just like, "Damn, this is why our shit is fucked up because they're not vested in our Black and Brown kids being successful."
>
> I was teaching in Watts when I first got out of college. It was a different context. It was a lot of [Black educators]. The babies were the same as the teachers. And so you could have a real conversation. People were on the same page because they were our babies. And I hear us calling them our babies. But when you move to a suburb, or a school that acts like it's in the suburbs, you don't hear that term "our babies." It's "those students." That disconnect was hard for me to deal with.
>
> And I saw that the teachers, if they weren't connecting with our kids, I'd tell them they can leave. You don't have to be here. And so they were my babies because the teachers would come and then go. And so I kept

having to hire people. And by the time the third year [of the school we started] came around, we had a solid staff. And they all didn't look like me, but through that vetting process of, "Why are you here? You know this is the hood, right? What is your experience with folks of color? Are you scared?" I had to really grill them because, if you can't make it, they don't need you.

Because he was in a leadership role of a school that was not held to district hiring protocol, André was eventually able to control which teachers were hired. His impact grew substantially through normalizing experience with and dedication to teaching Black and Latinx students.

The difference for André was that school districts did not focus on teachers of color, much less student-focused teachers. Implementing student-focused methods for recruiting, hiring, and sustaining teachers became one of André's non-negotiables. Yet André also became aware of how his commitment to children of color reflected another example of interest convergence, wherein his white colleagues would come to his school specifically to gain their own professional affirmation, using the school's population as a badge of pride. "I go to a lot of these conferences," André clarified, "And it's all about that turnaround story. And I know we all have a lot of them. And so we have to maintain that narrative, like who is saving the next year's school, or the next year's students."

Mainly, André had grown frustrated with educators who work at a school for a year or two, then go on to a higher leadership level, a tendency that reflected the whiteness of creating school systems to support non-responsive educators instead of children.

It's those folks that do not care about our kids [that we have to] have the ability to check them and their privilege every time. Even though you're in the principal seat, somebody thinks they know more than you. You know what I mean? And sometimes, you have to say 'Be quiet. Just be quiet,' to these [white] teachers. Last year, I didn't get no grievances because I'm the Black man that knows how to handle the kids that they can't handle. But now, when I start going to those classrooms and talking about we need to do a little bit more, and then, you got to make it palatable for them so they don't freak out and get scared because they're very comfortable in having very low expectations for our kids. And I have to be the voice and say would you want this for your kids? What can they do once they leave? Are they going to be able to survive? Can they write? Can they add? Can they work in group settings? Because you say they're not going to go to college, but well, if they're going to a trade school, which is school, they're going to have to be able to do math. They're going to have to be able to communicate with other people. So what are we doing?

André's frustration with teacher resistance to increasing expectations, to learning how to implement student-centered approaches within their classrooms led him to struggle for the right to hire and evaluate teachers. But district practice removed such power from his position, instead preferring to place teachers who were often removed from other schools into his classrooms.

As soon as she began serving in a formal leadership role, Raine elevated her staff development approach, focusing on helping adult-centered teachers learn to be student-centric. She clarified her approaches and values:

> I am coaching what we're not going to do to my babies. So I tell [the teacher] to watch me. Watch because she's a little, beautiful, chocolate, little thing. And she's bad as heck. Watch. I'm not chastising the teacher, I just want him to learn something. Watch me say the thing that you should have said in that moment. "Becky, did you not understand? This is what I was asking you to do. Do you see the difference between what you did and what I did because it didn't feel safe for me? Did it feel safe for you, Becky? That's okay, you don't have to answer that. It didn't feel safe. So all I'm saying is we could go around this circle of, okay, I want to check in with you after school. I want to blah, blah, blah." Or we could just name the thing. "You are mean, and that was evil. And you're going to break my kids." We can break behaviors, but we're not breaking babies.

Raine's example of "Becky," a white teacher representing many of the teachers Raine has coached, echoed with other participants, who expressed frustration with white teachers (and teachers of color) not committed to students.

But the deeper frustrations were the adult-centered systems that support teacher apathy and disengagement, including grievance processes that protected teacher racism. Raine clarified a specific incident of district alignment around adult-centered approaches over a focus on student growth:

> This morning I sent an email to the [district] behavioral team. I said, "There's a student at my school and he's a genius. He is six years old and they have sent five million people in to socially and emotionally help him. We're not going to get him an IEP because that's not how I roll. We are going to figure out how to support him in this or you can just leave. Like from the gate we need to get him into IEP. I'm telling you, he's a genius. I know, because he's in my office and I'm teaching him to read." When I sent the email, they sent in another behavioral specialist. Why is it behavior? And no, I'm not giving him an IEP. I don't know how many times I've got to say that, to tell mama to quit talking to them without me. They started calling her behind my back.
>
> People are coming to talk to Black families who [they identify as needing behavioral support] . . . I don't need behavioral specialists. I don't

know what that is. I don't want your district folks. I don't want your behavioral specialists. I don't want your "developmentally appropriate services" and whatever the hell else you think that we need in here that we didn't need before. I'm about kids and not adults. That's it.

Raine's frustration with a prescribed solution seen through the lenses of special education, without knowing the specific child, and without recognition that she was already in relation with the family, led her to continually challenge district decisions.

To note, district decisions were often made without consultation with site-based educators familiar with these particular students. Unable to provide input in the over-identification of Black children into special education, Raine was frustrated that she had teachers unwilling to learn to keep Black children in their classrooms. She was also aware that the district was aiming to address a problem that, seen through her daily interactions with the child and mother, was an adult problem. "We're trying to change the game for kids," Raine argued, "and if at the end of the day changing the game for kids is about the teachers and us working together as a team and figuring this out for our kids, then that's what we should do." Student behavior, Raine challenged, was an adult problem, and solutions that come from outside the team tasked with caring for and educating children, enabled structural racism to continue.

In addition to advocating for children, these leaders advocated for control over their own school sites. Efforts at creating local control to protect "our babies" created disjointed relationships between the leader and their privileged white managers, however, because Black leaders were seen as interrupting traditionalized district practice. Rosie argued that underlying racist teacher practice is a district commitment to teacher racism, in part because administrators see themselves in white teachers, because when they were teachers, they were also trying to remove Black children. Rosie clarified:

> The school is so teacher-centered. I've never been in an environment like that . . . it's in direct contrast with what I believe in. I believe it should've been student and family-centered, with teachers working as accomplices, not allies but accomplices, to fight oppression, to dispel oppression, to arrest oppression. But it's like, they all see the world the same way, see children of color as some burden to fix.

Jayson similarly challenged teacher disbelief in students and district support for such disbelief. "It's like I believe my students can do those things," Jayson argued, "And you talk to those parents, and they're like Jayson is the first teacher that talked to them about what college was like, what they need to do to get there, the supports we need to have here." The isolation of being the only educator seemingly talking to families about college helped Jayson create site-based structures that encourage more family communication. Yet with teacher expectations so low, Jayson can only create so many parallel structures that should be district practice.

Mason talked about how he is increasingly seen as a potential district leader because of his success at the school level. But he saw this institutional affirmation as false because ultimately, the district approach to recognizing good work was to stop that work from happening. Mason struggled with the potential opportunity to increase his leadership influence while seeing that there was no district plan to maintain the school culture he had built. He saw this as adult-centric, as the district was interested in rewarding a successful school leader by removing them from their position of influence with children, but not by investing in expanding what he was doing.

> I've got people saying, "You need to think about [moving up]"— no, I can't, because then, I won't sleep at night because I know there's some kids that are here that need that. They need to hear that because they wouldn't hear it any other place because of the traumas that they're going through. So, it's hard. I don't know what would happen if the district was like, "Hey, we need to you take this position." Well hold up now, a lot of people need some things. I could tell you what I need right now that I don't have.

Mason saw the lack of willingness to address the long list of needs to increase educator capacity to engage students as emblematic of adult-centrism. The district practice of affirming site leaders by removing them from the day-to-day of schooling was also seen as ignoring student need.

Alicia provided two examples of adult-centric approaches that prioritize educator perspective over student experience. The first was with an administrator who reported to her on recruitment and admissions procedures. Seen as a Black woman, Alicia's way of presenting the school was fundamentally different than the white woman with minimal experience at the school, and even less operating within communities of color. Alicia would speak to her directly, "If you want [your child] to go to a high school that is not an all-white high school, then you need to find a way to get some Black and Brown kids back in here." The administrator, however, was unwilling to be as upfront, particularly with children and families of color, yet still created a recruitment program. Alicia recalled:

> She was the one who really pushed to create this program, and to pilot it and to actually like go out and recruit kids. And I was the one, the squeaky wheel saying, "All of this is good, this is good stuff, let's do it." But we also have to think about what happens when these kids land on this campus. And so that's where the whole academic support thing kind of came from.

They kept calling it a recruitment push, and I kept adding the retention piece. And so it was a back and forth . . . but ultimately, [teaching children of color] is a harder conversation than they are ready for.

Alicia's frustration with recruitment-first efforts that did not engage the larger conversation of student experience paralleled the focus on white adults who benefit from the perception of a diverse school.

Ultimately, the willingness to do the work to retain students of color was not central to the school's approach. Alicia's second example clarified how a teacher who struggles with teaching children of color was provided support, but not in a way that reflects the students not being taught:

We have this English teacher who, for all sorts of really, really stupid, structural reasons, has a class of mostly children of color who are at below basic reading levels, who are not reading at Grade level in the tenth grade. And he has no idea what to do with them. One of the things that we tried to do was get a support teacher, an English teacher, who can go into that room and support him in doing real instruction in reading comprehension and fluency and these things that we know are the issue. But the teacher refuses to accept her support. It's like, "Dude, do you not fucking see how we are not serving these kids?"

This teacher was provided coaching support, essentially keeping two educators employed to do the job of just one teacher. Student-centered approaches, however, might instead address the problem from a student lens: the class still needed a teacher who can teach them, and the coaching was not addressing the teacher's approach.

In comparison, Shonda argued that internalized racism limits capacity to center students. "Our district is highly Latino, and the focus is often on our second language learners," Shonda argued, clarifying, "while our African American kids are failing. And so because I focus on all my kids and not just my Latino kids, I think sometimes my methods are called to question by some folks." Shonda identified that even when specific children who are rarely supported are the focus of culturally responsive approaches, other children of color are often ignored. When Shonda pushed against a particular district leader in trying to center all children as a focus, a white district leader essentially argued that a focus on second language learners was good for all children. Aside from not recognizing that not all Latinx students are second language learners and not all second language learners are Latinx, this district argument also ignored the large Black population that was being failed. One of Shonda's Latinx principal colleagues brushed this dismissal off, even as he recognized the racism, "He's white. They don't know how to deal with our kids. Just let it go."

Just letting go of the systemic collusion of anti-Black children, however, was not something Shonda, or the others in this book, could do. Shonda provided numerous examples of how adult-centric approaches maintained racial disparities while covering up the negative experiences students of color had across the district. She began to ask herself as a parent, "What could happen if they actually knew that we were screwing them up on a day-to-day basis?" Shonda's leadership approach increasingly centered families—and efforts to educate families—in the hopes that advocacy might be developed in ways that would push districts to do right. Shonda pointed out a caveat with parental and familial advocacy, recalling a recent graduation ceremony from elementary school where a family ordered a limousine to pick up their child from elementary school, over-celebrating what she felt should be a minor milestone, but ultimately, still advocates for empowerment strategies to help families better challenge school inequities:

> [My district] looks super good on paper. Like we're awesome with academics. But, if you disaggregate data, our Black and Brown kids are failing. We're doing really good with Asian English learners, but all of the Black and Brown boys are in the alternative school. All of them. But were not really talking about that because we're concerned about the more privileged, and really, the easier to deal with, Indian and Asian kids. So we have a support team for the relatively privileged students of color because they're killing themselves and they're depressed. And that's real. So the support team focuses on these elite students and we ignore the Black and Brown kids that are being killed, that we aren't serving, that our scores are terrible with. They are not given Algebra so they can't go to college. They're pushed out.

Shonda argued that even a predominantly Latinx district still failed to adequately support the Latinx students they have.

In one example, Shonda recalled the district providing a school with just one 50%-time language specialist, despite the school having over 70 first-language Spanish speakers. She helped the school find funds to support a full-time position, but had to advocate for removing reading specialists who only knew English; the district continued to hire and place English-only educators despite knowing the population was predominantly Spanish-speaking. The struggle to hire Spanish-speaking educators became a huge focus, despite the obvious student needs and Shonda's argument that "the data has to drive the decisions." While she was being told she was "sabotaging the school" because she was shifting resources to reflect student need, Shonda was continually reminded that adult-needs, such as an English-only reading specialist position in a majority Spanish speaking school, took precedent.

Shonda put her faith in children, in their capacity to identify, even at a young age, what teacher strategies work.

> When 10 kindergarteners come and grab me around the waist at one time and tell me what the teacher is doing wrong, when my sixth graders will say this person is screaming at us telling us we're stupid, I have to move.

The problem, as Shonda highlighted, is that leaving her school and shifting to a district role was easier than removing terrible teachers. Much of her work as a principal was spent trying to remove teachers who continually treated children horribly. "I've had to fire three people last year just because of how they're treating kids." Her efforts to remove teachers and district employees who cause children harm, however, are continually rebuked by district officials and the school board.

Shonda shared one particularly emotional experience with trying to fire a teacher who was verbally abusive to students:

> I had to fire somebody within two months for what she was saying. I thought I was being cool. I'm going to hire me an African American teacher, and we'll put her in this room with these Latino kids. She gets the struggle. "What are you stupid?" she tells the students. "What are you stupid or deaf? Your name is Juan. I'm going to call you John. I don't care what your name is." And my kids are crying. Boys, big, strong, the burly boys that usually are the ones fighting coming to my office crying. "I don't want to come to school anymore." I'm like she got to go. I'm on the phone with HR, and they're like you have to give her a letter. I don't—she got to go. She cannot be in my space.
>
> But she just out and out like, "You stupid." "What are you stupid?" When I walk in the room, there's an eerie silence. It's not like we're reading and engaged. It's like this "Help me" kind of face on kids. So I wrote the letter. I'll write another letter. How many letters do I need to hand you today based on how she's behaving? And so the fact that my kids know they can come to me for love. And even the ones who everybody is getting on, I'm like, "I love that kid." And they're like, "How do you love Enrique? How do you love Shantel?" Because I know her and I see her. And you don't know everything those kids are going through at home. And you don't seem to care . . .
>
> We're sitting here in the school. We hear gunshots. People running through the tunnel into my school. But we're just going to only talk about math? And my boss is like you seem like you do too much touchy feely. My kids are going through some serious shit that they should not be going through in this age. They should not have to. One of my kids was carrying a knife and hiding it on his way to school so that on his way back, he

would have it to protect himself from the woman on drugs that's begging him for money and chasing him down. We mad at the kid. "You're mad at the kid?" "We heard he had a knife." "Okay why did he have it?" Because this is like a really quiet kid who just lost his mom. So I talk to the kid: "Did you have a knife?" "It's not on campus, Ms. Shonda." "Okay. Did you have a knife?" "Yeah." "Why?" "You know the lady who blah, blah, blah, well, she's chasing me down asking me for money trying to stop me on the street." "Okay, baby. Let's see what we can do."

Shonda was extremely frustrated at how children in trauma are treated by systems enacted to protect educators. "My kids shouldn't have to be scared to walk home, shouldn't need a knife to go home, shouldn't be afraid," she argued. "And then, you're going to punish him because he had a knife to protect himself?"

Instead of being supported by teachers who help children survive the trauma they navigate at home and in the neighborhood, Shonda sees children of color being punished by having to engage with racist teachers. Racist teachers were supported by district practice, while Shonda was punished for trying to keep children of color in school, helping them talk through ways of navigating the violence they face when they walk to and from school. This alignment of adult-oriented approaches ignores the context in which children of color, particularly those in lower-income communities, struggle through, all while supporting adult racism and anti-children of color sentiments.

When she does find outstanding educators and administrators, Shonda continually encounters barriers to hiring them, demonstrating an irony in the difficulty of removing teachers and a parallel difficulty in bringing in educators of color. "So there's this one administrator I love," Shonda argued,

and growing up, he was kicked out of his home because he was gay. So he had been living in foster homes. He understands kids in a way that most teachers and administrators don't. But, everybody is like, 'He was never a teacher!' And I don't give a fuck if he was never a teacher. He knows how to come in and talk to children.

The difficulty in hiring and supporting educators who are familiar with and dedicated to children of color reinforce district policies that validate whiteness, protect teachers who harm students of color, and incite racially hostile school, district, and community contexts.

Conclusion

We conclude with a framing of Byron, to illustrate that Black leaders continue to cultivate student care in the face of anti-Blackness that attempts to silence and remove children of color while prioritizing the experiences of a predominantly white educator workforce. South High is a comprehensive high school, with over 2,000 Latinx, Black, Pacific Islander, Filipino, Asian, and white students. The tone of the school reflects many large Bay Area high schools in that a wide range of diverse, multiracial, and multilingual students have integrated themselves across campus and in individual classes. On one day, dozens of students of color wear duct tape over their mouths with the letters LGBT inked across. With his own mouth taped in solidarity, one student points to another whose mouth is not taped, and her role as appointed spokesperson becomes apparent. She clarifies how this is a campus protest started by a group of Black students, but soon included students from across the campus. They are expressing solidarity with LGBT students as continued anti-Trump protests on campus. Byron later clarifies that this ongoing protest was an extension of three walkouts students have coordinated at South High. The school board has urged him to stop these protests, but Byron defends student voice as "the whole point of school."

Byron makes his way around the school regularly; most teachers expect him in their classrooms at least once per week, just as students expect to see him in the hallways or pop into their classroom regularly. Rarely found in his office, Byron has a walkie-talkie that continually blurts out his name: "Mr. Garvey, a parent is here to see you," or "Mr. Garvey, a student is ready to see you." Walking the school grounds with him is a flurry of motion; he talks to everyone, seemingly remembers every single student's name, and chats with teachers, custodians, parents (who are often seen at the school), and security. He asks one group of students about their classes, then pulls a young man aside and asks specifically about his math class. Another student is pulled aside and asked about gym, while another is asked about art. He knows which students need which conversations about which classes, and ensures students continually stay focused on addressing their growth areas. As Byron talks to one group of students during lunch, he asks aloud how the entire group is supporting a particular student who has not come to school in a while. They look sheepishly around, and he chastises them, reminding them that this other student is part of their community. First one, then another, then all the students say something about their need to step up, and they end on a group hug before Byron heads on to another group of students.

A student rushes up to Byron while he is chatting with a security guard and, upon seeing that he is in a conversation, waits patiently for his attention. Byron concludes with the security guard, turns and thanks the student by name for her patience, and she bursts into excited conversation about how she did on a presentation. He reminds her how she was initially hesitant to volunteer for the competition and to reflect on how excited she is now that she did well. She thanks him for pushing her to go beyond her comfort zone, hugs him, and rushes off, almost skipping across the outdoor lunch area. Before Byron can blink, another student who has clear difficulty communicating verbally slides up next to Byron. The student just stares at Byron, who high-5s the student, holds the student's hand for a second, and then asks how the student is. The student offers a muddled response, and Byron talks with the student playfully. The student heads off with a huge smile on his face, with Byron demonstrating yet another of his many cultural shifts to respond to what students need.

Each Black leader moves in similar student-centric ways, reflecting their personalities, multiple identities, languages, cultures, and visions. They are engaging, well-respected by students, and have dynamic presence on campus, in communities, and across their district. Their commitment to students, and in particular, students of color, drives them to see their students, to know the communities in which their students struggle, and reflects their focus on student care. Yet they each operate within larger anti-Black, anti-people of color structures that diminish students. They see their work as equity-focused, while much of their work is dismissed as not aligned with district leadership. The approaches we validate in this book are precisely what districts dismiss, challenge, and fight against. Their inability to sustain safe learning opportunities for children of color remains an impossible-to-reconcile disconnect, even as they desperately try to increase student outcomes. Their efforts at creating student-centered systems of care are continually frustrated by the whiteness of their teachers, educators, administrators, district practice, and larger social context.

In Chapter 5, we clarify how these systems align to silence Black educational leaders and cause additional direct and secondary traumas. These traumas build upon the intersectional racism these Black educators previously navigated, requiring sustained commitment to developing and using coping strategies for survival.

5

THEY DON'T SEE ME

Coping and the Double Duty of Authenticity

It's not that they don't see me; they don't see anyone who looks like me.

—Shonda

There's a huge amount of stress that I would take in on my body, to the point that it rotted out my insides.

—Rosie

The previous chapter clarified some of the many ways in which Black educational leaders struggle to protect children of color from the intersectional racism that shapes much of their educational experience. In this chapter, Black educators wrestle with how bearing witness to the educational genocide of children of color impacts health and well-being. We begin with the recognition that the same systemic silencing that Black children face is used to similarly silence Black educators and leaders, forcing Black leaders to rely upon what Du Bois (1903/1989) called double consciousness, or what Rosie, some 115 years later, refers to as doing "double duty." Being made invisible through multiple levels of intersectional racism, through the isolation of being the only, and through having cultural strengths denied or appropriated leads to extenuating trauma. This trauma combines with the frustrating, complicated pain of participating in the oppression of children of color to create a need for coping mechanisms to heal while leading, setting Black educational leaders apart from their more privileged leadership peers who avoid living as systemic targets.

Throughout these interviews, participants took advantage of having a safe space to voice the daily struggle of racialized oppression that leaves African American leaders exhausted and angry. Individual and focus group interviews were occasionally interrupted by bouts of anger when participants retold stories of students being traumatized, and these interviews often then shifted to how leaders were traumatized, even as almost every leader downplayed microaggressions and outright attacks because they knew they were in the service of children of color. The attacks they faced were numerous, but were also seen as not entirely the point, as the focus continually was brought back to taking care of "our babies." When we were able to re-center conversation on the impacts of these attacks, and of the trauma associated with witnessing students be dismissed, that anger often shifted to a frustrated sadness, in recognition that these Black leaders were taking on additional stress that they were aware of had a cumulative negative impact. As they unpacked some of the causes of these intersectionally racist stressors, they knew that ultimately, their coping strategies would need to be increased, perhaps exponentially, if they were to maintain authenticity in their administrative positions.

Black Educator Silencing

The same context of silencing of children of color clarified in the previous chapter extended to African American leaders. While all participants nodded and voiced their assent when someone mentioned white inability to teach and reach our babies, participants were also vociferous when discussing the many ways in which they had to navigate leading while being actively silenced. Given global anti-Blackness leading to disposable notions of Black people (Harney & Moten, 2013), African American educational leaders' silencing should actually be expected, particularly when applying a critical race lens. The resulting trauma from leading within white oppressive structures lingers across each interaction, with students, teachers, administrators, and families, and can become cyclical triggering. This cyclical triggering was amplified by daily microaggressions and overt incidents of being overlooked, not invited to meetings, being ignored in meetings, and having ideas co-opted or directly stolen by lighter-skinned peers. The irony of being ignored when presenting ideas, only to later see those same ideas presented anew by a white colleague was an almost daily frustration for these leaders, as much research on African Americans leaders being silenced has demonstrated (hooks, 2013; Jones & Shorter-Gooden, 2003; Knaus & Rogers-Ard, 2012; Rogers-Ard, 2016; Rogers-Ard & Knaus, 2013).

All participants shared the ways in which they felt silenced in their work; some were silenced by being overlooked, undermined, or had their expertise or position directly questioned. Alicia assisted, "There's a thread of feeling silenced amongst people of color who are in administrative positions." She explained how she continually advocated for Black students, only to have her advocacy (and the students) dismissed:

> We have this one teacher—the dude is so rigid that he wanted us to create a policy where if kids were failing his class by the middle of the semester, they would drop the class and take the class online. I said to the principal, "So what you're telling me is this teacher is saying to you, 'Kids who can't pass my class, I am not willing to teach them anymore. I am not willing to figure out how to teach kids who are not currently passing my class.' And I am going to say to you that you need to make them pay $100 to take an online class so that they could pass this graduation requirement." I was like, "Yeah that's not gonna happen." At least I was able to make a difference. But it's like, "Dude, do you not see that the only people that you're kicking out your class are these Black kids? Do you not see that? Does that not register in your world that the only people you're saying that you don't get to take [this] class are Black kids?"

Alicia's positional authority enabled her to question a peer administrator, but when she raised these issues across the leadership team, there was no response. She was able to interrupt that specific racist practice but was unable to have the leadership team recognize that these sorts of exclusionary practices were normalized by the white principals.

Her role as intentionally challenging the day-to-day of schooling increasingly led to her being dismissed with eye-rolls shared across white administrators every time she spoke about an injustice. That her dismissal was not being addressed by other peer administrators or by the executive administrator reinforced her silencing, and while she continued to advocate by raising inequities, she realized her voice was increasingly marginalized. At this point in the interview, Alicia was emotional at the recognition of the systemic denial of her impacts:

> The part that hurts the most, the part that makes me tear up, is this idea of my blood, sweat, and tears is why the school still exists and has a reputation in the community. All of those things because for years, it was me. Sure we had a small team, but I was the rock. Unacknowledged rock, but still the rock.

As the "unacknowledged rock," Alicia recognized her decade of professional influence on the school and community were erased as if she had never been there. That meant the pain of being targeted by daily racism and sexism was unacknowledged, just as the students no longer had an advocate once she left the school community. Had she not had the positional authority to be around the leadership table, and been authentic in her continual insistence in raising critical questions that Alicia knew no one would be raising, Alicia knew that she would have been listened to: "But then," she argued, "I wouldn't have anything left to say!"

Trey echoed the dismissal of advocacy efforts, suggesting that he was never seen from the first interview to his last day, despite him trying to help others recognize that he grew up in the same communities that their students did. Trey clarified that he was asked in the interview "How are you going to relate to our students when they say you talk white?" His initial response was to almost ask: "Do you realize asking that is a violation?" Instead, he pulled back his honest gut reaction, and "proceeded to lay out my hood credentials." He continued, "I grew up next door to a drug dealer, crack heads, seeing all of that, dealing with all of that. So I have that experience and know that experience." Indeed, Trey's experience in leadership roles was based on him modeling how to be authentic in communities of color, but most of his peer administrators and teachers simply were not comfortable in such communities, leading them to continually question his street cred, since they had no real idea what that was, much less how to assess it. Trey kept urging educators to see him, continually reminding them: "Look, I'm here now," helping them see him as part of the team. Their resistance reflected an unwillingness to see him for who he is.

Trey further argued how navigating within racist systems silences Black leaders, above and beyond the educational sphere:

> I feel like you get silenced in terms of the moves that you have to make out of necessity, not just purely out of choice. We're silenced based off of our path out of necessity. This is how we have to maneuver. This is how we have to navigate because traditional doors aren't open. And that's the story of our lives as people of color, unfortunately. You always have to work twice as hard to get half as far.
>
> I've been in different industries where individuals had all the credentials in the world. I was in sales for a minute. And I had this brother fly in from DC, had an MBA, all the proper credentials. My manager at the time didn't have any degree at all. My manager! Let me say that again. My manager at the time didn't have a degree. Basically, he was moved over to our branch because we had a new district manager. And she pulled him in, pulled him out of a skateboard shop, and gave him a position in sales. Whereas, even in my path, it would be "How many years of experience do you have?" It's always the years of experience. How do I get experience if you're not going to give me the job? Yet, this other person who had no melanin, put it that way, got pulled up out of a skateboard and snowboard shop. And now, he's a manager over a division that was doing better than he did in his position previously.
>
> I've got supervisors who don't know what they're doing, but they're supervising you. So it's always this having to work twice as hard to get

half as far and always being questioned. And when you're successful, that's great. Let's move you on and have somebody else take over now. That's great. Let's move somebody else in that doesn't look like you to take over now. Once you've done all of the hard work, all of the leg work, start over somewhere else. Thank you very much. Put somebody else in.

Trey's range of experiences continually reflected silencing across systems. Not only is he not seen for who he is, where he grew up, and how he moves, Trey's experiences and advanced degrees were discounted.

Furthermore, even when Trey was finally hired into leadership roles, he endured continual questioned about his experience, his credentials, and he had his cultural strengths denied by the very teachers and administrators that caused the most harm to students of color. Once he was able to turn around the school culture, however, white educators would come in to claim the work he did, without having the experience, knowledge, or commitment to engage in the work required to turn around from the very whiteness they re-asserted.

Rosie's experience was also rooted in being authentic to who she is, being upfront about the way she moves, and hoping others recognize and support that. "I mean you go in there thinking, 'Yeah, I'm gonna institute change and this is gonna be great.' And then reality kicks you in the face and you're like, 'Goddamn dude; I just got bamboozled!'" In part, Rosie's frustration was because she allowed herself to believe that the school staff wanted her for who she was, but in reality, they were not committed to even seeing her. "So that is hard," she reflected, "Because you want to be hopeful. But even with support, trying to be Black and queer and a good educator is a set up. They don't want us there." Rosie recognized that the toxic climate that barely tolerated her presence led her to operate on her own, to build her own silos of support for a coalition of the willing—but recognized that this was not systemic.

André reflected on how his entire career was about being silenced by white educators: "The system silences me." Continually overlooked for leadership roles despite that he was the de facto school principal, André was frustrated by how he ultimately had to support white leaders who would only last "9 or 10 months, at most" in their leadership roles. He clarified one example of being overlooked while he was the assistant principal of a school and by far the most senior educator on campus:

> They had already vetted this little white woman about 5 foot nothing that don't know nothing from nothing coming from [a leadership program]. So they hired some outside person with all these credentials instead of someone [like me] who knew the school, the teachers, the students, the community.

André lived a systematic avoidance of hiring those with skill sets, cultural familiarity, and school experience.

Yet André was resolute in the transformative power he, and those like him, had on schools, school systems, and most importantly, children of color. "We cannot let the system silence you," he argued, standing his ground, "I'm damn sure not going to allow that." Continually asserting his values, André was adamant that educators of color, particularly African American, need to model engaging students while also struggling against colleagues who are not committed to children of color, or to systems alignment with supporting children of color. That commitment meant that while he may have been structurally silenced, his battles ultimately center children of color still having to navigate racist schools.

> I'll take the hit in the end because our kids need to know that there is somebody there that's going to speak for them because I was one of those kids. And I had a bunch of teachers that did not look like me. And I was disengaged. And that's what I'm trying to prevent and why I chose this profession.

Mason reflected on André's commitment and re-engagement after recognizing that he cannot allow the silencing to impact who he is and how he moves.

Mason's experiences directly paralleled the other administrators who, once they had developed positive impacts on their school communities, were ultimately silenced through systemic exclusion.

> I was silenced just by being ignored. My principal wouldn't even come into my classroom; I'm like, just come see what I do. She never came. And then, when I started talking about how can I take on bigger roles on the campus since I'm connecting with the majority of the students, there was silence. And it was hurtful to me. It was heartbreaking because I was at a school where I was one of the founding teachers. So I was like I put my heart and soul into this school; I took money out of my pocket to put into this school. My wife donated money on a regular basis to this school. And then, the minute I say I'm going to step up and do more, it was like, "Not only are you *not* going to do that, we're not even going to recognize that you want to do it." I was just like damn, how could somebody be in a position of change and see a person that has had and will continue to have a big impact on students that—even the students that don't look like him or talk like him or walk like him, just students in general. How do you sleep at night knowing you stifled that?

This stifling of Mason's impact echoed the thread of silencing across each Black leader's trajectory. Every classroom they taught, every site they led, and even their district-level impacts were met with structural resistance in the form of whiteness, and as they strategized to work through these anti-Black contexts, their successes were met with denial and, eventually, removal.

In addition to these systemic silencing mechanisms, all participants shared instances where they experienced microaggressions with white, Asian, and Latinx colleagues. They all agreed that daily microaggressions were designed to further silence them professionally, and felt like direct attacks layered the traumatic impacts of systemic silencing. The denial of degrees and experience was seen as a particularly common microaggression that challenged the core of these leaders' navigational strategies. Shonda, for example, relayed how close she was to completing her dissertation to a district administrator. He responded by saying, "Oh, I'll go on Amazon and get mine, too," as an attempt to diminish the quality of the university she attended. Shonda, shaking her head in frustration, clarified that, "The fact that even when you go to school and complete your doctorate, you're still the other, you're still not enough, you're still all of those negative things."

Jill echoed this dismissal:

> One of the white folks was talking about another colleague behind her back and was like, "I'm so glad, Jill, that you don't make me use your title." So then, it became this thing where I am seen as one of the more subservient dark people, because I don't remind white people that I have a doctorate. I said, "You know, the reason I don't do that has nothing to do with you; it's because I'm trying to be accessible to some people for whom my title might be a barrier."

Jill's rationale, however, was lost on the white administrators, who claim their titles but ignore the titles of Black educators. Trey situated this lack of being seen within a historic context, recognizing that white educators are intentional about their whiteness:

> You've been that person where the true leader is you. They may have the title, but when something needs to get done, who do they ask? Who do they come to? At one point in time, I'm dealing with white maleness all day long where it's like, "Make the kids do this; make the kids do that." But you, you get more money than me, you've got the title, but you're coming to me to make something happen. So, who's really leading? It's no different from a cultural perspective. Who really ran the plantation? Who ran the house? The madam of the house is looking to the servants to get stuff done to the point where the white children who were nursed at her tit, came to her to get values and everything else. It literally is the influence.

Byron spoke to a shared experience of insubordination as well, clarifying that his position is consistently challenged, most often passive aggressively: "I'm constantly under attack with all this white teacher insubordination.

I've learned to be consistent in inconsistent places, especially where teachers push against anything. Even when you do what they ask for, they push against that."

Shonda also explained that the isolation of being one of, if not the only, Black administrator encouraged microaggressions. "It's not just that they don't see me," Shonda argued, "but they don't see anyone who looks like me." The issue for Shonda is that in predominantly white-led schools and districts, even efforts framed as helping address racism are ultimately silencing to Black leaders:

> You know, all this implicit bias training and shit, that's not for leadership; like they think they are above that. And they just come to me, the Black-Black administrator and talk bad about the Black-Black administrator who is also gay, like somehow [these white administrators] think we're all on the same page, like they don't talk like that about all of us.

Shonda's recognition that she was seen as "Black-Black" and therefore, dismissed contrasts with white administrator avoidance of implicit bias training.

Indeed, efforts to help white administrators see Black administrator authenticity were seen as something white administrators intentionally avoided. The ways in which these educators were indirectly and directly silenced, through microaggressions, through racial isolation, through denial of their credentials, degrees, life experience, and cultural strengths, aligned explicitly with their dismissal as potential leaders. Thus, they were overlooked as practice because they represented potential solutions to the racism of school and district operations. This had a compounded affect, reducing the number of present, authentic Black educational leaders, which in turn, increased isolation, leading to even more reliance upon these educators.

Double Duty

There was a clear connection to participants being silenced in every role they occupied and the ways in which they were willing to advocate for students experiencing parallel silencing in the same school systems. Being a leader in predominantly white systems gave participants the ability to interrupt incidents and systems that targeted students of color, but also further isolated them from peers, often including peers of color. Except in rare instances where participants were able to replace disengaged teachers with culturally responsive teachers, they continually experienced the duality of having to lead educators whose personal and professional approaches created harsh, unjust, racially charged learning environments for students of color. Additionally, the unwillingness of teachers—many of whom were white—to teach to the students of color in their schools reflected the way leaders of color were viewed. Thus, these school leaders were presumed to echo the same silencing others before them engaged in, even as they crafted professional identities in direct opposition to such institutionalized racism. Leaders who cultivated successful schools by growing teachers and staff members in an effort to align around positive, student-centric school cultures were often tapped for new roles within central office, placed far from the very students for whom they continued to advocate, furthering their isolation.

While not all participants had that same type of influence, Rosie argued that being close to her students ultimately becomes an additional emotional burden. Her shared background with queer students of color enabled her to recognize why mainstream teaching approaches did not work and to recognize strategies that might effectively reengage students. This awareness was reflected in all participants, who translated their lived experience with racism and systemic oppression into advocating for children of color. But, as Rosie clarified, this translation and advocacy became a painful experience of seeing children struggle within oppressive schools that these leaders were at least partially responsible for, even as they could not fix everything.

> Because I was working with "those kids." I was one of "those kids" working with "those kids." So you're kind of segregated, you're kind of pigeonholed really. And your work doesn't really seem to be real or constituted as valuable because I wasn't working with teachers as much as I was working with kids . . . and that's heartbreaking. It brings up memories of my own childhood definitely. And I had a little bit more protection because my parents were white and educated and had certain expectations because they weren't abused by the educational system or neglected by the educational system that many parents of color were as well. But it's hard, it grates on you. You have that double stress of being an administrator and then looking like the children that you serve. You have that double entente of pain, that double duty.
>
> And it's emotional. It's hard. It's hard. Because you're not in a situation where you're in your classroom, you can shut your door and do what you wanna do, you're not in that situation. You're in a situation where you're holding an entire population. And you're in a situation where you can see things very differently. You can see how decisions are made, not just feel the impact. So it's very hard. It can wipe you out and it wiped me out. It messed me up emotionally and it screwed up my health physically. So it was, it's hard, it is hard.

Rosie's clarification of "double duty" reflects the notion of code switching or the shifting techniques African American women employ to navigate while challenging, to the detriment of their own health (Jones & Shorter-Gooden, 2003). These administrators felt responsible to students and families of color, even as they were often dismissed by these families because the person who was in the role previously may have been a person of color, but certainly was not authentic.

The difficulty of straddling these cultural divides, while also being targeted by educator whiteness attempting to maintain the status quo, enforced this double duty, a direct application of Du Bois's (1903/1989) double consciousness.

Nicole clarified how she tries to teach students about double consciousness, and how she is dismissed precisely because she moves in ways that are framed as culturally responsive:

> When I'm talking to my students, even though I know the teacher proba-
> bly initiated everything with the reason that they're in my office, I talk to
> them about, "How do we code switch? You're going to win that respect
> at the end of class when you speak about how you feel. And it's how you
> say it. It's what you say. It's how you say it and the timing." But I feel
> like I'm silenced in that the way that I'm building relationships with my
> students that isn't seen as appropriate, it isn't seen as how an administrator
> [should move]. It's not valuable. It's not how an administrator is sup-
> posed to be. You're supposed to be that disciplinarian. And don't get me
> wrong, I put my foot in my kids' behind when I need to all the time. But
> as with any discipline, there's that balance. That's where I feel like I'm
> silenced in how people perceive me to be as an educator.

Jayson frequently felt silenced because his authenticity did not fit the mold white educators wanted to force on him, as if his identity was up for their debate.

White educators ultimately projected an identity for him that better fit their expectations:

> I am silenced by the perceived exceptionalism and how I was raised. So
> when I say some things and it's like, "Jayson with the doctor dad and
> teacher mom, he doesn't know what he's talking about, about struggle
> and things like that." It's like my grandfather was a principal in Louisiana.
> My mom's house was shot up by KKK members that were police and
> mailmen and preachers. And since I don't fit what they think Black males
> should be able to do, my experiences are invalid. "When are they ever
> going to use Algebra II, Jayson?" "When are they ever going to use phys-
> ics?" So that's been my experience of trying to raise adult expectations so
> they don't lower the chances and expectations for students because I've
> had kids that would come here and fight, and the white adults love them
> so much that they just don't do anything with them.

Navigating these white spaces as one of the only heightens white identity poli-
tics, forcing educators to engage with projected stereotypes. These stereotypes not only target Jayson, they also lower expectations teachers have of students, causing additional psychic harm.

For district leaders, double duty is specifically problematic because unlike school sites that offer classrooms or buildings far from district politics, there is rarely anywhere to hide. District leaders must simultaneously navigate racist systems in transparent ways, provide leadership and modeling for other leaders, and maintain their own authenticity while being consistently silenced. Jill clarifies how the removal of culturally responsive administrators further adds trauma to Black authentic leaders.

> When they get good administrators who are doing really great jobs, the moment that they show any modicum of success we take them out of the schools and throw them in central office to work with other people. It would work if they were given the autonomy or if they really, really were about pushing principals. Just because you knew how to run a school doesn't mean you know how to train a principal.

Rather than increase the number of authentic leaders of color in district offices, or set up systems to nurture leaders into new roles, district practices of shifting administrators between sites and away from a role they were successful in contributes to racial isolation. This causes dissonance for central office administrators who recognize authentic leaders but cannot always support them in their new roles.

Ricardo shared this district-level lens and how double duty becomes more complicated when every leadership move is seen:

> Even now, I'm a district employee. Like, I don't belong to a school anymore, so I don't have a group of parents, all these students to empower me, to remind me why I do this work. So I have to make additional efforts . . . . And I try to stay fresh in classrooms, but a lot of these teachers get scared, like they are so used to principals getting them into trouble for not teaching well, so they think that's what I'll do. And then if I partner with a Black teacher—like I did this last year, tried to help out a new Black teacher. And all the other teachers—most of them were white, and they all got jealous, like "How come Mr. Ricardo doesn't volunteer in my classroom." And I was like, "What the fuck? You all just complained because I was in your classroom, now you are jealous cause I am chillin in a Black teacher's room? Ya'll can't have it both ways." But see, they can. That's how their privilege works. And the irony is, I just wanted to hang with children, to stay fresh in the lingo and youthfulness of the classroom.

Ricardo ultimately was reprimanded by the associate superintendent because he was seen as favoring Black teachers, even as he was getting grievances by white teachers for offering instructional leadership.

As a principal, Shonda was also frequently in classrooms, supporting teachers and ensuring adequate instruction was occurring. Her principal peers, however, did not believe she was in classrooms, discounting her commitment and instructional leadership:

> I was like I taught sixth grade twice this week and [a peer principal] was like, "Really? You were in a class all day?" "Yeah, I had three absent people and zero subs. I needed to go in the class and teach and because I'm educated to do so, I'm going to go into the classroom and I'm going to teach the kids and they're going to have a good time and we're going to learn about each other. It's going to give me time with them and I'm going to love it."

All of the Black leaders in this book shared Shonda's commitment to being in the classroom and had that commitment discounted and often challenged by teachers who tried to grieve their Black leaders for caring enough to help support their instruction.

While some teachers of color also aligned in trying to keep instructional leaders out of their classroom, Trey ultimately saw this exclusion as a whiteness problem:

> I'm at the district office, and it's a little bit better being removed. I feel like I let it beat me. I know what I'm doing, but seeing the school systems; you see this behemoth of a system that you're just throwing pebbles at. I feel like I didn't promote; play the game well enough to do what I needed to do. They don't get it. White folks read one book and think they know how to teach young people.

Conversations with our leaders yielded the idea that white managers must engage in continuous work around their limited experiences with educators and educational leaders of color. Rather than read "one book"—or make everything about their privilege—the white leaders these educators worked with needed deeper commitments to learn to manage African American leaders.

Rosie highlighted her frustrations being forced to work with unprepared white administrators:

> Sometimes I could use [the white principal's] inexperience to my advantage because he just didn't know. I mean we've had several strong conversations about equity and race. But it was always his refusal to do anything. And it really crushed me when we were, I was an equity coach, I was creating and facilitating equity professional development. And then the white co-equity coach that I had, white female couldn't take it anymore "emotionally." And he just canceled the whole program, and that really

upset me. He would promise me the moon and give me zero. You have the privilege to be reluctant to do equity work because of the challenges it may present. And I feel that our kids are more important than that and need more than that. Especially as an administrator I'm not gonna be part of a situation that supports that.

Rosie was frustrated by the privilege of white educator reluctance to equity work, recognizing how that avoidance negatively impacts children of color. Alicia also spoke to this frustration, complicated by her role as the face of recruitment for new families once they visit the school. As previously clarified, the decrease in students of color increased the discomfort students of color experienced, as their peer base and visible presence at the school diminished.

In turn, this led to parents and families seeking out Alicia as the *one* administrator of color at the school. Continually asked if the enrollment shifts would return to a more diversified population that reflects the local community, Alicia found herself having to publicly defend school practices that she disagreed with. This tension, reinforced by a predominantly white teaching staff and white leadership that did not see the transition as having long-lasting, negative impacts led Alicia to begin questioning the double duty role she felt forced into as the only woman of color in a leadership role.

After several years of increasing tensions, a number of students she had worked with for years left the school, and with a lack of concern and lack of recognition by the larger staff (and her direct supervisor), Alicia had had enough. The unacknowledged and unaddressed racism within the school had taken its toll and she knew it was time to leave. In addition, her current supervisor was caught squandering funds and was asked to resign. The proposed transition did not reflect her vision for the school, and there were simply too many changes away from the social justice mission that initially drove her into the school. Alicia stated matter-of-factly: "it doesn't feel like my school anymore. It feels like a different place, feels like a foreign place to me." This differential context, at a school she had worked at for 12 years, justified a shift, and, after much soul searching, Alicia accepted a position as assistant principal at a comprehensive local high school, in the hopes of being able to have a less complicated relationship with local families of color.

Byron reflected on the focus on working more with communities of color to help insulate Black leaders from the context of whiteness. Byron succinctly assessed the situation—"Sometimes it's even our own people"—and then clarified:

There's this Black woman teacher who is 100% anti-Black male leaders, and it's like she pushes against every single student-focused intervention and program. Instead, she's always trying to get students to go against me, like they can only support her or me. It just reinforces all the racist crap the white teachers already think.

As much as he centers students, Byron's leadership style reflects a relentless effort to support teachers and the related racialized resistance that the mostly white teachers react with.

While Byron is a regular in classrooms, he substitutes in new teachers' classrooms, provides one-on-one instructional coaching, meets with new teacher coaches from universities, and has monthly check-ins with most teachers. His engaging presence in these classrooms helps teachers see how presence is important to engage students, and he continually models culturally responsive teaching approaches, including call and response, caring-centered approaches, and student-focused lessons. A number of teachers offered unsolicited affirmations of Bryon's mentorship, and clearly enjoyed and benefited from his presence in their classrooms.

Yet the flipside was that a number of white teachers with decades of teaching experience saw Byron's presence in their classrooms as an affront. Byron clarified how these teachers "hate just seeing this culturally responsive, rooted Black male professional educator in their classroom, reminding them of what they don't do." The continual push back from teachers to his centering of students and providing the additional professionalism they interpreted as offensive resulted in incessant use of grievances and other union-supported methods of not having instructional support. The irony in Byron having received multiple district, statewide, and national teaching awards, but having white teachers push back against him as not being helpful reflected what Byron argued was an "anti-Black adult agenda." He continued, "They are fine with most of these students of color, as long as they can keep that 'student' part in front. But as soon as they see these students as men and women of color, they start disrespecting."

Byron often relied upon measurements he disavowed in order to push back against teachers who tried to exclude him from their classrooms, and he continually reminded all staff that any teachers with high disciplinary rates would have his presence more regularly. These were precisely the teachers who did not want him in their classrooms, and he was able to leverage their lower outcomes and higher suspension rates, despite that he had issues with both "outcomes and disciplinary measurements as inadequate to address race, class, sexuality, and other issues." The frustrations with being dedicated to supporting teachers that rejected support from Black leaders led all educators to think about how else to move authentically in ways that impacted classroom instruction.

Raine shared her experience implementing her school vision as a principal, and how that began with transitioning staff. Throughout her site transformation, she maintained authenticity to minimize having to do double duty, yet realized she still would need to code switch as she engaged with district administrators:

> At school last year I was allowed to just be me, and create the school that I envisioned, and we were hidden because the school has been

closing for many years. So, nobody showed up, and nobody was supporting. I fired a lot of people, and hired a lot of people, and built a team that I'm in love with. And, I feel joy in the building, and I feel happy, and I feel good.

If I feel like it's inequitable, if I feel like it's racist, I name it. I say it. It comes out of my mouth. It's just my truth. So what I was informed of is that what they thought was really great when I was a teacher is not so great as an admin. When you get in a different role, in a different capacity, you cannot talk like that. You're scary. You're the angry black woman. You are intimidating folks. And while I want the adults in the building to feel like they can come talk to me, I kind of enjoy some of that silence. So I'm the angry Black woman, and I get it. But I don't have the ability to be this, nor do I have the ability to not say exactly what they need to hear in order to understand this is not tolerated. It is in every other school. But where I am, and where I'm present, it's not tolerated. What I've been told is that I wear my history on my sleeve. I'm carrying the hurt child in me as I move forward in this. My voice and who I am and how I show up cannot change. And I recognize that I'm not going to be good in administration. I recognize that. I got to get the PhD. I got to do all of these things and navigate these systems in order for white people to accept me.

At some point, my voice is going to be so loud in this world that it's going to shake mountains. And then, the white people are going to be so excited about the black woman who is speaking her truth. That girl is bad. And then, maybe, possibly, some of them will hear me. And if they don't, so what? Because my babies will hear me. Their mamas will hear me. Their daddies will hear me. And we will move mountains.

Raine's recognition that navigational strategies are still required in "in order for white people to accept me," clarifies that double duty is not an option for those intending to transform sites, much less district-level systems. The trauma she carries as a "hurt child" is part of her authenticity, and while she recognizes that she cannot change who and how she is, she also realizes that she will not be able to stay, long-term, in administration being authentic.

As a principal watching what happens at the district senior level, Mason clarifies that part of the problem is that even when a Black authentic leader takes on an executive role, they are still discounted. Degrees and titles may accrue, but white racism still equates to a denial of respect for the leadership role:

[We have a] Black woman superintendent. My disappointment early on is when she walked into the room and I'm like, "That's a sister. Boy, I sure do want to get right behind her. Wow. This is really going to go down." So, when folks were in the room talking and we were in our little small groups it just kinda broke my heart. She got in front of the principals and executive staff, but everybody was talking. To me, when the Superintendent walks into the room, it's like, "What's up, pay attention." But they kept talking like, "Yeah, it's the Superintendent. So what?" And I'm like, at that point you can do one of two things. You can say, "Hey, folks. We're going to start this in 15 seconds. Finish up your last sentence and I need everybody's attention." Or, you can do what she did. She said, "I know all of you all want to get out of here because it's late and it's a Friday. You go ahead and continue your conversations and I'm going to talk over you." I was like, oh no. Hell no. She just gave up her power for no purpose.

André, who also had increasing experience at the district level, noted, "The function and structure of things at the district level are different." The toleration of whiteness—and the silencing of Blackness—were expected, just as Mason's superintendent exemplified.

André was clear that teachers rooted in whiteness needed to be removed, jokingly arguing to Jill during a focus group, "I've got some teachers I need you to retire." He was also aware that district operations reject the idea of removing teachers uncommitted to authenticity. André saw the status quo that tolerates ill-prepared white teachers as being enabled by a rotating shift in leadership, allowing Black principals and other authentic leaders to be exploited by white district administrators who control the day-to-day of operations:

Teaching and learning at schools are different than central office, and boards don't understand either. This shit happens by design. It gets exploited. They change superintendents. The board members are always at a clash with the superintendent after they try to make some kind of change. It boggles my mind that we are always the target of this kind of organizational behavior.

Jill's argument for a larger systemic accountability, particularly given urban district leadership turnover, would help address André's challenge; district ineptitude is often by design.

Yet districts are the next stop on the hierarchical leadership trajectory and the place that most of these Black educational leaders will eventually land. Jill elaborated on her experiences:

I'm finding that there is a lot of fear. No one teaches central office people how to run budgets. There is no business that you could work for if you were running a department and you had a $4 million budget and you spent $6 million. You would not still be working there. So, my question is, who's managing the person who ran over budget?

Jill is a district administrator who holds a position that interfaces with senior leadership, where she is at best marginally appreciated, and more often, simply tolerated.

While she regularly raises critical questions about systems of support for new administrators unprepared for their new roles, she recognizes a lack of willingness to listen and to see her as an outstanding leader:

> The new Deputy Superintendent, who has no melanin, sends me an email about my new program. Now, before I set it up, I went to the instructional folks, all of whom are white. I went to them and said, "How can we work collaboratively?" They all said, "I don't have any time. I can't possibly do it. I don't have any capacity." And I said, "All right, no problem. I'll get it together." Got the budget, got it together, got an email from the Superintendent this week: "Jill, we appreciate your willingness to put this together. We've looked at it. It's a really good program. And now, people are talking about it. We presented it to the board, and the board is excited about it. We presented it to a couple of funders; they might be excited about it. We're going to move it to the instructional side of the house and let them have it. So I appreciate what you did," get this, "because in your new role, you're going to be so busy. And I'm concerned that you may not have the capacity to do your new role and to support this work. So we're just going to move it away from you." Because when you have success, and when it looks good, we need to put some different faces on it. It was just way too Black; there were just too many Black people up in there. And so because I'm a woman of faith, before I cursed, first I prayed. And then, I cursed because He'll forgive me.

Jill's experience of having a program she created without white support ultimately be taken from her and given to white leaders paralleled all of the Black leaders in this book. When they moved collaboratively, their efforts were rebuffed. And as soon as their work came to fruition, they were removed from leadership, their work given to a white leader to co-opt.

This is precisely how double duty operates, with Black leaders moving authentically, creating programs without support and while facing direct barriers, and when successful, experiencing a critical race theory moment of interest convergence, where Black efforts are given to a white leader. This co-optation works only with white leaders who are not collaborative with authentic Black leaders, and relies upon the "unacknowledged rock" that becomes a normalized authentic Black leadership experience.

Ricardo clarified how navigating through leadership hierarchies is limited by white racism: "It's like I have institutional power, but only temporary." He pointed to his own experiences with the limited institutional power granted to authentic Black leaders: "I can only make [white principals] come to meetings, I cannot make them care enough to challenge themselves, to care more about our children, or to take classes or lessons in how to be around brown folk." Ultimately, Ricardo argued that this limited power reinforces the trauma associated with double duty and the continual need to challenge white leaders, who mirror the same white racism that these leaders grew up with:

> Sometimes it hurts, though. I try to get these principals to see that they are not "culturally competent" but they really have a hard time with that. It's like no one has ever told them they were wrong before. That white privilege hurts, cause it takes me back to my own childhood—that white privilege, the belief that white people, especially white men, are always right, is the reason why my mom was anti-Latino, anti-me speaking Spanish. So I get triggered a bit when I am in these meetings and these white principals dismiss me—even though they report to me.

The cumulative effect of always having to be on, of managing white teachers and white leadership in ways that minimize white privileged responses, of needing to challenge Black leadership in other nuanced ways, and of continually witnessing educational violence against children and communities of color causes trauma unique to Black educational leaders.

Rosie concludes this section by locating the impact of all of this strategic work in Black bodies:

> It got to the point where I would be pissed off in a meeting, pissed off by a white teacher who didn't do what they were supposed to and just basically ignored me, and then pissed off when I'd hear from Black teachers about the shit the admin said about them. It was like, everywhere I went I heard from frustrated Black parents and saw frustrated Black students, and then I was also frustrated, and I was like, "Fuck this. This shit ain't healthy."

Coping as Black Educational Leaders

Rosie's recognition that "this shit ain't healthy" names the impact of toxic professional climates on Black educational leaders. We have documented a systematic onslaught of traumatizing attacks through not being seen and through not having students of color be seen by a white educational infrastructure. The accumulation of these affronts, combined with witnessing the details of how oppression works while simultaneously trying to confront such systems, causes long-term frustrations that eventually negatively impact authenticity, health, and capacity to meaningfully challenge racist systems. As each participant realized the burdens they carried, they were also aware of how being a target eats at part of their soul. Each had witnessed critical colleagues of color become jaded, and as they internalized the oppressions they navigated, they became part of the infrastructure of intersectional racism, further excluding Black educators along with sexism, heterosexism, classism, religious, or other related social constructions. Authentic leaders' reflections within these racist and oppressive systems meant being intentional about taking care of personal health and well-being so that one does not become part of the anti-Black system.

One of the complications of being present to systemic racism is that racist educational systems nurture anger. As the popular saying goes, if you are not angry, you are probably not paying attention, and these leaders all forsake bliss for continued racial consciousness. Yet that consciousness also meant being aware of anger at a system one is dedicated to transforming, but which also pays the bills. Each participant was clear that, while anger is a valid emotional response to the many policies, practices, and pedagogies that leaders see and have to ignore; intentional reflection is required to manage that anger. Mason notes:

> It takes a minute. You've got to go through the angry. What works for me is I've got to go through the angry, and my angry could be at home, venting, out in the yard with my wife, or like with [this focus] group here. This group has been so helpful for me because, I can come here, and I can say what I want to say, how I want to say it, and it makes me feel better, and then I'm cool. Now I can go back Monday, and I can fight that fight. To me, it's productive, you go through the mad, get done with the mad, and reset. Okay, now, what do I have to do that's going to make me feel comfortable and continue fighting that fight for these kids that didn't ask for what they're getting?

Dawn further argued for the importance of the focus groups used in this research, reflecting on the rarity of connecting with trusted others:

> I actually don't have—aside from the people at this table I actually don't talk to other administrators. I don't engage with them. When I hear them talking or I'm in a room with them I find them to be unconcerned with what's happening with children, and so I just don't have time for it. My face tells it all and I'm going to be like; I think you're an idiot.

Most educators agreed with Dawn, talking about how continually wearing the mask required outlets for collegiality and to just be human. They laid forth the importance of trust and of having a community of critical Black educational leaders who understood their day-to-day and could just lend a compassionate ear.

Rosie reflected on strategy, arguing that being angry is important, but more important is moving through that anger to create with like-minded colleagues.

She began asking herself, "How am I gonna insulate myself and protect myself in a system that wasn't designed to insulate and protect me?" She answered her own question:

> It doesn't have to be super structured, it just has to be a safe space. There's an African-American proverb that says, "If you can't go through the front door, you go through a window." And I really think that we have to start going through windows because we know the front door is locked . . . . And we have to start leaning on each other to show that we love each other and that we support each other in this work.

Part of Rosie's notion of coping was to build up a collective community that could hold Black leaders when they were not moving as they should. "I think that [not trusting white people is] unhealthy," Rosie argued, suggesting that sometimes, she needs trusted others who can help her better strategize, "I think that I just have to be smarter about it, and play my cards a little closer to the desk, play the game a little smarter."

Furthermore, Rosie clarified how her most recent position was too much intersectional racism for her, and how this triggered her in ways that ultimately required her to prioritize her health over the field.

> You know this last round really; it broke me emotionally. I went into the job being my authentic self, letting them know my quote, unquote radical views. They asked some pretty radical questions in the interview about racism and stuff. So I figured I was in a safe spot where I could do my work and do what I do, and instigate and activate change, and have kids be successes and families be successes, academically and socially. And that didn't happen really. I mean it happened to a certain degree but it was an uphill battle. I think that's a price you pay to institute change. I think part of it's my responsibility; you can't serve from an empty vessel. And self-health and self-care is super, super important.

Participants in the focus group wanted to continue the group as a community network and support effort, and a few offered to expand the group to include other administrators of color they knew were down.

Several of our participants were hesitant, however, indicating that our space was "special" and "we got together because of you"; thus demonstrating the clear lack of trust with other administrators across race. For the participants who did not participate in focus groups, they wished for more conversations or groups to provide a safe space and argued that such spaces had to not be district sanctioned so they would not be taken over by a leader of color who wanted the affirmation.

Strategies African American leaders utilize to address the impacts of intersectional racism included leaving for presumably greener pastures, isolation—often heard as, "You know those folks won't mess with me!"—or not resisting specific issues to just ease personal tensions. Alicia suggested that critical awareness meant needing to isolate oneself: "Organizations paint such a picture of themselves and then you get in and you're like, 'Are you kidding me?' So I lock myself in the office and I disengage." Nicole agreed:

> Shut your shit down and go home. And don't bring it home; it'll be back here at 7:30 the next morning when you get here. That's the time for you to do you, do family, do whatever it is. Weekends, too. You have to find that balance. And then, also, still continue to always, no matter what the heck is going on, love what you do.

André also agreed, arguing that part of the problem is that some district leaders use their positions to not be at home, to not be in their family's lives:

> I got that one over there [points at his daughter], you know, I have to be present for her at all times, so those district folks—I think they lose touch, and then they've got weird hours. I'm not trying to be at a board meeting until 10:30, 11:00 at night. That's bullshit. You know what I mean? I'm not—that's not why I got into education.

When we asked Shonda how many days of vacation she has left, she replied, "Shit, I don't know," and could not remember having taken a day off recently. "I'm like 80 vacation days. I should just go home right now."

After additional conversation with the group, who urged Shonda to take breaks more seriously, she opened up more, recognizing that she does create space for her, in addition to extended vacations:

> Of course, work hard, play hard because I'll be at Disneyworld like I live there. Because I think it's cheaper than therapy. I can forget for those days and hang out with my son because he doesn't get the real me while I'm working. But I can go away and do that. And then, I can come back and be ready for the game. I'm using essential oils, diffusing them in my office. I am coloring in coloring books because, sometimes, you got to take your mind off of that. I am doing all of those things. And it's really hard to do in the spaces that we are working in. But it's essential.

Shonda then clarified how she is increasingly centering mindfulness as a coping strategy across schools, trying to help administrators of color see how toxic schools and districts are for people of color.

Raine concludes the focus on coping as a daily practice with what she framed as a healthy recognition of the privileges of being a credentialed, degreed Black educational leader, even within a toxic context.

> I can sit in my office and if I needed to cry a river, [a staff person I hired] will be there with her essential oils to kind of calm me down. And then I have a partner teacher and we've actually implemented mindfulness ourselves and not through district funding. We got our own grant and we used our own site money and we decided that we're going to train our parents because they're in a pretty difficult neighborhood right by where the kid was hit, right in that neighborhood where a lot of things are going on.
>
> I created this team, we basically are a reflection team, and we sit down, and we meet, and we talk about the past. And I did a training on trauma. I don't care about cycle of inquiry today. Today, our staff meeting is about trauma. And today, we're going to watch a video. And you're going to learn about trauma and how do you deal with these kids in the trauma.
>
> We need to take care of each other, and that's really the role of the leader, to get others to be okay at work, too. So that when I hear a kindergartener go, "Dr. Shonda!" it does something. It feels good. And for them to know, guess what, you guys can do this, for me to stand in front of my kids when they're graduating, and the parents have 1,000 balloons. Because when I walk into that space and 10 kindergarteners come and grab me around the waist at one time, and I'm like I'm about to fall, they hold me up!

Raine's focus on feeling good was based on her ability to prioritize the things that matter to her (the difference she is making in schools) and her ability to recognize, and not internalize, the traumatizing context she operates within.

She summarized all participant commitment to the work, illustrating that as long as there is a belief in doing good work, she, and the others in this book, were able to sustain their roles and presence:

> I'm not afraid to be fired. I don't even care. If you fire me, I still can get a teaching job. I got a credential for the rest of my life. This is my belief. I went home that night; I had a big old steak. And I felt good about it. Came in the next morning to the grievance, and I felt good about it because that piece of paper says to me that I'm doing what I said I would do. I'm making the difference that I said I would make. That is what matters to me. If I get enough grievances to put all over my wall where it looks like that, right, I'm feeling real good. I'm feeling real good.

But for when they were unable to see the impact, the trauma became too central, and like Rosie, they needed to step away, at least from their current role.

We conclude this chapter, then, with a critical reminder that school and district leadership turnover is high for many good reasons. For authentic Black educators, positional leadership roles within schools and districts committed to intersectional racism cause trauma, and require a number of personal and professional approaches to mediate that toxicity. The educators in this book were clear that the longer they operated within leadership roles, the higher their leadership climbs took them, and consequently, the more they were targeted *and* the more toxicity they faced. Their successful navigation leads to several takeaways relevant for districts and professional leaders. The first is that positional leadership roles should not be seen as permanent, but as temporary stops in a career dedicated to transform educational systems. The second is that Black educational leaders should strive to be as authentic and healthy as possible, and this requires commitment to coping mechanisms that work for the individual. This also requires a commitment to being Honest, to maintaining Empathy towards Equity, to being Accountable to critical communities of color and other Black educators, to establishing daily Reflective practice that helps center professional purpose, and to fostering Trust in self and others. In the next chapter, we outline these commitments through clarifying the HEART model, as a tangible set of reminders of how to maintain authenticity for as long as one can remain whole while leading within fractious, intersectionally racist educational systems.

6

THIS IS HOW WE DO

Authentic Leadership

Walking into Jill's office brings an instant feeling of warmth and welcome. From the numerous posters and reflective quotes on the walls and whiteboard, to books spilling out of her overburdened bookcase, to snacks on the guest table, Jill has a knack for continuously making people feel comfortable. She attributes part of this intentionality to growing up in her grandmother's home watching a stream of visitors always being welcomed in. As she grew into professional leadership roles, she also increasingly implemented her value of providing a welcoming place for those around her. Jill frequently and openly discusses faith and family as guiding values that guide her efforts to reach back, mentor, and lead. Jill reflects that she loves to support people and has been doing that in a variety of educational and spiritual spaces since she became actively involved in her local church when she was 11.

Born and raised in the Bay, Jill is proud of her East Bay lineage and frequently discusses being from the Bay as her "brand." Indeed, Jill leverages the cultural capital gained from working almost two decades within the same district, combining that with local knowledge from being involved in faith and activism communities. Jill is known for welcoming people with hugs and a warm smile, although she describes herself as an "extroverted introvert." On a recent visit, Jill was wearing skinny jeans with her signature heels, a black blouse with ample cleavage, and a blue suede jacket. Her first question is an inquiry about how the researchers are doing, and we pause to talk through personal realities prior to engaging in any work or research-related conversations.

As mentioned earlier in this book, Jill taught for several years, then became a district teacher-leader, which led to a position several years later as a central office administrator. Operating from a positional leadership role within central administration, Jill was immediately confronted with intersectional racism and sexism. During her tenure at the district, Jill reported to several white managers who all experienced challenges for which they were unprepared when faced with leading a Black female leader with a depth of localized experience, and often, more education. White women's lack of readiness and unwillingness to supervise a more experienced, more educated, and more-locally conscious Black woman, became a theme throughout Jill's leadership journey. Jill was uniquely positioned within the district to speak to educational challenges; her ability to create trust across racial and gendered contexts is one of her greatest strengths. Despite her cultural strengths, decades of experience, and commitment to that particular district and community, Jill ultimately left the district, frustrated by the accumulation of her work being undervalued, under-resourced, and underappreciated.

We open this chapter on leadership with Jill, a Black senior-level educational leader who chose to struggle against racism as schooling at the district level, to illuminate systems-level oppression detailed in previous chapters. This chapter connects critical race theory lessons from participant experiences to a systems-based model of leadership development. We offer the resulting HEART framework not as a salve, balm, or band-aid for what Black leaders and those of color will experience when choosing to lead within P-20 systems. Rather, the HEART framework is a reminder of the ways in which Black leaders must differentiate themselves from white, mainstream leadership if the goal is to dismantle and rebuild affirming educational systems. We do not offer this framework for white leaders to use against Black leaders, nor do we offer these approaches as ways to retain Black leaders; we are clear that Black leaders must leave toxic work spaces to heal in order to remain alive. Indeed, we argue that the experiences of the 13 Black educational leaders suggest that tenure within racist systems must not be permanent if the goal is also to survive and live healthy lives. CRT becomes a lived experience through our framework to help ensure that Black leaders remain self-aware and increase their capacity to fight against the silencing of Black children and educators while modeling healthy survival.

In this chapter, we combine the findings from the first five chapters, uniting themes into a leadership model that takes into consideration who and how we are, the always present intersectional oppressions we operate within, and the impacts of those oppressions on organizations, ourselves, and others. We return to Bettina Love's notion of abolitionist teaching, offering a leadership life-preserver as reminders for critical educators, Black or otherwise, to continually grow, while also remaining committed to being who and how we are. And we continually remind systems thinkers, educational leaders, and those committed to systems transformation that the work of intersectional anti-racism and decoloniality causes physical, emotional, psychic harm that accumulates over lifetimes. Operating in traumatic spaces, particularly while trying to confront and dismantle so we can create and build has a timeline, after which our bodies and souls require nourishment to continue on. In what comes next, we re-imagine leadership orientations around a commitment to authenticity and clarify the components of the HEART model as a way to tether our values to systems transformation.

Re-imagining Leadership

We readily admit that leadership is difficult, especially when pitted against the white mainstream leadership frameworks that abound on YouTube, TED Talks, and in academic and professional leadership associations. Leadership tradition-alized by mainstream publishing houses is framed by a white, patriarchal lens, most often demonstrated in K-12 contexts by site-based and district leaders bat-tling for resources to "save" Black children by measuring standardized test gaps. For Black leaders, these battles are conducted on a backdrop of increasingly nefarious racialized barriers that deny intersectional racism and the colonial purpose of schools. Leaders are expected to model inclusivity into racist systems and multicultural sensibilities not taught (or supported) at the professional level, while celebrating linguistic diversity when dealing with neighborhood issues, gentrification, and power struggles related to racism at the regional level. These struggles are compounded when Black leaders challenge systemic racism to interrupt the white supremacy of schooling.

We define leadership as "The deep understanding of one's self that forms the sum totality of one's personal life, empathy, perspective and experiences" (Rogers-Ard, 2007, p. 22). Thus, leadership is about knowing who you are, how your past, present, and future life impacts how you are, and how you oper-ate within systems of intersectional racism. Brown (2018) simplifies, "Who we are is how we lead" (p. 11). If leadership is the sum totality of our experiences and self-perceptions, then a keen sense of self-awareness will help ensure lead-ership effectiveness; indeed, our leadership perfectly reflects who we are. Our leadership is our mirror and how we lead is a reflection of our values and lived experiences. What happens, then, when a leader's experiences have been rooted in and regularly attacked by whiteness? Based on our participants' responses, our own scholarship, and personal experiences, we argue that the centering and grounding of personal and professional identity and purpose is necessary for Black leaders to navigate the tumultuous waves of systemic oppression. We refer to this grounding as *Authentic Leadership* which requires the intentional, continuous process of self-awareness as a strategy.

When asked about their leadership, our participants discussed how they move differently from most of the K-12 leaders they see; they continually discussed that who they are is central to their roles as leaders. As Rosie notes, "They just wasn't ready to partner with a strong Black woman like me, and definitely weren't ready to take orders from me." Who these leaders were seen as directly impacted their capacity to lead. The reason our participants move differently from the whiteness of K-12 leadership is because they have become increasingly aware of their own values, who they are, the reasons behind tough decisions, and their commitment to voicing unpopular opinions. Jill reflects this self-awareness: "I believe so much that we lead from our values; we lead from who we are. I believe that to my heart, to my core." This is not to suggest that Black leaders need to be destructive forces, however, interrupting racist oppressive systems requires the courage to speak to power, the strength to stand in one's own integrity, and the bravery to leave systems that are not in alignment with one's own values. This is especially difficult because Black educators are continually positioned (and ironically celebrated) as martyrs for "our babies." Our goal is not to encourage more martyrdom; instead we argue for a more healthy, sustainable way to lead against the grain of oppressive systems. We must recognize the difference between making a systemic improvement and making a mess; between being at the apotheosis of one's purpose and purposefully portentous as we fight for children intentionally positioned furthest from opportunity.

Jill's insight is particularly important as a systems-level leader who saw numerous initiatives come and go, witnessed continued disparities despite the many (many!) proclamations to address them, and continually observed the systematic pushout of conscious, dedicated educators. Despite the systemic exclusion of Black people, Jill did not believe that educators were ill-intended:

> I don't think that a lot of people who are in central office roles got there because they were like, "Forget kids, I don't care anything about children." I'm thinking about other folks who I remember as teachers. I remember them doing phenomenal jobs as APs and principals. When you start to veer and drink the Kool-Aid, you have to have people who can pull you back and be like, "That Kool-Aid is tainted; here's some water." That's how you stay grounded, and that's how you stay on purpose, and that's how you stay on task.

Jill's point about staying grounded includes having teams of rotating colleagues of care, who are trusted to call out inconsistencies in our behavior, to remind us of the day-to-day harms Black educational leaders operate within, and to hold leaders in confidence to help sustain purpose.

Being an Authentic Leader means fusing the professional and personal masks leaders of color wear. Leaders of color must be aware of their own duality; Authentic Leaders are so aware of the masks, they begin to create intentional spaces where the masks are fused into one consistent person. With respect to the necessity of code-switching that has been highlighted here and elsewhere (Bell Edmonson & Nkomo, 2003; Jones & Shorter-Gooden, 2003; Smith & Nkomo, 2003), Authentic Leaders work to develop a way to speak and move that remains constant in the face of oppression. Trey reflected on his own leadership growth in relation to his voice:

> I've learned from other previous negative situations in which I tried to play the game, I tried to code switch, and still had the same result. What I realize is, "Oh, I'm gonna say what I want to say" because, at the end of the day, I'm not going to go home with the same result, feeling like, "I should've said . . . I should've done . . ." I'm going to make those moves, and still be me.

All participants ultimately reflected on the same recognition that who they are was actually a tremendous strength, even as they were targeted because others rejected their identities.

Understanding intersectional racism, however, suggests recognition that people of color are not targeted just because they are people of color; rather, they are targeted by people enacting racism. Ricardo echoed this strengths-based reflection:

> I'm the only Black man, the only Spanish speaker, the only person from middle school, the only person who quotes Tupac. There's other Black people, but they don't move like I do—they have integrated that code-switching into their identity. They only let it down after work. And that just reinforces all of this racism.

This recognition helps personal identities be reframed as strengths. Rosie also reinforced this recognition, restating her own embrace of identities as strength, but adding in a caveat that in order to protect herself, she also masks who she is, and some of the work she does:

> I'm of color, I'm a woman, I'm a lesbian, I'm of African descent, I have a Jewish last name; I mean I don't fit in anybody's mold. So it's much more challenging for me to wear a mask. There's a lot of clandestine, covert work going on. That to me is wearing the mask: where I'm preparing children how to live and thrive not just survive in this world. So that's the mask work that I do. I don't do that in front of white people.

We readily admit and understand that the work of fusing multiple masks is a lengthy process, one that requires consistent work and courage.

"We wear the mask that grins and lies," begins Paul Laurence Dunbar's (1913) famous poem, a 100-year-old reminder that navigating whiteness and white supremacy has long been a survival strategy. "With torn and bleeding hearts we smile," Dunbar's poetic reminder challenges, suggesting the need to hide the personal impacts of systemic and historic traumas. The battles, struggles, and pain highlighted by Black educational leaders clarify the continued historically rooted navigational strategies of wearing a range of masks to traverse intersectional racism. And just as relevantly, proximity to privilege correlates directly with the need for fewer masks, but also, fewer cultural strengths that align with the navigational strategies of the students served by US schools. Thus, as white educators require fewer masks to operate within school systems, Black educators require many more. These masks increase exponentially when one traverses the leadership hierarchy, adding in systems-level masks to negotiate and navigate towards increasing leadership.

André extended the conversation beyond the masks we wear to survive, arguing that being an Authentic Leader requires being brave, but also recognizing that you may have more privilege than you think.

> Man, it is about your level of courage. At some point, you've got to say, "I can always get another job, but I'm going to stand on my values," and sometimes that gets kind of lost when you're paying bills, and you're going through your daily routine, and you start thinking logically about your situation. But again, it comes back to your heart and your intentions.

André was ultimately suggesting that leaders need to recognize the reality, particularly when operating within impoverished communities, that school leaders make a lot more money than people struggling through poverty.

Even as educational leaders can struggle through very real middle-class economic issues, especially when being one of, if not the only, professional income supporting an extended familial community, the recognition of privilege affords the opportunity to stay rooted in values. These are not opportunities that previous generations of Black communities excluded from college-based professional jobs allowed. These relative privileges can be parlayed, André argued, into the courage to "stand on your values." Brown (2015) shares that courage is actually a word that means "heart"; thus, when people are courageous, they are acting, responding, and moving from their hearts and souls.

As Black educational leaders climb leadership ladders, their increased access to systems-level analyses is mirrored by an increased exposure to witnessing systemic intersectional racism. Maxwell's (2002) definition of leadership as influence provides an opportunity for Authentic Leaders to shape the way in which they move through and within these racist systems, especially as the goal to increase power aligns with the capitalistic goal of increasing income and always rising. Jill helps leaders stay rooted in thinking about movement:

> The power that you're looking for is influence. You're going to have to figure out who are those key people; as my grandmama would say,

"You've don't have to be the head, but the neck that turns it." So, how are you the person who influences the person to get you what you need to get? This is a chess game; everybody else is playing checkers. What is your ask? When you have that clarity, then you leverage your cultural capital to move other people to move for you. That's how we have to move in these spaces. I know I'm placed where I am for a reason, so I have to be systemic and move all the pieces on the board. And that's influence; not power.

Jill shifts the focus on obtaining power to thinking about leadership aspirations as increasing influence. Increasing influence within intersectionally racist systems, however, requires staying true to who you are as a leader of color, and that means continually reflecting on who and how you are, your values, and surrounding yourself with critical others to keep you grounded.

Authentic Leadership: The HEART Model

How do we become Authentic Leaders? We offer a framework for Authentic Leadership that is based on HEART: **H**onesty, **E**mpathy towards Equity, **A**ccountability, **R**eflection, and **T**rust. Key to this framework are guiding questions that help each of us grow and develop as a leader; we were purposeful in creating initial questions rather than statements as levers towards self-awareness. It is crucially important to understanding that no one ever "gets" leadership in the same way that no one is forever "woke"; we are always in the process of learning and re-learning how to be ourselves within violent, anti-people of color societies. Just as we cannot be shielded from the impacts, messages, and knowledge construction processes of white supremacy, there is never a point where one is a perfect leader because leadership is based on who people are and context matters. As people cannot be perfect, leaders are similarly imperfect. Thus, HEART offers a leadership framework as a way to continually grow and develop ourselves and others.

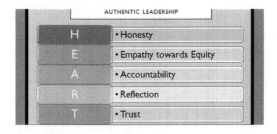

AUTHENTIC LEADERSHIP

H	• Honesty
E	• Empathy towards Equity
A	• Accountability
R	• Reflection
T	• Trust

FIGURE 6.1 HEART Model.

Honesty

We define honesty as the willingness and courage to live and demonstrate one's core values. Naming one's core values allows for transparent clarity about personal and professional purpose in relation to vision for society, the organization, and your current role within education. This also sets a foundation for implementing boundaries. While people generally have a list of values that apply to them, Authentic Leaders narrow their focus to two or three concrete core values that support the way they move and map out professional purpose. Making and justifying difficult decisions becomes much easier when one's values are crystal clear.

The Black educational leaders in this book all attempted to move increasingly honestly about their core values and purpose as educators. The longer they stayed in educational leadership roles, the deeper their commitment to honesty rose. Trey clarified the connection to honesty and sleep patterns: "Your conscience—I mean for me I sleep better at night knowing that I did the right thing as opposed to what was the politically correct thing." Mason agreed:

> You have to be so wedded to your principles and your vision; you can't be swayed by the minutiae and the bullshit. If you take the job, you're like, "This is what you guys hired me to do, and I'm going to do it."

Raine reflected on a growing dissonance with her values not aligning to district practice:

> I just feel like a lot of what's happening in our district is against my own core values, and in order for me to exist in this world, I need to move based on my values. I was told that I was moving from a place of fear and frustration. My response to that was I'm moving from a place of love for kids, and integrity, and if this is where our district is headed, this is not something I can be a part of.

The notion of honesty requires leaders to be aware of their own needs and to seek resources and support to help them meet those needs. Being in community and in affinity with others who understand similar struggles helped each leader meet the need for safe conversations to de-stress; being in safe spaces with like-minded individuals was seen as extremely necessary to ensure Authentic Leaders remain grounded. André rejoiced in having critical community: "Just glad to be around some other brown folk, talking about their struggle. Because we all try to lead a lot of white folks to care for our kids, and it's tough."

Jill further clarified the benefit of leading from values as a way to help insulate against the many pressures that align with larger processes that are contrary to one's purpose. In those cases when Authentic Leaders are isolated, being honest means recognizing when they are in a place that does not support authenticity:

> I believe that you must lead from who you are, from your values, with purpose. Otherwise, you do make a shift. So, some leaders who have made that turn, they drank the Kool-Aid, they moved away from their values and knowing who they were. The way to stay grounded in that is to have people around you. We have to find those places, and they may not be at work; work might be super-isolating. So then you create spaces. You allow people around you who can let you be authentically who you need to be, and then your modeling shows other people it's possible to show up as who they need to be.

When we are dishonest about our needs, we receive institutional affirmations for aligning with the team (and often, with white supremacy), and/or our emotional and physical health suffers from dissonance.

The accumulation of racist experiences and the growing frustration of trying to transform racially hostile work environments led to Rosie developing a justified growing rage. While she was able to control this rage within professional settings, her rage had physical impacts: she was ultimately hospitalized and had several severe surgeries from trauma directly related to the toxic, stressful work conditions she had begun to internalize. Rosie clarified how being angry was "a natural reaction to all these fucked up people who just cannot tolerate any fucking differences" but that holding onto such anger was also not healthy. At the time of this study, Rosie had taken a year off from educational work while trying to map out next professional steps. Her physician suggested she try less stressful work, though she knew that avoiding the underlying cause of workplace trauma would be difficult, as she ruefully lamented: "Oppression is fucking everywhere."

Sometimes even when we are honest with our needs, the toxic work environment threatens our mental and emotional health. At the beginning of this study, Nicole was serving as an assistant principal at a high school with many like-minded individuals in leadership; she enjoyed her role and was not considering leaving; insight through many of her comments suggests she was supported institutionally. Recently, Nicole's district administrator tapped her to lead a small, struggling middle school; she instantly agonized over the decision, not because she was scared of the work, as she loved the idea of the challenge, but because she knew the culture would be a 180° change. Nicole reflected on this transition and its impact on her:

> The challenge enticed me! The ability to do culture-building the way I wanted to do. I took it . . . but I'm rethinking my life choices only six months in. The people! FUCK! But the kids are great. [The school]

was the dumping ground for horrible staff and teachers. The office man-ager had been moved around and bullied teachers for the past 20 years. FUCK! THIS bitch! She was horrible and took advantage of me being new. I wanted her to create an office space that was happy and improve the culture. I spoke to my boss: "What the fuck did you get me into? Can I get my [former] job back?" Five people planned open attacks on me. My staff is now divided. It has been miserable for the last six months. I'm not sleeping at night. My wife was like, "I wish you had never worked there," because I'm so stressed. Their unions protect people who are ma-licious, mean and evil. Why do we keep horrible people? Fuck documen-tation; how will you protect me as an administrator? These people are intentionally fucking with me, because my spirit fucks with their demons.

While Nicole's release was safe in the context of our focus group, the pain she experienced was traumatic. Going from a well-supported leadership context to an isolating, toxic community that intentionally caused violence to those who aimed to interrupt their site-based power was demoralizing. Her commitment to staying true to her spirit is precisely what enabled her to wrestle with the decision to stay or not, and reflects the critical honesty of Authentic Leadership.

Because we cannot outrun or outdistance oppression, Authentic Leaders must be clear and honest about work-life balance, needs, boundaries, and our actual verbiage. Ruiz and Mills (2010) discuss being "impeccable" with our words. One of the ways we followed up with Nicole was to remind her of her purpose and need for healthy boundaries. We recommended Nicole control only what she can as she struggles to remain in a tenuous position; we also invited her to share within the focus group as a safe place to vent, to receive support, and to be reminded of some ways for her to move through difficulty that she understands was intentional. At the same time, being in a challenging situation does not remove one's authenticity; those situations are exactly when authenticity is tested and when we must be extremely clear with our words, actions, and feedback to others.

A local pastor provided a metaphor for engaging with those who claim to be supporters: "Real believers are like teabags; if you want to know what's inside, drop them in hot water" (W. Coleman, personal communication, August 2, 2018). Nicole is in a "hot water" context; this is when her Honesty, Empathy, Accountability, Reflection, and Trust are being tested, and her community increasingly is developed around those who recognize and provide support. Raine extended Nicole's desire to maintain her authentic presence, arguing that "My voice and who I am and how I show up cannot change," no matter the leadership situation. Dawn also argued that, as long as we can continue to be who we are, "We have to stay in the space where we can make those changes, where we can sit at those tables, and we can create change." When we cannot be authentic, she argued, we must step away from the table.

André shared his experience of being excluded systematically because he kept to his core values:

> I found myself being somewhat black balled because I was bringing that same intensity and advocacy to folks that have been in these situations for 30 years . . . I ended up getting moved because I was too strong for these white teachers in this situation to deal with.

While frustrated with being removed because he was adamant about treating children and families with respect, André preferred being pushed out to him accepting the passive embrace of white supremacy. We are most honest with ourselves and others when we seek opportunities to demonstrate leadership at the highest level or to leave when we are out of alignment. Alicia further aligned with this authenticity:

> I could've still been principal had I wanted that, but I didn't want that in that context. I just didn't want to be a fake principal. I didn't like being in a position that people's perception of what a principal dictated what I could do. And the reality of my principal-ship sometimes was consistent with their perception and sometimes it was not. And it didn't feel good and I just didn't wanna do it anymore.

In addition to self-honesty about our capacity to be authentic in specific contexts, another aspect of critical honesty is in the way we provide feedback to others. Being honest and judicious with our feedback, especially to those who continue to be challenging can be a powerful way to disrupt expectations and confrontations. Proximity also matters. Brown (2018) indicates that when we are most ready to provide honest feedback, we are okay with sitting next to the person instead of opposite him/her, often with a desk serving as a barrier between. Being physically honest—asking if we are physically oppositional or on the same side—helps model work and provide excellent feedback, requiring an awareness of our own limitations, boundaries, and values. Steps such as these can help bridge divides, but giving honest feedback requires doing some internal work first.

Raine provided an example of the tension of not doing this self-work: "I'm carrying the hurt child in me as I move forward in this leadership. When people say, 'Who was your favorite teacher?' I'm like F- all teachers. I don't like any of them. Never have, never will." This painful set of emotions obviously will impact the way Raine engages with teachers. She continued: "I remember them talking about my Mama. I remember them calling my mom a crackhead. I remember." Raine was still carrying the lived trauma caused by some of the teachers from her formative years. Her transformative honesty helped her reconcile this:

What I won't do is be in an environment where you do the same thing. I didn't come into education to be anything but who I am . . . . And if the hurt little girl shows up in moments like that, fire me.

Recognizing that the cause of her trauma is still being enacted can be a powerful strength as long as Raine is fully honest about her capacity to balance trauma with her core goal to transform educational spaces to nurture her babies' growth.

These Authentic Leaders became particularly incensed when trying to help staff of color by providing honest, intentional feedback. Their goals were to provide honest feedback in ways that teachers, most often white, could hear. But being honest does not mean teachers or others will hear that feedback. André shared experiences with leading a challenging staff person and how being critically honest may not always be enough to transform a school site (hence it is only one of the five components), but it is how we should lead as a foundation:

I'm Black-Black; this dude is white-Black. I realized this wasn't a good fit [at our school]. He fractured my staff. He has an issue with Black women. If I ever see him on the street, it's going to be bad. He's always saying thank you for this opportunity, but he's fucked over this opportunity. He took me two, three steps back with the culture of the school. Staff began siloing up and not wanting to authentically collaborate. They were doing it with gentle nudging. They were trying to do the work; they were having conversations about the work, but now it's a struggle. That wore me down. It wasn't supposed to be like this; you can't steal when you don't know the game.

André spent tremendous energy and resources trying to coach this teacher, bringing in and mentoring someone who otherwise might not have had a chance to become a teacher. He was repeatedly honest in his assessment, but the teacher increasingly rejected the opportunities André provided.

Trey had a similar experience, further echoing the importance of honest feedback, despite potential, and predictable, outcomes.

I fired a brother—I tried Cornell West, Malcolm X, whoever you could think of to motivate this dude. He's teaching my [special education] class and just watching videos. Now, I get that the students have severe disabilities but that does not mean that they cannot learn. I've got parents complaining that their kid is just sitting there staring at the wall; I've got parents passing by the school and seeing him smoke a cigarette down the street or walking to McDonald's when he's supposed to be in the classroom, right? But he's in a credential program, and he started as a paraprofessional. So I said, "Listen; your job is predicated on you taking care of that, so if you don't, you can't work here. SPED is the Holy Grail; it's like talking derivatives in finance. Nobody really gets it, so if you halfway know what you're doing and you're an African American, you've got it made. Do what you've got to do." At the same time, I was conflicted, cause man, it's a brother! We need more Black males on campus, but I would rather not have somebody than have a bad example.

Like André, Trey spent significant time and energy committed to promoting a Black male educator into a culturally responsive, outstanding teacher. He provided extensive feedback and space for the educator to take his work, and their babies, more seriously. Trey would do the exact same thing again, even knowing that his efforts may backfire, because he'd rather be the educator who cares, who provides feedback, then the one who does not. Providing such feedback honestly and in alignment with his values, however, means modeling his greater commitment towards societal equity. Such honesty provides a foundation required to lead authentically in contexts of drastic intersectional oppression.

Questions to Ask about Honesty

1   In what ways are you authentically living and demonstrating your core values within your leadership?
2   In what ways are you critically honest about your needs by implementing true boundaries?
3   In what ways are you honest and impeccable with your word?
4   In which ways do you clearly, honestly, and fairly provide feedback to others?

Empathy towards Equity

We unapologetically speak of equity from a critical racial lens, with the underlying presumption that racism is everywhere and all the time. Using the word "equity" to simply describe giving everyone what they need when they need it does not reflect historical, ongoing, and future intersectional racism. The notion of equity without a critical race lens also downplays the colonial purpose of schooling. Therefore, **we define equity as a condition that would be achieved if intersectional racism was not a major predictor of people's outcomes.** This definition of equity is dependent upon recognition of critical race theory tenets, including the willingness to challenge systems of oppression. We also believe that all people need to become more aware of equity perspectives; in other words, just because a leader is Black does not mean the leader has an equity lens that recognizes systemic oppression, intersectionality, and the permanence of racism. Thus, Authentic Leaders must continually hone empathy skills as a means of leading towards equity.

We look to Brené Brown (2015) and her discussion of empathy to further clarify the focus on equity. As Brown delineates, empathy and sympathy are often seen as the same, but they are different. Empathy is a skill that allows people to connect and provide inclusion across difference; sympathy creates an uneven power dynamic which leads to isolation and disconnection. Authentic Leaders strive for real connection across difference; they value collaboration across positional and identity-based differences, and center multiple voices and perspectives in decision-making processes. Site-based Authentic Leaders often connect with other leaders and students across difference because they empathize with shared backgrounds and experiences that transcend location, place, and time. All of the leaders in this book spent a great deal of time discussing the necessity of connecting across difference with their students; they shared backgrounds that allowed for empathetic responses to their students' lives and stories while modeling the importance of connecting across difference for teachers, staff and faculty.

Shonda recognized early on as a teacher that her lived experience mirrored many of the poor families of color she is committed to supporting. That similar lived experience cemented a foundation for empathy:

> The only thing that sustains me in this setting is thinking about where I came from. And yeah, growing up in LA, living in South Central, not having a door that locks, literally understanding what that feels like to have your home broken into night after night. And no one knows that about me. Everyone thinks I grew up in a suburb, but we lived in South Central in a little shack that was falling apart where I'm sitting on my trike, and the ceiling starts collapsing. And we were scared, and there were rats. And the landlord wouldn't take care of it.
>
> Remembering where I came from and knowing that it's a privilege to be able to work with my students every day, and it's a privilege to be able to actually close my door and be like, look, when I was little in South Central. I know about gangs. And I remember that parts of that place is now gone because of the riots. So those memories, for me, I can connect with my kids. I know what it feels like to be hungry sometimes. I know what it feels like to eat the wrong foods because that's all you can afford. I know what it's like to not have a refrigerator, so every morning, we get a honey bun. And I know that stuff. Or never going to the dentist until I'm an adult with a job of my own. I know that. And because I know that, I can talk to our students tell them that they can make it.

Shonda's reflection on how her empathy came directly from her family poverty echoed André's earlier point about knowing what struggle feels like.

Though he did not grow up in poverty, Ricardo shared a similar foundation of how lived experience helped him develop a deep sense of empathy, in part developed because students saw themselves in him:

> I was reading all these books during my Teacher Ed program that said teachers should code-shift, but none of the professors and none of the so-called master teachers I was paired with could, so I learned early that I could offer something that most teachers couldn't, and that was myself. But as I was learning to teach, I was always told that my approach was too Black or too Latino or too strong in some racist way. Like I was always too ethnic for these white professors and teachers and principals. But I saw the impact I had as soon as I walked into the classroom. My students were all Black or Latino or Black *and* Latino. So they were like, "Snap, that dude is like my dad or my uncle." So I had students the second I walked in there, especially cause their teachers were unrelatable. From there, I just had to figure out how to teach, but I already had the benefit of the doubt from the students, and if I didn't, I just switched to Spanish, and then the Latino students would perk up, and the Black students were like, "Wait, what just happened?" And then they were like, "We should learn Spanish."

While Ricardo was able to rely upon his multiracial, multilingual, and multicultural identities as foundations for reaching children and setting higher expectations than they had previously set for themselves, he also saw the importance of learning how to be with the students he had.

Consequently, that empathy aligned with Nicole, who also helped students just see who she is, and in that authenticity, students came to trust her more because they knew she saw them:

> Isn't it funny how even the kids begin to believe we are different. And when they see us in these leadership roles, they're like, "Well, you must have gone to a white school. I can't never be you." And then, when you sit, and you roll out this is what I came from. I might not have been poor, but the expectation was you're going to college. It wasn't about how much money my mom made or we had. It was about what you were going to do to be a better person. And having that conversation, to actually have that conversation with a kid, and they look at me like, "Yeah, right. You super-human. You're a unicorn."

Having to dispel being seen as this super-human unicorn became a commitment for Nicole to ensure students of color saw her in all of her many facets while acknowledging that she also sees them.

This is one of the ways Authentic Leaders use empathy towards equity to provide spaces for underrepresented students who not see others like them. Our leaders discussed being authentic as inherent to their character and their values, especially when leading in the midst of racialized systems that framed them as unicorns. Raine argued that if "you don't want to be about my kids, then I'm going to push you up or push you out." For Raine, authenticity required "being honest that I need to do the same work at a higher level" to have increased equity influence. Dawn agreed that authenticity meant centering a critical notion of equity, arguing that she needed to be able to ask teachers for honest answers to: "What is your trajectory around education?" Dawn's point was

> Everybody can't be a 35-year teacher, and that's cool, because I swore I thought I was going to be one. But, what is your trajectory? If social justice and equity is really the lens of how you look at teaching, how are you going to do that in the classroom?

At the beginning of this study, Shonda was still a principal and shared a focus on improving classrooms. But she shifted within the first year, and as a cabinet-level administrator for her district, she shares racial and cultural data with leaders in hopes of creating spaces for students of color, particularly those who are being systematically failed. Shonda's shift to systems-level thinking within a predominantly white district was demanding, difficult, and devalued, yet this simply deepened her equity resolve:

> I'm doing rollouts about equity: gender-spectrum is difficult; now [they think] I hate all Christians. I felt like I was at a Trump rally when doing gender-spectrum work. It is not our job to teach morals and values at schools, but it is our job to make sure everyone feels loved and welcomed at school sites. The level of bashing that I've gotten this year about stupid shit [crying]. This whole thing we're doing around gender spectrum is to save lives. We have children killing themselves! How can teachers be mad about that? I'm trying to save the life of a child.

In part because Shonda saw equity work as potentially life-saving, she recognized that she could leverage student-centric approaches in ways to instill teacher empathy.

Recall that Alicia set up a site-based program to diversify the student population by recruiting students of color from targeted communities; facing initial resistance, when the program began showing success, a white administrator co-opted the program. Yet Alicia maintained her focus on equity, and leveraged her leadership to foster educator empathy through telling stories about students with current data:

> All these people in the suburbs heard about the program and they're like, "Oh we want that." And so now there was a whole thing around,

"Wait, who are these applicants?" We got almost 200 applications and like 100 of them were not the kids that we were targeting. And so we had to say no, and we did. People kept talking about how, "Oh our population is still 60 percent kids of color." When I showed our leadership team the fact that our Middle School, our sixth grade, was like 80 percent white, and our twelfth grade was like 80 percent black. And when you average out all of those numbers it looks like we're doing a fine job. But when you split it up that way, that tells a whole other story.

Promoting empathy towards equity for students is as important as continually pushing white colleagues to engage in equity work for students they may invisibilize. The Black leaders in this study frequently lamented the difficulty of pushing white teachers to accurately and expressly teach with love and care for "our babies"; our discussions clarified that the tensions of challenging white adults happen at all levels within educational systems.

Given the whiteness of teachers, site administrators, and district personnel, Authentic Leaders have no choice but to become equity warriors fighting to push white people in their systemic and internalized racism. As Raine mentioned, "The system is working, and some of us have been called to get in and break it. Until we break this system, it will continue." While we argue this breakage has to happen with empathy, the ultimate goal, systemic transformation, requires recognizing that breakage may be needed along the way.

Rosie shared her tensions with the notion of transforming with or without white people:

In theory, that's something that white people have to do on their own. And to a certain degree, I agree with that, but to a certain degree, I don't because how are they gonna do it? When most white people are insulated, all their friends are white, their communities are white, their schools are white, their work is white. I'm not on this planet and I don't feel that I exist to appease white people, at all. So it's, how do I ease them into equity work, not appease them? That's a challenge.

While Raine expressed extreme frustration with white teachers throughout this book, she also continually modeled, in practice, working alongside with and mentoring white educators.

When she was able to lead with empathy, moreover, the white educators around her often more closely aligned with her critical notion of equity:

I realize I have a gift of getting white people to do things that they wouldn't normally do in opposition to their ethics which are sour and poisonous. They do the right thing sometimes because I ask them to. And I just think, if every now and again we can get some people to do the right thing, it's well worth it for me to stay in it. I just know they're not always going to do the right thing, but if every now and again I get something, then it's worth it. But, the color of your skin—you know, it's the value of your heart. Our purpose and intent is tied to how our hearts move. At some point, you recognize that there's a white person in that room that you can be allied with. Until you get to a place where you create enough white allies to break the system, we'll still be in this place. I plan to get in there and get them all. I'm going to have enough white allies to break the system.

As the goal of breaking a system all leaders saw as intending to "break babies," the longer these educators talked with each other, the more they transitioned from naming racism towards strategizing on creating empathetic coalitions.

While the notion of empathy towards equity for students and systems was seen as extremely important, Authentic Leaders must also remember to create spaces for often overlooked staff members. Jill's work allowed her access to many classified staff across the district; she worked with clerical and attendance clerks, nutrition services, custodial services, and facilities staff. A prevailing theme across each division was the way these staff members felt unseen and mistreated by site administrators who demonstrated a lack of empathy towards equity. To be clear, this was also a racial equity issue, as more than 80% of employees in these divisions were people of color. In a district workshop populated almost entirely with administrators of color, Jill shared:

> I just want you to know that even as you're speaking, there's a group of individuals who may be seeing you in the very same role that you see white folks. I know you're all about kids, but when's the last time you talked to your custodian? I know this is all about we want to improve schools, but when's the last time you had a meeting with classified staff and went to the cafeteria, helped clean up and helped serve food? Because to that group of people, *you* look like the oppressor.

As Jill was arguing, building coalitions of colleagues from across sectors, communities, and social divisions requires empathy and a continual centering of equity. The HEART model thus presumes Authentic Leaders commit to promoting empathy for the specific purpose of working towards equity, and that such coalitions can, in turn, lead to critical accountability.

Questions to Ask about Empathy towards Equity

1   In what ways do you consider, reflect, and connect with the perspectives of people who differ from you?
2   In what ways do you refrain from judgment of others?

3   How you demonstrate empathy across race, class, gender, sexuality, ability, religion, and other core aspects of social identities?

4   In what ways do you leverage your leadership to ensure the equitable representation of marginalized groups at every level of decision-making processes?

Accountability

We define accountability as the primary way in which Authentic Leaders model collective and community responsibility for equity. Leaders must hold others accountable towards honest, empathetic efforts towards equity, while also demonstrating the integrity to be accountable to those most targeted by intersectional racism. Part of equity work is understanding the importance of mentorship not just for others but to ensure those who come after have a slightly easier road. Our notion of accountability requires that Authentic Leaders create affirming, community affinity spaces for themselves and others. The difficulty of creating spaces for mentorship amidst an already overwhelming plate of responsibilities cannot be overstated; creating space for others when there is not enough space for you seems an impossible task. While we are mindful of not adding more upon leaders' full plates, we argue that Authentic Leaders must understand and build community: others' success relies in part upon learning from critical race theory-informed voices that clarify personal and professional struggles, successes, and cautionary tales of lessons learned.

As a concrete example of collective and community responsibility, Byron serves multiple communities largely through his dual focus on local business incubation and athletics. He has been a high school football assistant coach, head coach of a middle school team, and has mentored a number of the region's coaches, including participating in, and then leading, coaching seminars. He serves on a number of regional business councils and when his evenings are not filled with sports, he attends citywide business council meetings to advocate for support for local business endeavors that students can benefit from, or better yet, participate in. Byron has particularly meaningful relationships with parents and families, in part due to his presence throughout the community. He is continually stopped at grocery stores and in pickup basketball games by parents eager to check in with him. Similarly, because he regularly attends local athletic events, he is seen by students and their families alike as approachable.

> If we don't see these families as our own, then it's a battle between us, our students, and their families. Our job is to be a positive influence in everyone's lives, and that means we gotta be in and about the community, being who we are so they can see: "Hey look, Byron is at the game," or "Hey look, Byron goes to the same happy hour we do," and "Hey look,

Mr. Byron shops at the same places we do, Mom." The principals who don't do that, who don't live here, who don't know what popped off the other night cause they aren't around or didn't chat with the gas station attendant, or the old dude on the corner, they just have a much harder time connecting.

At the school, this translates into parents trusting him before they even formally interact with him. In fact, numerous other district administrators often look to Byron for advice on engaging parents or navigating complicated issues with particular parents.

In addition to being present and seen in students' local community, our notion of collective and community responsibility extends to mentorship and creating space for those who have limited opportunities.

Rosie reflected on the importance of community, and of leaders' roles in fostering such:

> I think there needs to be professional learning communities and affinity groups. There needs to be partnerships and mentorships between administrators of color and aspiring administrators of color. So much of life is experience based and motivated by experience. And if you don't have the experience, if you don't have the human connection, you're alone, and that's a really hard place to be, especially when you're asked to be of service every day and give a lot of yourself emotionally and physically every day, spiritually every day . . . . We need to be working out, going to the gym, taking a walk, taking a drive, surrounding yourself with people that have a like mindset and bouncing things off one another or just venting is important. It's important to have those accomplices in your career. So I think that, like the Black Teacher Project,[1] there should be one for administrators. I would structure it a little differently but the concept is incredible, a place to heal and to exhale emotionally and just leave it there. We gotta do it on our own.

While Rosie argued that the creation of Black administrator affinity groups might need to happen on "our own," she did not know that Ricardo, whom she had not met, had already helped create a local Black principals group.

Ricardo ultimately demonstrated the impact of professional affinity groups, which serve as a space of release, but also a place to rethink the type of leadership he wants to model:

> I feel like when I get with my homies, like the Black principals' group or the Black statewide educator professional network, we all bash on these white folk, and at times I wonder, are there any good white educators? And then I think for a second and every school I have been at had some

kick ass white teacher. But they never seem to get tapped for leadership either. And maybe I should be mentoring them, too, but I'm just tired, you know. And can I mentor all these Black and Latino brothers to get them ready for the hustle of leadership positions, and then take on some white folk? I just don't know if I have that capacity, or that patience.

Similarly, Jill echoed Ricardo's focus on supporting others, though in part because of her deeper systemic lens, she had already decided she was committed to nurturing a range of educational leaders:

For me, it's about how do I move authentically? How do we coach up? How do we continue to mentor those around us so that *they* can move authentically? And then, how do we create support systems for ourselves so that we can move? How do you ensure that you're ultimately keeping your number one goal, which is to do the right thing for students, and for the adults who serve those students? Creating spaces where a group of like-minded leaders can come together and provide support and have conversations is a critical first step.

In part through Jill's mentorship, André has started to consider ways he can improve his accountability to others through expanding his influence:

I noticed the county office of education has these side jobs where you can be a mentor to other administrators. And so, I've been looking into that because we need more of us, and we need to school more of us on the process and the business of how to navigate it, what to expect in terms of the personalities that come in the door, and how to maintain your spirit through all of that so that you don't get run down and say, "Screw it, I'm going to go back," either to the classroom or wherever else.

Our definition of accountability includes the notion of seeing, respecting, and growing those who report to us as well as adults around us.

Authentic Leaders lead horizontally and vertically; our leadership is not defined by the people who report to us. Rather than rely upon power bestowed by a hierarchy designed to oppress, we define accountability as leading from where we are, aware of positional boundaries, modeling integrity and authenticity with communities intentionally excluded by school and district practice.

Here, Jill shares an example of the importance of being accountable to all staff:

So, this custodian comes to see me, and is like, "I've been here 14 years. I love the Bay; I went to school here. I'm treated like shit by everybody at my school site." And I was like, "So, your principal . . . ?" And he was like, "My principal, she don't know me except when there's something wrong." He was like, "From the admin to the teachers, to whatever, nobody sees me. Nobody knows me. They want me to come in and do something, but they don't see me. Like, I'm invisible." And that tore at my heart. And so, as site leaders, how are you modeling that ALL adults are important because they are leaders for children?

So, I was able to work with him. I was also able to reach out to his boss, and be like, "You need to do some work there," but then, I also took that information to the other district leaders, and gave them that. And of course, they were like, "Well, I feel like they need more professional development," but I was like, "Let's talk about what you're doing with your principals to make schools more inclusive." Those things are important to me in terms of my values, and I'm embedding them. That is not in my job description. I'm making those connections because that's important to me. That's mentoring up; it's more than up and down. It's more of a conjoined alignment.

Collective and community responsibility becomes a reminder for Authentic Leaders that our leadership does not end with ourselves; rather, we are opening portals through which other leaders should pass.

This intentional commitment to lead beyond our positional role, to embody what being an "educator" means, to let authenticity be a guiding virtue, reclaims the notion of accountability from standards and checklists to being in community with all employees, students, and families. Jill expanded on leading as mentorship:

> The reality is, each one of you should be having a circle just like this with the next five people that you are mentoring and taking care of the same way we have tried to mentor and support you because that's how change happens, and that's how movements are created. So, part of your work is to continue to find those people who don't think that they want to be leaders. By bringing them under your wing, they're seeing leadership done differently. What are you creating for the next leaders? What's your succession plan? Who are you mentoring? Your responsibility as Black people is to get back in there and figure out who we can bring along.

Accountability is thus reframed as a commitment to transforming from intersectional racism through leading with honest, empathic efforts towards equity that engage those around us, those intentionally excluded from us by hierarchy and power, and through mentoring.

This mentoring can take on affinity groups, support for those in other sectors, as well as shared commitments to privileging others' critical voices. Through increasing personal leadership accountability to a range of others, Authentic Leaders can mentor across positional roles, dramatically expanding community resources and reinforcing those that can help encourage reflection on purpose, strategy, and outcomes.

Questions to Ask about Accountability

1 In what ways are you accountable to your own community through reaching back and mentorship?
2 In what ways do you model mentorship of others within your leadership?
3 In what ways do you sustain relationships with critical colleagues who actively hold you accountable to your lived values?

Reflection

During his doctoral studies, Chris presented on the importance of critical reflection about race, racism, and racial identities for teachers. An audience member, the director of the university's teacher education program, objected to Chris's argument that personal reflection was essential for teacher growth around racial understanding. The director of teacher education remained adamant that reflection was not something teachers need to do; rather, they needed to learn how to teach. Defining adult learning as if reflection is not a central aspect of the learning process ignores learning theories (Gay, 2000; Knowles, Holton, Elwood, & Swanson, 1998), but deeper, this myopia mirrors a lack of investment in preparing educators to think through how (and why) they engage those they aim to teach. Similarly, the preparation of school leaders rarely centers the practice of personal reflection around oppressive systems, and national leadership standards consistently exclude reflection as a skill set (National Policy Board for Educational Administration, 2020). These structural exclusions reinforce a teacher and leadership profession seemingly divorced from the need to reflect on purpose, approach, and outcome.

Within the anti-adult learning context of schooling, Authentic Leaders recognize the importance of personal reflection, whether written in a journal, online, or in critical conversation with peers, friends, family, or even strangers. **We define reflection as the intentional, consistent time set aside to be in alignment with one's purpose.** Intentionality is key to this work, and as a wave of mindfulness approaches spreads across schools, we argue regular, ongoing reflecting on personal and professional orientation is essential to transforming from oppressive systems. Jill clarified this point:

> How do you make [reflection] part of your work? Are you writing? Is it built into the way that you structure your job? You have to structure it so it becomes part of your work. If you're waiting to have time, you're never going to really have time to do it.

Creating spaces for personal reflection, whatever formats that can take, as well as mentorship and affinity spaces for critical colleagues allows Authentic Leaders to continually ground themselves in answering the reflective question of

"Why do this work?" Why push in the midst of racially difficult and oppressive systems? Why lead when leading is incredibly painful and difficult?

Our participants discussed their "whys" at length; for some, the ability to try to transform as a site administrator was predicated on a capacity to keep firm boundaries. This discussion echoed participant reluctance to become principals. Now firmly ensconced in the roles, however, our leaders were able to be accountable to themselves and others by reflecting on how they were (or were not) living up to their "why." As Mason noted, "What keeps me grounded here is I enjoy being a principal. My biggest fear is if I go to a larger school or the district offices, I will lose the joy that keeps me going every day."

Raine shared her fear of being removed from that joy:

> So if I say, "You know what would really help our students is if we just had PD like this or we did it like that, right?" I have a million plans and a million ideas and I'm highly intelligent where instruction is concerned. If I share that, I won't get to lead my school. I won't get to be there for my family. I'll always be asked to go to this meeting or do this thing. They just start pulling at you and pulling at you and no part of that is for kids.

Jill extended Raine's reminder that work that is not linked to students may not be a personal and professional focus, unless your leadership context is based on adults, such as at the district level.

During a workshop for teachers, Jill clarified the importance of aligning to purpose:

> When you were teachers, people often asked you to handle student that no one could handle because they saw that you had that skill-set—whatever they called it, like classroom management. Really, you were like, "I'm going to take these kids because no one else can handle them and I don't want them pushed out." Then, you became administrators, and I see you creating spaces in your schools for the children that others don't want or don't know how to handle. And then, when the teachers don't know how to teach them, I see you doing that same movement: "What do I need to do to try and create safe spaces for those teachers?" And where I am, there's this space where I'm like, "How do I create support systems for the people who are supporting the people who are teaching?" It's all the same purposeful work.

As a concrete example of the necessity of knowing your "why," we previously shared Nicole's journey from being an assistant principal who thoroughly enjoyed her job and the people with whom she worked to becoming a first-year principal in an extremely challenging situation.

Through both contexts, Nicole was able to answer her "why" and remain grounded. In the first situation as an assistant principal, Nicole shared:

> I think it goes back to leading from your core. And my core, what I figured out, is that I'm a genuine person, and I want to see every one of my students survive or every one of my teachers be who they can be because that makes me feel good. I know my why: I'm just going to keep it real: it makes me look good; my name is attached to this. So if my name is attached to it, then it has to be the best that it can be regardless of what's going on. We're still doing what we're doing because we love it. We love it. We love our students. We love what we're doing. And so that keeps me motivated. And the fact that I can go to work and have fun doing my job; I can smile at the end of each meeting with my student who just cussed their teacher out? At the end, we're laughing about it. I love this work.

Because our interviews were spread across several years, we were able to engage leaders before, during, and after leadership transitions.

While Nicole had been extremely happy in her previous role, her reflections after her first year as a middle school principal were revealing:

> This has been a horrible first year. I'm a new principal; I'm not going to know everything; I'm going to make mistakes. My entire respect for unions is gone because there is no reason we continue to keep horrible people. I respect my boss as a Black woman, but I can't play the game and play a role instead of being authentic, cause I'm Black-Black. In order to be who I am, I'm continuing to do the things I love to do. I'm building on the reasons why I believe students will be successful; building up social-emotional items, creating a functional student activities program. Bringing in programs and mentors. Going to feeder schools; lead all the rallies; do dress-up days. *I have to remind myself constantly not to let them take me out of my character.* I have to keep reminding myself of my "why"; these public school systems are unhealthy for my life. I refuse to change and comply with what I'm supposed to look like and how I'm supposed to act.

Despite the drastic shift in school contexts, from a supportive environment to where she is directly being confronted and challenged, Nicole modeled the importance of regular reflection on her purpose. The notion of purpose is designed to push Authentic Leaders past the "why" we discussed previously, into the idea of leadership as purpose-driven work.

Burrus (2015) clarified, "Your purpose isn't just what you do, but it's who you are . . . your job is what you are hired to do; but your [purpose] is what you were born to do" (p. 60). Just as fusing the masks required to navigate together can be a survival strategy, finding job settings that align with purpose can enable authenticity. When leaders are out of alignment with purpose, being authentic becomes even more difficult, and leadership suffers. Illustrating this alignment, André reflected on purpose driving his next professional steps:

> Whatever it is that's next for me has to be purpose-driven. It can't just be, "Oh, you'd make a good . . . . What's-her-name's leaving. You want that seat? You want to apply for that?" The money's not huge for me. It's what it is that I'm doing. That's what I'm thinking right now.

In previous chapters, Raine has shared her desire for invisibility to create space to do the work that she most values. To note, though, Raine's primary purpose is to do whatever is necessary to educate children; if that means being invisible, moving teachers, making adults angry, or getting grieved by the teacher's union, she is reflective enough to tolerate those outcomes as long as students are getting what they need. Raine shared her strategy for purpose:

> The other day in the principal's meeting I just chose somebody and whatever they said I said because right now we're in the budget crisis and everybody is in panic mode. I'm really not because I'm like, "Well, we don't have any money anyway, so I'm not panicking. We're just going to do what we've been doing." And so, the person next to me was a white woman and she was panicked and was like, "I'm overwhelmed. I'm just overwhelmed." I mean really though! I just went to my staff, and I was like, "Hey, whatever, it's like the end of the month, we're broke out here in these streets, and whatever, you plug your electricity into somebody else's, and keep pushing." And they were like, "All right, we with you." And we've been working with purpose. We're just working for kids, having fun, and enjoying life.

Raine's reflective orientation allowed her to focus on the aspects over which she and her staff have control. Mason agreed on staying positive in the face of oppression:

> I think I'm really fortunate because I have an all African American teaching staff. And we just sat down, being me, being real, said, 'Look, brothers, we're going to win this. If we win, our kids win, and nobody else can take this away from us as a group. Losing is not an option.'

Being intentional about reflection creates an opportunity to strategically plan responses and future moves given the oppressive nature of educational work and the many ways in which Authentic Leaders have to push against systems. Those moves might include taking time away from a current role for health reasons. As mentioned throughout this book, Black educational leadership takes an emotional and physical toll that is rarely discussed. Reflection must push beyond coping and self-care as we are in a larger societal struggle for Black bodies and Black health. While Rosie needed to leave administration as a concrete example of prioritizing her health over professional commitments, others in this book have left or are making plans to leave their positions because the toll professional struggle takes on their bodies, minds, and hearts. Nicole reflected, "I think that if I'm looking at longevity in administration, it would be something that really brings emphasis and focus and importance back to what also is being silenced in education."

In order for Nicole to sustain in administration, however, she knew she would need her authenticity enabled: "If I was ever forced to change [being me], I will cut. I will cut because I need to be me. I've just got to be me, and if I can't, it's going to be a wrap." Jill warned Black educational leaders of the need to be intentional around reflection:

> Whenever you're trying to move authentically, be about community, be about folks who are serving children and the adults who serve them, folks are going to come for you. You just need to know that. There's never going to be a position where folks aren't going to come for you; because of who you are, how you move, and because of what's important to you, people are going to come for you. But, it's a matter of who will you be at that moment?

Alicia recognized the toll her current toxic environment was taking—she echoed Jill's warning that "people are going to come for" Authentic Leaders.

Alicia's reflection helped her recognize that the context she dedicated herself to increasingly caused harm to her, and any shift would require taking care of herself more fully:

> I don't know that staying in education is taking care of me, I honestly do not know that. Which is why I've been ambivalent about looking for a job. Because if I'm gonna convince somebody to give me a principalship, I need to be engaged. And I don't know that I am. And then I cry. And I kind of half ass look for a job. Because I don't even know if I can do this education thing anymore. I don't know if I wanna take that on like, it's hard ass work. I can't imagine a context in which it would feel good again. I don't have the space to care right now. The school used to be everything, and now it's not.

Alicia also recognized that she was unable to support children as much as she wished to, and that further encouraged her to leave that context. Mason agreed with the need to be present, or to leave if not: "I always bring it back to, what do I do every day that's in the best interest of the kids that I'm serving right now?" Mason's point was that if not able to honor the best interest, it is time to leave.

Rosie further corroborated:

> It is an added responsibility and it is a pain in the ass, it's a pain in the heart! But I'll do what I have to do to make sure that the kids in my school are learning at the best, at the best ability and not have their dreams deferred. You do what you gotta do, you plant seeds and you leave a legacy.

As these Black educational leaders demonstrate, reflection is an essential aspect of building, enhancing, and maintaining authenticity. The type of legacy one leaves is entirely based upon capacity to reflect while present, and to know when one needs to leave. Reflective practices can look very different, but the key for these leaders was having ongoing spaces to be challenged, to be honest about struggles, and to be vulnerable. Only with ongoing reflection could these leaders accurately weigh if they were having a powerfully positive impact on children of color and if that impact was worth the life harm they were sustaining. Reflection, on professional purpose, on effectiveness towards that purpose, and on the real impacts of operating in toxic oppressive contexts is required to lead authentically.

Questions to Ask about Reflection

1   What is your purpose on this earth?
2   In what ways do you answer your "why" each day?
3   In what ways are you intentional about personal reflection?
4   In what ways are you consistently working on your spiritual, emotional, and physical well-being?

Trust

The final element of the HEART framework is trust, which is the foundation of all relationships. There are many definitions of trust; we honor Brené Brown's Braving Inventory[2] as a concrete tool to help teams and leaders break down the steps needed to understand trust. **Therefore, we define trust as the ability to be vulnerable within relationships.** Due to multiple levels of historic and ongoing intersectional oppression, trust, however, is a minefield for Black leaders. We asked a few Black men over 40 years old who were not involved in this study about trust at work. At first, the responses were surface comments around trusting employees and direct reports to do the work. Eventually, however, all of the Black men responded that trust was really difficult because it meant letting down their guard—something they had been trained by years of negative responses not to do.

From the never-ending assault on Black bodies (Coates, 2015) to consistent micro-aggressions like clutching purses and bags on elevators, Black men understand that trusting others can lead to extreme violence. Black women also understand the danger of trust, as historically, white women acted largely as co-signers to rape and abuse throughout US slavery and with the suffrage movement intentionally excluding Black women. Centuries of broken promises and passive acceptance of oppressive conditions have forged a rarely discussed mistrust (hooks, 2015). Indeed, much has been written about the feminist movement as a white appropriation of Black women's labor and how these appropriations continue to exploit Black women's trust (Collins, 2009; hooks, 2015). Historically, Black women and white men also have not been in authentic, honest friendship with each other; the chattel slavery system where white slave owners freely, regularly and repeatedly raped Black women (McGuire, 2006) created a chasm of mistrust based on stereotypes of hypersexuality. These stereotypes continue to be met with anti-Black violence to punish Black women for trusting white women and men.

As authors of this text, we had to look at our own personal relationship to authentically include trust in this framework. We also readily acknowledge that this element of the framework requires time and patience; as co-authors, we have been developing our relationship for almost two decades. As we discussed earlier, as our professional working relationship turned into a friendship throughout the years we began to name and assert the different ways that our collegial bond should not work, and why we felt it did. While we have been colleagues across a range of experiences (co-teaching, co-writing grants, academic papers, traveling across the US to conferences, facilitating workshops, conducting research), we are continually asked, incredulously, how we could possibly know each other. The presumptions are clear: A Black woman and a white man, both moving authentically, could not possibly be friends, and given societal segregation, certainly could not live within the same social circles. As others continually enforce boundaries that exist for them, we knew we had to develop a depth of trust as our work would continue to confront the intersectional racism of people invested in challenging cross-racial, cross-gender professional relationships.

We come to trust work through very different pathways but continually end at the same place: to enact the world we wish for, and to enable our professional purpose, we see a critical need to collaborate in honest ways across every imaginable barrier. We had already built internal foundations for such engagements, demonstrated by hooks' (2003) example of a friendship between a Black woman and white male who are colleagues and friends:

> When I walk out into the world with Ron, clearly indicating closeness by our body language and our speech, it changes how I am seen, how he is seen. This is yet another way race matters in a white-supremacist patriarchal context. It is still important for us to document these border crossings, the process by which we make community. (p. 106)

Though every time we are together, we experience discord and microaggressions associated with cross-racial and cross-gender relationships, two examples illustrate the need for trust as we navigate the racist world that actively targets authentic relationships that aim to challenge intersectional racism.

The first is an experience traveling on the conference circuit in Chicago. Chris found a great soul food restaurant a few blocks away from the hotel. When we saw only Black folks in and around the restaurant, Rachelle knew it would be difficult sitting there with a white man. As we walked in, a silence came over the dining room, as seemingly every head turned to look and gasp. The covert looks, comments, and sly glances made her uncomfortable, and the presumption that we were a romantic couple was clearly jarring for the Black patrons who had been enjoying their meal. For Rachelle, Chris' apparent lack of awareness for the situation combined with her own response was triggering. When Rachelle mentioned the obvious tension—patrons continued to stare—Chris responded that this was the way to push.

Later, we had conversations that deepened our understanding of each other and forged bonds, talking through the ridiculousness of others' expectations, the historically rooted violence against interracial couples, and the lack of exposure most people have to a Black woman and white man comfortably eating together. Rachelle was able to understand that part of Chris' approach to challenging racism involves him leaning into uncomfortable situations where he is usually the only white person within communities of color. Chris was able to understand that Rachelle was triggered by generations of Black men talking about Black women who prefer white men; she almost wanted to shout, "We're just friends!" but nothing would soothe the tensions. Over time, we recognized that our ability to be open to each other was a necessary element to create trust, and we continue to challenge our own comfort and others' expectations.

A second example reflects our shared enjoyment of food, and a similar discomfort projected onto us. At a restaurant with colleagues that at that point Chris had thought were close friends and colleagues with Rachelle, a Black woman across the table from Chris interrupted a group conversation to ask a pointed question: "Are you white?" Everyone immediately turned to Chris, the only non-Black person at the table. While Chris brushed off the question, the effect was awkward. Often presumed to be a person of color—he is frequently one of the only racially white people in the room—Chris continually reminds people that he is, in fact, white. But at dinner with friends, Chris also let down his guard. Rachelle later helped remind Chris that operating across race and gender lines means our guard can never be let down, especially not in public, even with those we think we know. The conversation shifted to focus on our roles beyond allyship, as what has increasingly been referred to as co-conspirators. Love (2019) clarifies: "Too often, though not always, our allies are eager White folx who have not questioned their whiteness, White supremacy, White emotions of guilt and shame, the craving for admiration, or the structures that maintain White power" (p. 117). This conversation reminded both of us that while most often, people uncomfortable with our cross-racial, cross-gender friendship will target Rachelle; as a co-conspirator, Chris would also be targeted. Trust requires both of us to open up to each other, to support each other, and to be ready for microaggressions and attacks with the intent to cause harm.

We share these experiences as a cautionary tale for Black leaders and the white folks who intend to operate as co-conspirators. Racism is always present and always impacts the way in which leadership happens. We lead based on the sum totality of our life experiences. If a leader has limited experience with people of color (watching television, YouTube videos, or films does not count), trust across racial lines will be difficult, regardless of how often that white person claims to be an ally. Recall Raine's experience the first year she did not have an African American woman mentor; "[My manager] is cool," Raine said, "but she's white. She hears things through a white lens." Not doing the work to recognize and challenge this white lens becomes a professional barrier to trust. Jill asks "What do you do when you have a leader who checks all of the boxes, but is still not leading from values?" Her answer reflects the need for honesty: "You cannot trust [this person]." We cannot control who is trustworthy, but we can do the work to be so ourselves.

Shonda shares this story:

> I sat down with my superintendent and told him that people don't feel safe. I said, "No one feels safe. None of us. Especially your females, especially your people of color. And we're not treated appropriately." Now he is super white. He keeps coming to the African-American-centric things trying to dance, and clap his hands. And I only felt like I could talk to him like that because I know I have another damn job. And he's like, "Well, what we'll do is we'll do a survey." I said, "No one's going to do your survey. You need to change the conversation around what you came in to do." As a white person, he has fear around being seen as not culturally relevant, even though he has no freaking idea what that is. Cultural responsiveness hasn't been in you, which is why you got promoted in the first place. And part of the problem is that so many of these white teachers and administrators won't admit they do not know something. It's like, if they admit it then that means that a Black woman has more knowledge than me.

Shonda's superintendent was not committed to being a co-conspirator (and likely not an ally, either), and that meant leading without a context of trust, particularly for educators, families, and students of color.

In contrast, Rosie recalls:

> I was reading an article that Ta-Nehisi Coates wrote about Obama. And he pointed out that one of Obama's biggest challenges as a president and

as a Black man, was that he inherently trusted white people because he was raised by them. And that struck a chord with me and resonated with me because I inherently trust white people because I was raised by them. And I can't tell yet if it's a help or a hindrance. I think it's both, because my antenna may not go up as fast as other people of color. Once they're up, they're up, but it takes me a little while longer and that's where damage comes in. I think it's important to trust. I think that if we're ever gonna heal transcultural divides and problems, we need to trust each other.

Authentic Leaders must be generous with employees' intentions, using vulnerability to both demonstrate trustworthiness and to build trust with others.

And trusting white educators may be easier for some than for others. Mason reflected on trust as central to authenticity:

> I look at it as continuing to build relationships with people. That's how I model it; that's what works for me. Teachers see me walk with the custodian through their classrooms on the grounds, the custodian sees me walk with the admin assistant through the grounds. They see me in meetings where everybody comes to the table. That's what gets me through my day-to-day, being authentic like that.

As Shonda reminds us that our school systems prioritize leaders who are not culturally responsive, Jill understands this causes very few educators to lead authentically:

> The one thing I've learned is that no one freaking knows how to do this. No one knows how to educate our children except like 12 people who are not in the space to do it. So, when I finally came to that, I realized that our leaders really need a lot of grace, and we have to extend some compassion. Imagine how scared you would be if you did not know what in the hell you were doing but you were getting paid a lot of money to do it, and everybody was looking at you.

Trust is an essential yet extremely complicated concept to grasp and implement. For Authentic Leaders, developing trust with students is much easier, and often more rewarding, than with adults.

Indeed, many leaders have spent years working on building trust within classrooms and schools. For example, Ricardo's relatability to children of color, particularly African American and Latinx, is clear within the first five minutes of a conversation. He clarifies that part of his orientation to teaching began when he realized that he could be himself in the classroom, and his teaching always incorporated a multicultural blend of music. In his first few years of teaching, Ricardo realized that his ability to switch between multiple worlds (corporate America, elite graduate school, and growing up with a single mother in low-income African American, Latinx, and Colombian communities) and multiple languages (Spanish and English) allowed students to trust him.

Similarly, Mason builds trust with his students in concrete ways:

> Brother, sister, you are having an issue. Bring your behind up here. You need to eat? We'll get you some breakfast. You need to take a nap? Go take a nap. You need to get cleaned up? We've got hot water down in the high school. Go take a shower. We've got you. It helps me sleep really good at night if I can put a couple wins together for some kids that look like me.

The difficulty lies in shifting our trust frameworks from students to adults. We argue that in order to build the connective tissue to transform educational systems, Authentic Leaders must demonstrate vulnerability and develop trust with the adults who serve those students. We must guard against creating silos that have long-lasting impact when trust is destroyed; our students are looking to us to model the relationships they can create across difference to fight oppression daily.

Jill thoughtfully summarized the importance of trust as a systems value:

> When I look at [all of the leaders I've supported], I see my leaders doing different things, and taking on different roles. That's what systemic change is—it's long-term, and it's not quick, and in fact, it's unbelievably slow. Leadership is about knowing what you don't know, and surrounding yourself with people who know the things you don't. You get a couple of people around the district that you trust; you get a couple of principals, you go talk to a couple of teachers. You create the vision; without vision, the people perish. I believe I can lead differently based on what I know now.

Questions to Ask about Trust

1   In what ways do you demonstrate being trustworthy?
2   In what ways do you consistently extend generosity to the intentions, words, and actions of others?
3   How do you engage with those whom you do not trust?
4   How do you demonstrate vulnerability and self-compassion?

Applying the HEART Model

We conclude with an encouragement to apply the HEART model to schools, districts, and as a reminder for individuals to strengthen their own leadership practice. While much of the leadership preparation and evaluation world focuses on skills and dispositions, the HEART model reminds that who and how we are is the foundation for our culturally rooted strengths. With continual investments in deepening voice, in exercising personal identities in relation to professional orientations, in modeling our multicultural, multilingual, multi-faceted identities, we model that authenticity is a survival mechanism. Indeed, the effectiveness of school systems that challenge their original colonial intent requires a critical commitment to maintaining honesty, empathy towards equity, accountability to each other and ourselves, reflection as daily practice, and trust as a foundation to enable healing relationships. The HEART model is designed to remind educational leaders that commitment to transform educational systems is extremely painful, traumatizing, temporary work, and that for Black leaders and leaders of color, the intersectional racism is dramatically exacerbated by longevity within the system. Thus, while we wish we could argue for sustainable, long-term leadership strategies, our goals are for culturally thriving Black communities, and that requires leaders who remain alive, healthy, and balanced.

At the core of systems transformation rests the efforts of those who have come before, most of whom have died younger than they should have. We argue that although strategic authenticity as a leadership approach is needed as a professional coping mechanism, being authentic will not replace the need to take breaks, to breathe, and to create the space to be human in the face of inhumane, toxic conditions that are schools and school systems. The longer one stays within toxic environments, the greater the chance that such environments leech into our souls; the HEART model is designed to be an individual and systemic reminder to soothe ourselves back to healthy practice while in the war against the souls of our children.

Notes

1 www.blackteacherproject.org
2 http://www.brenebrown.com

EPILOGUE

Where Are They Now?

The interviews that informed this book were carried out over two years, followed by another year for coding and writing. During that time, a few participants changed positions, mostly increasing their hierarchical influence. Since the conclusion of the book, however, many participants had significant shifts, with some in their second or third position in three years. This reflects the tumultuous nature of educational leadership within districts, as leadership turnovers in urban schools remain extremely high. The bulk of the transitions echoed Jill's reflection about her shift from a district to a state-level position: "I left one system of oppression, and landed in another." What follows provides a quick update about participants' current positions.

Byron

Byron has maintained his role at the same school site, serving as assistant principal to an almost annual rotation of temporary principals. While he continues to be passed over for the principalship, his work within the community, direct engagement with students and families, and his business relationships keep him grounded in this role.

Raine

Raine is completing her doctorate and preparing to leave the district to implement her vision around literacy leadership.

Dawn

At the time of the interviews, Dawn was an assistant principal at a district high school. She became an assistant principal at a high-poverty school serving children of color and is currently the site-leader for a district-approved grade 6–12 charter school.

Jayson

Jayson has maintained his role as the same school as a site-based Teacher on Special Assignment.

Mason

At the time of the interviews, Mason was a site-leader enjoying having created an all-Black staff to serve students at his alternative school. Recently, Mason accepted a district position supervising other site leaders. As he mentioned via phone, "I didn't know what I didn't know."

Trey

At the time of the interviews, Trey was an assistant principal in a high-need school serving Black and Brown students. When the district surreptitiously closed the school, Trey took a district-level leadership position supporting principals in a neighboring district. As Trey mentioned via phone, "I'm not sure being a principal is in the cards for me right now; I'm loving the flexibility."

Nicole

We have discussed Nicole's most recent moves; now that her office manager has been moved, she is diligently working on improving culture at her school and has reconnected with her purpose and joy. Her concluding thoughts were

> The kid energy energizes my soul. I always say, you build relationships with students by hanging with them in their safe spaces or free zones. Get out of the office/classroom and spend time on the black top, in the gym with them doing things they love to do. It's that simple.

André

Currently finishing his doctorate, André remains the principal of an alternative high school, a position he has held for the past five years.

Shonda

Shonda is still the Equity Lead at her predominantly white district, but she is actively seeking other employment. When discussing her health challenges, Shonda said, "I've got to get my life together . . . this ain't it! I need to make a move—SOON!"

Alicia

Alicia left the magnet school to become an elementary school principal, a role she stayed at for three years, before shifting towards higher education roles. "I am leaving not because of the people here, mostly white," Alicia clarified, "but because of the institutional disaster that is [school districts]." "Being a principal is backbreaking and soul hardening work and there is no acknowledgement of that. That's what makes it unsustainable and why I am choosing to walk away from it."

Rosie

Rosie relocated back East after a significant health issue led her to leave school administration. This relocation enabled her space to re-focus on health, and she now serves as a consultant to education-focused non-profit organizations, school districts, and charter schools, with a focus on centering Black and Brown youth within regional LGBTQ centers. In this role, Rosie controls who she works with and the terms of the engagement, something she could not do as an administrator.

Ricardo

Ricardo has been the director of school improvement at a large urban school district for the past three years and was recently accepted into a superintendent certificate and doctoral program so that he can apply for the superintendency.

Jill

Jill left the district and accepted a state-level position. She is enjoying her extended reach and is clear that the work continues across multiple levels.

REFERENCES

Adams, D. (1995). *Education for extinction: American Indians and the boarding school experience, 1875–1928*. Lawrence: University Press of Kansas.

Allen, Q. (2010). Racial microaggressions: The schooling experiences of Black middle-class males in Arizona's secondary schools. *Journal of African American Males in Education, 1*(2), 125–143.

Angrist, J. D., & Guryan, J. (2008). Does teacher testing raise teacher quality? Evidence from state certification requirements. *Economics of Education Review, 27*(5), 483–503.

Assari, S. (2018a). The benefits of higher income in protecting against chronic medical conditions are smaller for African Americans than whites. *Healthcare, 6*(2), 1–11. doi: 10.3390/healthcare6010002

Assari, S. (2018b). Life expectancy gain due to employment status depends on race, gender, education, and their intersections. *Journal of Racial and Ethnic Health Disparities, 5*(2), 375–386.

Au, W. (2009). *Unequal by design: High-stakes testing and the standardization of inequality.* New York, NY: Routledge.

Au, W. (2013). Hiding behind high-stakes testing: Meritocracy, objectivity and inequality in US education. *The International Education Journal: Comparative Perspectives, 12*(2), 7–19.

Au, W. (2016). Meritocracy 2.0: High-stakes, standardized testing as a racial project of neoliberal multiculturalism. *Educational Policy, 30*(1), 39–62.

Au, W., Brown, A. L., & Calderón, D. (2016). *Reclaiming the multicultural roots of US curriculum: Communities of color and official knowledge in education.* New York, NY: Teachers College Press.

Au, W., & Ferrare, J. J. (Eds.). (2015). *Mapping corporate education reform: Power and policy networks in the neoliberal state.* New York, NY: Routledge.

Austin, R. (1998). "Not just for the fun of it!": Governmental restraints on Black leisure, social inequality, and the privatization of public space. *Southern California Law Review, 71*(4), 667–714.

Baldwin, J. (1985). *The evidence of things not seen.* New York, NY: Holt and Company.

Banks, J. (2006). *Cultural diversity and education: Foundations, curriculum, and teaching* (5th ed.). Boston, MA: Allyn and Bacon.

Barbian, E., Gonzales, G. C., & Mejia, P. (Eds.). (2017). *Rethinking bilingual education: Welcoming home languages in our classrooms.* Milwaukee, WI: Rethinking Schools.

Bell, D. (1992). *Race, racism, and American law* (3rd ed.). Boston, MA: Little, Brown and Company.

Bell, D. (1998). *Afrolantica legacies.* Chicago, IL: Third World Press.

Bell, D. (2004). *Silent covenants: Brown v. Board of Education and the unfulfilled hopes for racial reform.* New York, NY: Oxford University Press.

Bell, L. A. (2002). Sincere fictions: The pedagogical challenges of preparing white teachers for multicultural classrooms. *Equity & Excellence in Education, 35*(3), 236–244.

Bell Edmondson, E. L. J., & Nkomo, S. M. (2003). Our separate ways: barriers to advancement. In R. J. Ely, E. G. Foldy, & M. A. Scully (Eds.), *Reader in gender, work and organization* (pp. 343–361). Malden, MA: Blackwell Publishing.

Bennett, C. I., McWhorter, L. M., & Kuykendall, J. A. (2006). Will I ever teach? Latino and African American students' perspective on PRAXIS I. *American Education Research Journal, 43*(3), 531–575.

Brooks, J. S. (2019). The unbearable whiteness of educational leadership: A historical perspective on racism in the American principal's office. In J. S. Brooks & G. Theoharis (Eds.), *Whiteucation: Privilege, power, and prejudice in school and society* (pp. 35–51). New York, NY: Routledge.

Brown, B. (2015). *Daring greatly: How the courage to be vulnerable transforms the way we live, love, parent, and lead.* New York, NY: Penguin.

Brown, B. (2018). *Dare to lead: Brave work. Tough conversations. Whole hearts.* New York, NY: Random House.

Brown, M. C., II, & Davis, J. E. (2001). The historically Black college as social contract, social capital, and social equalizer. *Peabody Journal of Education, 76*(1), 31–49.

Brown, M. C., II, Donahoo, S., & Bertrand, R. D. (2001). The Black college and the quest for educational opportunity. *Urban Education, 36*(5), 553–571.

Burrus, D. (2015). *The pursuit of purpose: 21 truths for discovering your why.* Long Beach, CA: Doxa Global Group.

Capper, C. A. (2015). The 20th-year anniversary of critical race theory in education: Implications for leading to eliminate racism. *Educational Administration Quarterly, 51*(5), 791–833.

Cartledge, G., Gibson, L., & Keyes, S. E. (2012). Special education and disciplinary disproportionality of African American students. In J. L. Moore, III & C. W. Lewis (Eds.), *African American students in urban schools: Critical issues and solutions for achievement* (pp. 75–93). New York, NY: Peter Lang.

Caton, M. T. (2012). Black male perspectives on their educational experiences in high school. *Urban Education, 47*(6), 1055–1085.

Coates, T. N. (2015). *Between the world and me.* New York, NY: Spiegel & Grau.

Collins, P. H. (1987). The meaning of motherhood in Black culture and Black mother/daughter relationships. *SAGE: A Scholarly Journal on Black Women, 4*(2), 3–10.

Collins, P. H. (2009). *Black feminist thought: Knowledge, consciousness, and the politics of empowerment* (2nd ed.). New York, NY: Routledge.

Collins, P. H., & Bilge, S. (2016). *Intersectionality.* Cambridge, England: Polity Press.

Crenshaw, K. (1989). Demarginalizing the intersection of race and sex: A Black feminist critique of antidiscrimination doctrine, feminist theory, and antiracist politics. *University of Chicago Legal Forum, 1*(8), 139–167.

Crenshaw, K. (1991). Mapping the margins: Intersectionality, identity politics, and violence against women of color. *Stanford Law Review, 43*(6), 1241–1299. doi: 10.2307/1229039

Crenshaw, K. (2009). Mapping the margins: Intersectionality, identity politics, and violence against women of color. In E. Taylor, D. Gillborn, & G. Ladson-Billings (Eds.), *Foundations of critical race theory in education* (pp. 213–246). New York, NY: Routledge.

Dancy, T. E., II. (2013). Sociohistorical contexts of African American male education: An analysis of race, class, and gender. In M. C. Brown, II & T. E. Dancy, II (Eds.), *Educating African American males: Contexts for consideration, possibilities for practice* (pp. 1–21). New York, NY: Peter Lang.

Dantley, M. E. (2009). African American educational leadership: Critical, purposive, and spiritual. In L. Foster & L. C. Tillman (Eds.), *African American perspectives on leadership in schools: Building a culture of empowerment* (pp. 39–55). New York, NY: Rowman & Littlefield.

Darling-Hammond, L. (2010). *The flat world and education: How America's commitment to equity will determine our future.* New York, NY: Teachers College Press.

Davis, D. B. (2015). *The problem of slavery in the age of emancipation.* New York, NY: Random House.

Davis, J. E., & Madsen, J. (2009). African American leadership in urban schools: Implications for organizational structure and improved educational outcomes. In L. Foster & L. C. Tillman (Eds.), *African American perspectives on leadership in schools: Building a culture of empowerment* (pp. 115–139). New York, NY: Rowman & Littlefield.

Delgado, R. (2011). Rodrigo's reconsideration: Intersectionality and the future of critical race theory. *Iowa Law Review, 96*, 1247–1288.

Delgado, R., & Stefancic, J. (2012). *Critical race theory: An introduction* (2nd ed.). New York, NY: New York University Press.

Delpit, L. D. (1997). Foreword. In M. Foster (Ed.), *Black teachers on teaching* (pp. ix–xii). New York, NY: New Press.

Delpit, L. D. (2012). *"Multiplication is for white people": Raising expectations for other people's children.* New York, NY: New Press.

Derman-Sparks, L., & Phillips, C. B. (1997). *Teaching/learning anti-racism: A developmental approach.* New York, NY: Teachers College Press.

Donner, J., & Ladson-Billings, G. (2018). Critical race theory and the postracial imaginary. In N. Denzin & Y. S. Lincoln (Eds.), *The SAGE handbook of qualitative research* (5th ed., pp. 195–213). Los Angeles, CA: Sage.

Du Bois, W. E. B. (1903/1989). *The souls of Black folk.* New York, NY: Penguin Books.

Du Bois, W. E. B. (1935/2004). Does the Negro need separate schools? In E. J. Sundquist (Ed.), *The Oxford W. E. B. Du Bois reader* (pp. 423–431). New York, NY: Oxford University Press.

Dunbar, P. L. (1913). *The complete poems of Paul Laurence Dunbar.* New York, NY: Dodd, Mead, and Company.

Dyer, R. (1997). *White.* New York, NY: Routledge.

Echols, C. (2006) *Challenges facing Black American principals: A conversation about coping.* Retrieved from http://cnx.org/content/m13821/1.1

Ellis, W. F., & Epstein, K. K. (2015). Tactics and strategies for breaking the barriers to a diverse teaching force. In C. E. Sleeter, L. V. I. Neal, & K. Kumashiro (Eds.), *Diversifying the teacher workforce: Preparing and retaining highly effective teachers* (pp. 139–150). New York, NY: Routledge.

Epstein, K. K. (2008). *A different view of urban schools: Civil rights, critical race theory, and unexplored realities.* New York, NY: Peter Lang.

Evans-Winters, V., & Twyman Hoff, P. (2011). The aesthetics of white racism in pre-service teacher education: A critical race theory perspective. *Race Ethnicity and Education, 14*(4), 461–479.

Fairclough, A. (2007). *A class of their own: Black teachers in the segregated South.* Cambridge, MA: Harvard University Press.

Falck, C. (2012). Equitable access: Examining information asymmetry in reverse redlining claims through critical race theory. *Texas Journal on Civil Liberties & Civil Rights, 18*(1), 101–119.

Farzan, A. N. (2018). BBQ Becky, Permit Patty and Cornerstore Caroline: Too "cutesy" for those white women calling police on Black people? Morning Mix, *Washington Post,* October 19. Retrieved from https://www.washingtonpost.com/news/morning-mix/wp/2018/10/19/bbq-becky-permit-patty-and-cornerstore-caroline-too-cutesy-for-those-white-women-calling-cops-on-blacks/

Foster, L. (2005). The practice of educational leadership in African American communities of learning: Context, scope, and meaning. *Educational Administration Quarterly, 41*(4), 689–700.

Foster, L., & Tillman, L. C. (2009). Introduction. In L. Foster & L. C. Tillman (Eds.), *African American perspectives on leadership in schools: Building a culture of empowerment* (pp. 1–13). New York, NY: Rowman & Littlefield.

Foster, M. (1997). *Black teachers on teaching.* New York, NY: The New Press.

Freire, P. (1970). *Pedagogy of the oppressed.* New York, NY: Continuum.

Garrett-Walker (in press). *Healing our own spines: Black women school leaders subverting ideological lynching.*

Gay, G. (2000). *Culturally responsive teaching: Theory, research, and practice.* New York, NY: Teachers College Press.

Gillborn, D. (2008). *Racism and education: Coincidence or conspiracy?* New York, NY: Taylor & Francis.

Gillborn, D., Dixson, A., Ladson-Billings, G., Parker, L., Rollock, N., & Warmington, P. (2018). *Critical race theory in education.* New York, NY: Routledge.

Ginwright, S. (2016). *Hope and healing in urban education: How urban activists and teachers are reclaiming matters of the heart.* New York, NY: Routledge.

Gist, C. D. (2017). *Portraits of anti-racist alternative routes to teaching in the US: Framing teacher development for community, justice, and visionaries.* New York, NY: Peter Lang.

Gist, C. D. (2019). For what purpose? Making sense of the various projects driving grow your own program development. *Teacher Education Quarterly, 46*(1), 9–22.

Gist, C., Bianco, M., & Lynn, M. (2019). Examining grow your own programs across the teacher development continuum: Mining research on teachers of color and non-traditional educator pipelines. *Journal of Teacher Education, 70*(1), 13–25.

Goldhaber, D., & Hansen, M. (2010). Race, gender, and teacher testing: How objective a tool is teacher licensure testing? *American Educational Research Journal, 47*(1), 218–251.

Gooden, M. A. (2013). Exploring the property rights and liberty interests of African American males in public schools: Confronting the denial of education under the guise of maintaining order. In M. C. Brown, II, T. E. Dancy, II, & J. E. Davis (Eds.), *Educating African American males: Contexts for consideration, possibilities for practice* (pp. 89–103). New York, NY: Peter Lang.

Goodman, G. S., & Hilton, A. A. (2013). Urban dropouts: Why persist? In R. Brock & G. S. Goodman (Eds.), *School sucks: Arguments for alternative education* (pp. 199–212). New York, NY: Peter Lang.

Harney, S., & Moten, F. (2013). *The undercommons: Fugitive planning and Black study.* London: Minor Compositions.

Harris, A. (1990). Race and essentialism in feminist legal theory. *Stanford Law Review, 42*(3), 581–616. doi: 10.2307/1228886

Heitzeg, N. (2016). *The school-to-prison pipeline: Education, discipline, and racialized double standards.* Santa Barbara, CA: Praeger.

Herron, R. (2018). I used to be a 911 dispatcher. I had to respond to racist calls every day. *Vox*, October 31. Retrieved from https://www.vox.com/first-person/2018/5/30/17406092/racial-profiling-911-bbq-becky-living-while-black-babysitting-while-black

hooks, b. (1994). *Teaching to transgress: Education as the practice of freedom.* New York, NY: Routledge.

hooks, b. (1996). *Reel to real: Race, sex, and class at the movies.* New York, NY: Routledge.

hooks, b. (2003). *Teaching community: A pedagogy of hope.* New York, NY: Routledge.

hooks, b. (2013). *Writing beyond race: Living theory and practice.* New York, NY: Routledge.

hooks, b. (2015). *Ain't I a woman: Black women and feminism* (6th ed.). New York, NY: Routledge.

Howard, T. C., & Milner, H. R., IV. (2014). Teacher preparation for urban schools. In H. R. Milner, IV & K. Lomotey (Eds.), *Handbook of urban education* (pp. 199–216). New York, NY: Routledge.

Hudson, M. J., & Holmes, B. J. (1994). Missing teachers, impaired communities: The unanticipated consequences of *Brown v. Board of Education* on the African American teaching force at the precollegiate level. *Journal of Negro Education, 63*(3), 388–393.

Hutchinson, B. (2018). From "BBQ Becky" to "Golfcart Gail," list of unnecessary 911 calls made on Blacks continues to grow. *ABC News*, October 19. Retrieved from https://abcnews.go.com/US/bbq-becky-golfcart-gail-list-unnecessary-911-calls/story?id=58584961

Ignatiev, N. (2009). *How the Irish became white.* New York, NY: Routledge.

Jones, C., & Shorter-Gooden, K. (2003). *Shifting: Based on the African American Women's Voices Project.* New York, NY: HarperCollins.

Jones, N. (2014). "The Regular Routine": Proactive policing and adolescent development among young, poor Black men. *New Directions for Child and Adolescent Development, 2014*(143), 33–54.

Jordan, E. C., & Harris, A. P. (2006). *Beyond rational choice: Alternative perspectives on economics.* New York, NY: Foundation Press.

Khalifa, M., Dunbar, C., & Douglas, T. (2013). Derrick Bell, CRT, and educational leadership 1995–Present. *Race Ethnicity and Education, 16*(4), 489–513. doi: 10.1080/13613324.2013.817770

Knaus, C. B. (2006). *Race, racism, and multiraciality in American education.* Bethesda, MD: Academica Press.

Knaus, C. B. (2011). *Shut up and listen: Teaching writing that counts in urban schools.* New York, NY: Peter Lang.

Knaus, C. B. (2014). Seeing what they want to see: Racism and leadership development in urban schools. *The Urban Review, 46*(3), 420–444.

Knaus, C. B. (2018). "If everyone would just act white": Education as a global investment in whiteness. In J. Brooks & G. Theoharis (Eds.), *Whiteucation: How privilege, power and prejudice is destroying school and society* (pp. 1–21). Charlotte, NC: Information Age Publishing.

Knaus, C. B. (2019). "If everyone would just act white": Education as a global investment in whiteness. In J. S. Brooks & G. Theoharis (Eds.), *Whiteucation: Privilege, power, and prejudice in school and society* (pp. 1–21). New York, NY: Routledge.

Knaus, C. B., & Brown, M. C., II. (2018). The absence of indigenous African higher education: Contextualizing whiteness, post-apartheid racism, and intentionality. In M. C. Brown, II & T. E Dancy, II (Eds.), *Black colleges across the diaspora: Global perspectives on race and stratification in postsecondary education* (Advances in Education in Diverse Communities: Research, Policy and Praxis, Vol. 14; pp. 263–288). New York, NY: Emerald Publishing.

Knaus, C. B., & Rogers-Ard, R. (2012). Educational genocide: Examining the impact of national education policy on African Americans. *ECI Interdisciplinary Journal for Legal and Social Policy, 2*(1), Article 1. Retrieved from http://ecipublications.org/ijlsp/vol2/iss1/1

Knowles, M., Holton, E. F., & Swanson, R. A. (1998). *The adult learner: The definitive classic in adult education and human resource development* (5th ed.). Houston, TX: Gulf.

Kohn, A. (2000). *The case against standardized testing: Raising the scores, ruining the schools.* Portsmouth, NH: Heinemann.

Ladson-Billings, G. (1999). Just what is critical race theory, and what's it doing in a *nice* field like education? In L. Parker, D. Deyhle & S. Villenas (Eds.), *Race is . . . race isn't: Critical race theory and qualitative studies in education* (pp. 7–30). New York, NY: Routledge.

Lipsitz, G. (1998). *The possessive investment in whiteness: How white people profit from identity politics.* Philadelphia, PA: Temple University Press.

Lomotey, K. (1993). African American principals: Bureaucrat/administrators and ethno-humanists. *Urban Education, 27*(4), 395–412.

Lopez, G. R. (2003). The (racially neutral) politics of education: A critical race theory perspective. *Educational Administration Quarterly, 39*(1), 68–94.

Love, B. (2019). *We want to do more than survive: Abolitionist teaching and the pursuit of educational freedom.* Boston, MA: Beacon Press.

Macedo, D. (1994). *Literacies of power: What Americans are not allowed to know.* Boulder, CO: Westview Press.

Macedo, D., & Bartolomé, L. I. (1999). *Dancing with bigotry: Beyond the politics of tolerance.* New York, NY: Palgrave.

Madaus, G. F., & Clarke, M. (2001). The adverse impact of high-stakes testing on minority students: Evidence from one hundred years of test data. In G. Orfield & M. L. Kornhaber, (Eds.), *Raising standards or raising barriers? Inequality and high-stakes testing in public education* (pp. 85–106). New York, NY: Century Foundation Press.

Madda, C. L., & Schultz, B. D. (2009). (Re)constructing ideals of multicultural education through "grow your own teachers." *Multicultural Perspectives, 11*(4), 204–207.

Maxwell, J. C. (2002). *Leadership 101: What every leader needs to know.* Nashville, TN: Thomas Nelson.

McGuire, D. L. (2006). "It was like all of us had been raped": Sexual violence, community mobilization, and the African American Freedom Struggle. In J. Appleby (Ed.), *The Best American History Essays 2006* (pp. 123–150). New York, NY: Palgrave Macmillan.

McLaren, P. (1999). Unthinking whiteness, rethinking democracy: Critical citizenship in Gringolandia. In C. Clark & J. O'Donnell (Eds.), *Becoming and unbecoming white: Owning and disowning a racial identity* (pp. 10–55).Westport, CT: Bergin & Garvey.

Mills, C. W. (1997). *The racial contract.* Ithaca, NY: Cornell University Press.

Moore, A. B. (1977). The disturbing revelation of the predicament of Black principals in Southern school districts. *Urban Education, 12*(2), 213–216.

Mullen, C. A., & Robertson, K. (2014). *Shifting to fit: The politics of black and white identity in school leadership.* Charlotte, NC: Information Age Publishing.

Murtadha, K., & Watts, M. D. (2005). Linking the struggle for education and social justice: Historical perspectives of African American leadership in schools. *Educational Administration Quarterly, 41*(4), 591–608.

National Policy Board for Educational Administration. (2020). *Alliance for advancing school leadership.* Washington, D.C.: National Policy Board for Educational Administration. Retrieved from http://npbea.org/psel/

Orfield, G., & Joint Center for Political Studies. (1983). *Public school desegregation in the United States, 1968–1980.* Washington, D.C.: Joint Center for Political Studies.

Payne, Y. A., & Brown, T. M. (2010). The educational experiences of street-life-oriented Black boys: How Black boys use street life as a site of resilience in high school. *Journal of Contemporary Criminal Justice, 26*(3), 316–338.

Perry, T., Steele, C., & Hilliard, A. G. (2003). *Young, gifted, and Black: Promoting high achievement among African-American students.* Boston, MA: Beacon Press.

Petchauer, E. (2016). Shall we overcome? Self-efficacy, teacher licensure exams, and African American preservice teachers. *New Educator, 12*(2), 171–190.

Peters, A. (2011). Leading through the challenge of change: African-American women principals on small school reform. *International Journal of Qualitative Studies in Education, 25*(1), 23–38.

Pierce, C. (1970). Offensive mechanisms. In F. Barbour (Ed.), *The Black seventies* (pp. 265–282). Boston, MA: Porter Sargent.

Pierce, C., Carew, J., Pierce-Gonzalez, D., & Willis, D. (1978). An experiment in racism: TV commercials. In C. Pierce (Ed.), *Television and education* (pp. 62–88). Beverly Hills, CA: Sage.

Randolph, A. L. W. (2009). The historical tradition of African American leadership in African American schools: 1830–1955. In L. Foster & L. C. Tillman (Eds.), *African American perspectives on leadership in schools: Building a culture of empowerment* (pp. 17–37). New York, NY: Rowman & Littlefield.

Reed, L. C. (2012). The intersection of race and gender in school leadership for three Black female principals. *International Journal of Qualitative Studies in Education, 25*(1), 39–58.

Ricard, R., & Brown, M. C., II. (2008). *Ebony towers in higher education: The evolution, mission, and presidency of historically Black colleges and universities.* Sterling, VA: Stylus.

Roberts, D. (1997). *Killing the Black body: Race, reproduction, and the meaning of liberty.* New York, NY: Pantheon Books.

Rogers-Ard, R. (2007). *The burden of admission: Profiles of African American female educational leaders; understanding self through others' journey* (Unpublished doctoral dissertation). Mills College.

Rogers-Ard, R. (2016). The burden of admission: Profile of an African American female leader. In N. N. Croom & T. E. Marsh (Eds.), *Envisioning critical race praxis in higher education through counter-storytelling* (pp. 71–85). Charlotte, NC: Information Age Publishing.

Rogers-Ard, R., & Knaus, C. B. (2013). From colonization to RESPECT: How federal education policy fails children and educators of color. *ECI Interdisciplinary Journal for Legal and Social Policy, 3*(1), 1–32. Retrieved from http://ecipublications.org/cgi/viewcontent.cgi?article=1020&context=ijlsp

Rogers-Ard, R., Knaus, C. B., Bianco, M., Brandehoff, R., & Gist, C. (2019). The grow your own collective: A critical race movement to transform education. *Teacher Education Quarterly, 46*(1), 23–34.

Rogers-Ard, R., Knaus, C. B., Epstein, K. K., & Mayfield, K. (2012). Racial diversity sounds nice; systems transformation, not so much! Developing teachers of color. *Urban Education, 48*(3), 451–479.

Rollock, N. (2012). Unspoken rules of engagement: Navigating racial microaggressions in the academic terrain. *International Journal of Qualitative Studies in Education, 25*(5), 517–532.

Ruiz, D. M., & Mills, J. (2010). *The four agreements: A practical guide to personal freedom* (Vol. 1). San Rafael, CA: Amber-Allen Publishing.

Rumberger, R. W. (2004). Why students drop out of school. In G. Orfield (Ed.), *Dropouts in America: Confronting the graduation rate crisis* (pp. 131–155). Boston, MA: Harvard Education Press.

Saltman, K. J. (2003). Introduction. In K. J. Saltman & D. A Gabbard (Eds.), *Education as enforcement: The militarization and corporatization of schools* (pp. 1–23). New York, NY: Routledge.

Sanchez-Hucles, J. V., & Davis, D. D. (2010). Women and women of color in leadership: Complexity, identity, and intersectionality. *American Psychologist, 65*(3), 171–181.

Singh, N. P. (2004). *Black is a country: Race and the unfinished struggle for democracy.* Cambridge, MA: Harvard University Press.

Sleeter, C. E. (2001). Preparing teachers for culturally diverse schools: Research and the overwhelming presence of whiteness. *Journal of Teacher Education, 52*(2), 94–106.

Sleeter, C. E. (2012). Confronting the marginalization of culturally responsive pedagogy. *Urban Education, 47*(3), 562–584.

Sleeter, C. E., Acuff, J. B., Bentley, C., Foster, S. G., Morrison, P., & Stenhouse, V. (2019). Multicultural education or ethnic studies? In R. T. Cuauhtin, M. Zavala, C. Sleeter, & W. Au (Eds.), *Rethinking ethnic studies* (pp. 12–16). Milwaukee, WI: Rethinking Schools.

Sleeter, C. E., & Milner, H. R., IV. (2011). Researching successful efforts in teacher education to diversify teachers. In A. F. Ball & C. A. Tyson (Eds.), *Studying diversity in teacher education* (pp. 81–103). Lanham, MD: Rowman & Littlefield.

Smith, E. L. B., & Nkomo, S. M. (2003). *Our separate ways: Black and white women and the struggle for professional identity.* Boston, MA: Harvard Business School Press.

Solórzano, D. (1998). Critical race theory, race and gender microaggressions, and the experience of Chicana and Chicano scholars. *International Journal of Qualitative Studies in Education, 11*(1), 121–136.

Solórzano, D., & Yosso, T. (2001). Critical race and LatCrit theory and method: Counter-storytelling Chicana and Chicano graduate school experiences. *International Journal of Qualitative Studies in Education, 14*(4), 471–495.

Solórzano, D., & Yosso, T. (2002). Critical race methodology: Counter-storytelling as an analytical framework for education research. *Qualitative Inquiry, 8*(1), 23–44.

Spring, J. (2018). *The American school: From the Puritans to the Trump era* (10th ed.). New York, NY: Routledge.

Steele, C. (2011). *Whistling Vivaldi: How stereotypes affect us and what we can do.* New York, NY: W.W. Norton & Company.

Stovall, D. (2016). Out of adolescence and into adulthood: Critical race theory, re-trenchment, and the imperative of praxis. *Urban Education, 51*(3), 274–286.

Taylor, E. (2009). Critical race theory and interest convergence in the backlash against affirmative action: Washington state and Initiative 200. In E. Taylor, D. Gillborn, & G. Ladson-Billings (Eds.), *Foundations of critical race theory in education* (pp. 117–130). New York, NY: Routledge.

Taylor, E., Gillborn, D., & Ladson-Billings, G. (2009). *Foundations of critical race theory in education*. New York, NY: Routledge.

Taylor, K. Y. (2016). *From #BLACKLIVESMATTER to Black liberation*. Chicago, IL: Haymarket Books.

Theoharis, G. (2019). White privilege and educational leadership. In J. S. Brooks & G. Theoharis (Eds.), *Whiteucation: Privilege, power, and prejudice in school and society* (pp. 52–61). New York, NY: Routledge.

Tillman, L. C. (2004a). African American principals and the legacy of Brown. *Review of Research in Education, 28*, 101–146.

Tillman, L. C. (2004b). (Un)Intended consequences?: The impact of the *Brown v. Board of Education* decision on the employment status of Black educators. *Education and Urban Society, 36*(3), 280–303.

Tillman, L. C. (2007). Bringing the gifts that our ancestors gave: Continuing the legacy of excellence in African American school leadership. In. J. Jackson (Ed.), *Strengthening the African American educational pipeline: Informing research, policy and practice* (pp. 53–69). Albany: State University of New York Press.

Tolley, K. (2016). Slavery. In A. Angulo (Ed.), *Miseducation: A history of ignorance-making in America and abroad* (pp. 13–33). Baltimore, MD: Johns Hopkins University Press.

Valenzuela, A. (1999). *Subtractive schooling: US-Mexican youth and the politics of caring*. Albany: State University of New York Press.

Vega, D., Moore, J. L., III, Baker, C. A., Bowen, N. V., Hines, E. M., & O'Neal, B. (2012). Salient factors affecting urban African American students' achievement: Recommendations for teachers, school counselors, and school psychologists. In J. L. Moore, III & C. W. Lewis (Eds.), *African American students in urban schools: Critical issues and solutions for achievement* (pp. 114–139). New York, NY: Peter Lang.

Walker, V. S. (2000). Value segregated schools for African American children in the South, 1935–1969: A review of common themes and characteristics. *Review of Educational Research, 70*(3), 253–285.

Walker, V. S. (2001). African American teaching in the South: 1940–1960. *American Educational Research Journal, 38*(4), 751–779.

Watkins, W. H. (2001). *The white architects of Black education: Ideology and power in America, 1865–1954*. New York, NY: Teachers College Press.

Watson, D., Hagopian, J., & Au, W. (2018). Black students' lives matter: Building the school-to-justice pipeline. In D. Watson, J. Hagopian, & W. Au (Eds.), *Teaching for Black lives* (pp. 17–31). Milwaukee, WI: Rethinking Schools.

Williams, H. A. (2005). *Self-taught: African American education in slavery and freedom*. Chapel Hill: University of North Carolina Press.

Woodson, C. G. (1933/1990). *The mis-education of the Negro*. Trenton, NJ: Africa World Press.

Wright, R. (1956). *The color curtain: A report on the Bandung conference*. Jackson: University Press of Mississippi.

Wright, R. (1953/1995). *White man listen!* (1st HarperPerennial ed.). New York, NY: HarperPerennial.

Yellow Horse Brave Heart, M., & DeBruyn, L. M. (1998). The American Indian holocaust: Healing historical unresolved grief. *American Indian and Alaska Native Mental Health Research, 8*(2), 60–82.

Zamudio, M., Russell, C., Rios, F., & Bridgeman, J. (2010). *Critical race theory matters: Education and ideology: Education and ideology.* New York, NY: Routledge.

Zeichner, K., & Pena-Sandoval, C. (2015). Venture philanthropy and teacher education policy in the US: The role of the New Schools Venture Fund. *Teachers College Record, 117*(6), 1–44.

INDEX

Note: **Bold** page numbers refer to tables, *italic* page numbers refer to figures and Page numbers followed by "n" denote endnotes